Challenges to
the Humanities

Challenges to the Humanities

Edited by
Chester E. Finn, Jr.
Diane Ravitch
P. Holley Roberts

With an Epilogue by
William J. Bennett
Secretary, U. S. Department of Education
Formerly Chairman,
National Endowment for the Humanities

Holmes and Meier
NEW YORK   LONDON

A project of the Educational Excellence Network of
Vanderbilt University's Institute for Public Policy
Studies, undertaken with support from the National
Endowment for the Humanities

First published in the United States of America 1985 by
Holmes & Meier Publishers, Inc.
30 Irving Place
New York, N.Y. 10003

Great Britain:
Holmes & Meier Publishers, Ltd.
Unit 5, Greenwich Industrial Estate
345 Woolwich Road
Charlton, London SE7

Book design by Ellen Foos

Library of Congress Cataloging in Publication Data
Main entry under title:

Challenges to the humanities.
    1. Education, Humanistic—United States—Addresses,
essays, lectures.   2. Humanities—Study and teaching—
United States—Addresses, essays, lectures.   I. Finn,
Chester E., 1944–   . II. Ravitch, Diane.
III. Roberts, P. Holley.
LC1011.C43   1985   370.11'2'0973   84-29065
ISBN 0-8419-1017-0
ISBN 0-8419-1018-9 (pbk.)

Manufactured in the United States of America

Contents

Challenges to the Humanities

Introduction

Chester E. Finn, Jr., Diane Ravitch, and P. Holley Roberts

American education is not doing right by the humanities. In many of our schools, history, literature, and foreign languages are retreating before an onslaught of basic skills, minimum-competency testing, vocationalism, trendy social science, computer technology, public apathy, intellectual confusion, and squeamishness about studying Western civilization during an era of multicultural sensitivity.

That the humanities face potent challenges in our schools is a statement unlikely to set off alarms in the citadels of scholarship and the chambers of the mighty. Unlike the celebrated allegations of the National Commission on Excellence in Education—that a rising tide of mediocrity is flooding the American schoolhouse, that if an unfriendly foreign power had done this to us we would have deemed it an act of war—the problems that concern us here have little direct bearing on the nation's economic vitality or its technological prowess. Instead, the problems limned in the following pages affect our spirit, our understanding of ourselves, our capacity for discernment and wisdom, the visions we hold of individual and shared purposes, our awareness of our own past and that of others, and our ability to understand great

3

achievements of the imagination, as well as great debacles of the soul and paralyses of the will.

Amid the "hard-nosed," "tough-minded," "high tech" pragmatism of our time, such concerns seem recherché, a bit precious, perhaps even a little embarrassing to discuss. "The humanities" is not a phrase that rolls lightly or frequently off many tongues, and a lot of people— including, it turns out, a number of educators—are not entirely sure what it means. If what we are worried about is thus slightly obscure as well as a little bit odd, and in any case is not the sort of thing the public is hopping up and down about, why not leave it be? Those who like to worry about problems can find plenty that are more tangible, more easily defined, more readily solved. Those who prefer to suppose that everything is basically copacetic can handily exclude from their consciousness the dilemmas and challenges that beset the humanities.

Curiously, perhaps perversely, that is why this book came to be written. But first we must say a word about its predecessor.

In the autumn of 1982, at the behest of Chairman William Bennett of the National Endowment for the Humanities, we undertook to organize a pair of national conferences designed to call attention to and encourage support for the humanities in the schools. We did this with no particular sense of urgency, much less alarm. While we knew that there were shortcomings in the ways that many American schools and school systems organized and taught the humanities, and while we knew that university-based scholars and education experts were not as attentive to these shortcomings as they might be, we still assumed that relatively straightforward remedies were to be found in the familiar domain of "public policy." We supposed, in other words, that what dogged the humanities were problems of resource allocation, competing priorities, low rank among the concerns of school boards and administrators, inadequate materials and obsolescent curricula, ill-schooled teachers, and apathetic colleges.

Problems of this genre are not necessarily easy to solve, but they are certainly common ones in every policy domain. One solves them first by drawing attention to them, then by asking wise and influential people to ponder solutions to them, then by enlarging the constituencies that want such solutions to be carried out. The pattern would be much the same if we were dealing with poor housing, unsatisfactory prisons, or polluted streams.

But as the 1982–83 school year unrolled, as our first two conferences were held, and as the thoughtful and creative individuals who had agreed to help us ponder solutions did their pondering, we began to suspect that, with respect to the humanities and the schools, we might be facing large problems of an altogether different nature.

And as we followed those conferences with work on the volume based on papers presented and deliberated there—*Against Mediocrity*, published in 1984—we became more certain. There was, to be sure, no dearth of "policy" problems bearing on the condition of the humanities in American schools, and it was not impossible to imagine solutions. But lurking in the background were challenges of quite another order.

We shared our surprise with the National Endowment for the Humanities (NEH) in the early summer of 1983 in the text of a proposal for support of a successor project—a project that by then we knew ought to have been the antecedent. We explained that we had encountered "widespread resistance to the very idea that high school English, social studies and language courses should embody a vision of the humanities as repositories and sources of an intelligible body of questions and knowledge about, and canons of inquiry into, 'the human predicament.' We have found resistance to the idea that through the schools we should initiate students into the Western cultural tradition and its intellectual achievements. And we have found profound confusion over the very nature of the humanities."

The most important problems, in other words, did not lie in the "policy" domain at all and were not apt to respond to solutions crafted there. The primary challenges to the strength, the vitality, and the quality of humanities instruction in the schools stemmed from intellectual and moral uncertainties, cultural ambivalence, irresolution, self-consciousness, loss of spirit, and failure of imagination. The humanities were indeed under siege. But many whom we expected to be staunch defenders had lost their nerve, forgotten their mission, clouded their vision, or, in some instances, defected altogether and begun to offer aid and comfort to the attackers.

This is a serious charge, and we do not mean to overstate it. We also found dozens of educators, scholars and—more often than we expected—laymen who were perfectly clear about what the humanities are and why they are important, and who continued year in and year out to teach, study, and support them. Some of these people were heroic, others quiet pluggers. All were defenders, to be sure, but mainly they were confident practitioners, which turns out to be the best kind of defense the humanities can have. For the most insidious "challenges to the humanities," as we came to think of them, turned out not to be frontal attacks or purposeful campaigns waged by canny opponents; rather, they took the form of a generalized disposition among the putative defenders—arising, we suppose, from exhaustion, insecurity, and confusion—to lay down their own weapons and abandon the field. The result of such abandonment is that the terrain one had once held is slowly encroached upon by idlers, squatters, unfriendly bands, wild beasts, and the tangled underbrush and odd sediments that nature deposits when one isn't watching.

The humanities, in short, have been engaged in a kind of preemptive surrender to a set of challenges that grow ever stronger and more apt to encroach precisely because of the weakness of the defenders.

In this book, we undertake to identify a number of those challenges, to examine them closely, to strengthen the morale and the armaments of the resistance, and to explain once again why the humanities matter and why the forces that would weaken them must be countered.

To the extent that we succeed in this ambitious undertaking, we owe it to several factors. The National Endowment for the Humanities, instead of chiding us for trying to do second what wiser folk would have done first, agreed to support the preparation of another round of papers and the holding of another pair of conferences at which those papers could be reviewed and discussed by thoughtful and concerned people from across the country. The authors did as we had hoped and more; starting from different institutional and intellectual perspectives, they went right after the fundamental issues underlying what we had tentatively identified as "challenges," and in so doing both improved our identification of the problems and profoundly deepened our understanding of their origins. Finally, the participants in the two national conferences, held in Phoenix and Minneapolis in the spring of 1984, were in no sense passive audiences. Thoughtful, sometimes argumentative, often lively, always alert, they transformed our examination of these "challenges" from an academic exercise into vivid reality fraught with the most powerful implications for our schools, our colleges, and our society.

The remainder of this introductory chapter divides into three parts. We endeavor first to outline the actual and potential impact on the humanities of the educational reform movement that has been shaking the United States in the mid-1980s. Then we set forth with greater specificity the "challenges" that beset humanities education in particular. Finally, we supply a partial guide through the rest of the book, identifying some important themes, a few unresolved dilemmas, and a selection from the many keen insights and arresting observations proffered by our fellow authors.

The mid-1980s are likely to be remembered as a remarkable era in the history of American education, for it was one of those rare times when the public and the education profession joined in scrutiny of the performance of the schools. After publication of *A Nation at Risk*, the report of the National Commission on Excellence in Education, in April 1983, nearly a dozen other reports critical of the schools appeared. In response to demands for change, school reform went to the top of the legislative agenda. For the first time in many years, there was sustained attention to the condition of the schools in national magazines and on national and local television. Some educators were unwilling to grant that there was a "crisis" in the schools, and many others were genuinely concerned about the danger of "quick fixes" and illusory panaceas that might be foisted on them by outside forces. Although there was a tendency among school officials to castigate the workings of the political process as a form of undue interference in education, the fact that public schools are publicly funded granted a certain legitimacy and inevitability to the oversight activities of governors, legislatures, and other public officials.

For the humanities, however, this attention to "educational excellence" gave new cause for alarm. Those concerned about the humanities had reason to worry that the new era of school reform was based on premises that might actually weaken these subjects, which were not all that strong to begin with. In the drive for school improvement, subjects like English language and literature, history, and foreign languages—the major humanistic disciplines taught in the schools—might be ignored. They might be ignored because they are not manifestly useful in the way that mathematics, science, and even vocational education are "useful." They might be ignored because their contribution to the nation's economy is not as obvious as is the contribution of the technical subjects. They might be ignored because their value is not easily quantified, inasmuch as there are no test scores to reveal a collapse of historical or literary knowledge comparable to the decline of basic skills or scientific information. Humanities teachers and scholars observed that political leaders talked incessantly of the nation's need for scientists and engineers for defense or economic productivity, but rarely mentioned the parlous condition of cultural literacy as a national problem or the tenuous condition of language study and history in the nation's schools as a focus for urgent reform.

Though they might not know it, reformers of American education in the mid-1980s have cause for grave concern about the actual condition of the humanities in our nation's schools. These subjects are today often in a marginal position, even when they exist as requirements within the curriculum. The mandatory "English" course may be, in fact, a course in mass media or science fiction or the humor of Woody Allen; are these to be the literary experiences that will shape our culture or stimulate expressions of critical intelligence? Do we not have a literary heritage that should be taught in our schools? The required "history" course may be equally unpredictable; it seems that every American student will learn a history different from that learned by every other American student. Is there no common heritage that belongs to us all? As for the study of foreign languages, this is so seldom required by school (elementary or secondary) or college that, in consequence, few students avail themselves of those opportunities for language study that do exist.

How have the humanities fallen to this low estate in our nation's schools? Before describing the challenges to which they have been succumbing, let us briefly sketch our vision of the place of and rationale for the humanities in the curriculum of our schools—a vision that is developed more fully in several of the succeeding chapters.

Mindful that such a statement will appear hubristic to anyone who does not already believe it, we assert that the humanities are central to the entire educational enterprise, that they must be seen as the heart and soul of the educational process and not as leisure-time studies with only slight payoff to the individual and to the economy. Without the humanities, the schools may provide various cognitive skills and technical training, but no education worthy of the name. The disciplined study of history, literature, and language shapes individual consciousness, makes people aware of their common humanity, and provides the tools for the communication and self-knowledge that make our shared social life possible. Because they are typically taught—when taught well—by dialogue, discussion, debate, and reflection, the humanities necessarily build critical intelligence. These are not peripheral considerations; they are the very essence of education.

That these claims on behalf of the humanities have seldom been heard in the numerous commission reports, scholarly studies, and legislative deliberations about how to renew and upgrade education is not adequately explained by inattention or oversight. Rather, as we came slowly to realize during the four national conferences we led between 1982 and 1984, it is because the humanities are indeed so beset by challenges and enveloped in discord that contemporary "reformers" are understandably a little skittish about them. One is not likely to get into trouble if one talks about better-paid teachers, keener principals, or more attention to computers, chemistry, and basic skills. But when one gets into matters that bear on the interpretation of our national past, our current culture, and the best ways to impart values and ethics to the young, one may be into very deep controversy indeed.

What, exactly, are the "challenges" that in combination have produced this loss of consensus, this welling up of controversy, and the resulting avoidance of the humanities by contemporary education reformers?

First, there is the all-important question of the role of the schools in contributing to the common culture in America. There *is* a common culture, largely served up by the mass media, but is there not a national heritage or cultural tradition that should also be a part of every person's knowledge and that should be taught in the schools? The belief that we possess no shared cultural heritage—whether true or not—leads to the disintegration of the humanities curriculum in the schools. If there is no common cultural heritage, the argument runs, then it really doesn't matter what is taught in literature or social studies classes. There was indeed a time not long ago when it was fashionable to assail the concept of a cultural heritage as though this were the exclusive province of white Protestant males. But can we not imagine a course in American literature or one in American history that represents the true richness and diversity of our heritage without becoming merely a numbers game based on gender, race, and ethnicity? Should not the humanities, as taught in American high schools, carry the weight of what we believe is a common cultural heritage, transmitting a core of common knowledge, rather than serve as the vehicles of ethnic, racial, and gender particularism? At one of our 1983 conferences, a teacher who was outraged by past neglect of women's history insisted that her students needed to learn about "domesticity, not the Constitution." Can she not be convinced that, however strongly she may feel about women's history, her students must also learn about the Constitution, even though it was written by men, since women's claims for equality are based on its letter and spirit? How these questions are answered will prove strongly determinative of the nature of the humanities curriculum.

Second, our nation's fascination with science and technology poses a direct challenge to the humanities. Officials at every level are worried about teacher shortages in science and mathematics, and there are plans in Washington and in state capitols to provide special funding for those who teach these subjects. While humanists harbor no animosity toward technical studies, there is considerable fear that the humanities will end up as the dispensable subjects in the curriculum, that federal and state mandates will extend protection to teachers in every area of study except the humanities. The nature of the school reform movement of the mid-1980s provokes such fears; the overwhelming absorption in issues of productivity, national defense, and international competition lends support to the claims of the technical subjects. Defenders of the humanities are challenged to make a case for cultural knowledge and literacy as powerful as the claims presented for science and mathematics. They find this difficult because of the false assumption that the humanities are "soft" and deal with the "affective" domain, while the sciences, somehow, are "hard" and "cognitive."

Third, every teacher of the humanities at some point has faced the questions, "But what use will it be for me? Will history or English or foreign language help me get a job? What are they good for?" The insistent utilitarianism by which educational studies are judged gnaws at the consciences of humanities teachers. Some respond directly to these concerns; they strain to be relevant, to tie their teaching to adolescent problems or to contemporary issues, often with remarkable success. But sometimes such linkages are not possible, and sometimes they are not even desirable. Much great literature and many historical events speak to the present only indirectly. Yet detachment from the day's headlines does not make them less relevant to human beings, less illuminating to the growing mind. Still, teachers of the humanities cannot simply shrug off the challenge of utilitarianism: Unless students plan to teach, the study of history and literature will not prepare them for the marketplace. The best that can be said in their defense may be that such studies bolster students' sense of dignity and sharpen their wits. In response to this challenge, humanities teachers should not be afraid to assert that knowledge and understanding are legitimate ends in themselves, not only for the rich and wellborn but also for the laborer, the shopkeeper, the technician, and the parent. There is no determinate cash value to be placed on such outcomes, but they are valuable nonetheless. Unfortunately, it is often the teachers themselves, accustomed to skeptical students and unpersuaded parents, who are unsure of the value of their contribution.

Fourth, we perceived a challenge from the social sciences. At the college and graduate school level, historians teach history enlivened by the social sciences, and social scientists teach economics, psychology, anthropology, sociology, or political science. The high school teacher of social studies feels compelled to bring almost all of these disciplines to bear in the classroom, usually without adequate training to do so. In reality, no college teacher would presume to be master of so broad a range of disciplines. The social sciences have been expanding rapidly in the high schools, even though few teachers are trained as economists or sociologists or psychologists. Though the school day may be stretched a little, for the most part the curriculum is a zero-sum situation; if a new subject is introduced, some existing subject must be reduced in time. Usually, the time allotted to courses in social science is taken away from the study of history; and often, what history is taught is taught by someone with little or no training in that discipline. For children and adolescents, the best introduction to the concepts of sociology and psychology is through the study of history and through literature, which offer limitless examples of the applications of sociological and psychological principles (and exceptions). How could one read a Jane Austen novel, for example, without considering the sociology of a nineteenth-century provincial English village or the psychology of her characters? Mustn't one consider such issues and perspectives when learning about the abolitionist movement, for example? Yet the reality is that history and literature have lost ground to the insistent claims of the social sciences, which have entered the school curriculum in part because they carry with them an authority that the traditional humanities have foolishly conceded.

Fifth, teachers of the humanities have been warned off from dealing with troublesome questions of values. Whose values are to be taught? is a rhetorical question that serves frequently as an excuse for avoidance. Yet it is hard to imagine a humanistic subject that contains no values; literature and history are freighted with judgments about right and wrong, good and evil. Should anyone teach the Civil War or World War II in a completely neutral fashion? Can any work of literature be taught without coming to conclusions about the behavior and motives of characters? It is true that many questions have more than a single answer; almost all *interesting* questions have multiple answers. And teachers of the humanities have the unique burden of struggling to explain the values implicit in a literary work or a historical situation without imposing a simplistic interpretation; it is in the presentation of dilemmas that teachers can engage the imagination, curiosity, and empathy of their students. We do not suggest that this is an easy task. Indeed, the appearance of groups who want to purge the curriculum or the library shelves of controversial books attests to the difficulty of treating questions of value. But without treating these questions, the humanities cannot be taught in an honest or engaging fashion.

The sixth and most painful challenge to the humanities, we believe, is the confusion among those who teach them about what they are. Are the humanities a singular or a plural subject? Is someone who studies them a humanitarian, a doer of good deeds, a social worker armed with apt quotations? Do the humanities consist of knowledge, of attitudes, of judgments, or simply of feelings? One way of defining them is by listing the subjects that they have traditionally included: history, literature, language, philosophy, and so on. These disciplines should be seen, we believe, not as airtight boxes into which subject matter is locked, but as different ways of fathoming the complex whole of human experience. To study them is to learn the story of human struggles to survive, to dominate others, to live together, and to reflect on life; the humanities, collectively, represent the efforts that people have made to understand and interpret their experiences. But in American public education today, we have learned, there is no shared conception of "the humanities." There are schools that offer a course labeled "humanities," usually an interdisciplinary stew intended to nourish creative self-expression. When our conferences were announced and teachers were invited to apply for them, some wrote to say that their school offered no courses in the humanities. Presumably, they did not regard English or history as courses in the humanities. Some teachers evidently don't know what the humanities are or think of them only as the stuff of a special innovative course, which may or may not be included in the curriculum in any given year.

These, then, were the challenges to which we sought to respond, with the support of the National Endowment for the Humanities, and with the help of an extraordinary group of scholars, educators, and laymen. These challenges shaped the agenda for a pair of exciting national conferences and furnished the issues that are discussed in the following pages.

Apart from the more fundamental character of the intellectual dilemmas with which it grappled, this project differed from its predecessor in two respects. This time, conferees included journalists and policymakers—school-board members, legislators, and state officials—as well as school-based educators and university scholars. Also, the conference "presenters" included schoolteachers, administrators, and business leaders as well as academics. This greater variety seemed to us important—and in retrospect the hunch was confirmed—because the challenges with which we were dealing are by no means solely the concern of the academy. Indeed, they are the more formidable because their roots extend far into the general culture. Yet we were also powerfully impressed by the ability—and the determination—of some teachers quietly to transcend these challenges on their own, and we judged that it would be valuable for us and our fellow conferees to leaven the general solemnity of the scholarly presentations with some demonstrations of fine teaching and with visible proof that individual practitioners of the humanities can overcome the obstacles in their paths. Furthermore, teachers had—we think justly—criticized the previous project for not trying hard enough to see the problems of the humanities from the perspective of the classroom. As the reader will presently see, this volume is immeasurably enhanced by our resolve not to make that mistake twice.

The essays that follow are organized into three clusters. The first and largest of these contains seven chapters, each by a distinguished university scholar and each responding to, or helping to explicate, at least one of the major challenges to the humanities that we have sketched above.

Paul Gagnon of the University of Massachusetts at Boston was a veteran of the first round of conferences, which he had attended as part of a school-university team based in Cambridge. He understood the malign power of the allegation that there are no important reasons for the humanities to be part of the education of every young American. If we cannot answer the primal question, "Why study the humanities?," then we have surrendered before even encountering the other challenges. Hence we asked Professor Gagnon to set forth the reasons for studying the humanities and to do so within a historical framework so that it would be clear what has happened to these reasons at the hands of the education profession in the United States during the twentieth century. Gagnon's paper—which was prepared first so as to serve as background reading for the Phoenix and Minneapolis conferees— makes a strong case for the inseparability of the humanities from the fundamental purposes of education in a democracy, but explains as well how some very foolish ideas that took root within the profession have—like ivy climbing a once-solid wall—penetrated and weakened this relationship.

E. D. Hirsch, Jr., of the University of Virginia extends the rationale for universal study of the humanities in a very important direction. He shows that true literacy requires not only technical proficiency in the handling of the language but also "cultural literacy," or familiarity with a wide range of shared background knowledge, a very large portion of which is supplied through study of the humanities. Developing insights he first presented in a pair of seminal essays in *The American Scholar*, Hirsch wrestles with the challenge posed by "educational formalism": the assumption that literacy is content-free and can be taught as a set of technical skills. He demonstrates that this view—widely popular within the education profession and in many academic circles as well—is fundamentally unsound, and that even so seemingly simple a task as reading a newspaper article with understanding becomes virtually impossible if the reader has not previously absorbed a substantial amount of specific knowledge and made at least the casual acquaintance of a great deal more. But not just any knowledge will suffice. The essential purpose of acquiring literacy is to become able to communicate, and Hirsch powerfully explains that successful communication across a large and variegated nation demands universal acquisition of a common core of knowledge and cultural reference points that are shared by everyone in the society.

Stephan Thernstrom of Harvard University addresses the role of history as source and vehicle for that body of shared knowledge and common cultural understanding. He argues that it is a national tragedy to be losing consciousness of a shared past and mutual heritage that, while sometimes harsh and often ignoble, are nonetheless the bases for nationhood itself. Particularly noteworthy is the conclusion by Thernstrom, himself a social historian keenly sensitive to the distinctive sagas of various ethnic groups, that history as taught in our schools no longer pays sufficient heed to the commonalities in our past or to the central institutions, events, and principles that build *unum* from *pluribus*.

Diane Ravitch of Teachers College, Columbia University, examines in greater depth the reasons for the decay of history as a fundamental element of the curriculum in American schools and for its replacement by the hodgepodge known as social studies. She traces the evolution of the curriculum from the period in the late nineteenth century, when history won general acceptance as an important (if uncomfortably "modern") subject, into the era of educational progressivism, when it began to lose favor with the education profession. The "social studies" that replaced it was never a well-defined or intellectually coherent subject, but did offer the appeal of superficial usefulness and relevance as well as the optimistic hint that it would foster progressive social reform.

Joseph Adelson faults contemporary "social studies" for a truly basic shortcoming: much of the "social science" that comprises these courses, he finds, is erroneous, grossly oversimplified, or presented in ways that imply far greater confidence in its methods and conclusions than is actually warranted. A social scientist himself (professor of psychology at the University of Michigan), Adelson eloquently argues for banishing the social sciences from the elementary and secondary schools and replacing them with greater attention to the humanities, which he judges to be richer sources of understanding of character development, the stages of moral maturity, and the elements of social and political consciousness.

The next essay in this section takes up the challenge that mathematics and the natural sciences pose to the humanities within the nation's schools. Bernard Gifford of the University of California at Berkeley was trained as a scientist but is also a professional educator of great repute and an amateur historian to boot. He does not content himself with comforting anxious aficionados of the humanities that their subjects are important, too. Instead, he embarks here on a far more challenging but ultimately rewarding course: explaining how the tension between the natural sciences and the humanities parallels the centuries-old division between what C. P. Snow termed the "two cultures"; why and how that rift appeared in the intellectual history of the West; and how the two types of knowledge embodied in the sciences and the humanities are at once different and mutually reinforcing, twin approaches to thinking, knowing, and understanding that must *both* be included in any "liberal" education worthy of the name. Dean Gifford's essay on the challenge posed to the humanities by the natural sciences is in some respects a companion to Professor Adelson's examination of the challenge posed by the social sciences. It should be noted that their conclusions regarding their respective specialties are quite dissimilar. While Adelson advocates the abandonment of social sciences in favor of the humanities, Gifford argues for the legitimacy of the natural sciences in the school curriculum—not that they have been in much jeopardy—but also demonstrates how the humanities are fully as important even though their intellectual methods and the kinds of knowledge they impart are different in many ways.

Among the challenges to the humanities that we set forth above is ambivalence about values: whether to teach them and, if so, whose, when presenting material that can scarcely be examined at all without encountering profound value conflicts. These vexing issues receive straightforward and cogent attention from Joel Kupperman of the University of Connecticut in the final essay of this section. The essay propounds two theses: that there is no reason for uncertainty about the place of values in the study of the humanities, for the adequate treatment of these subjects demands attention to value issues; moreover, studying the humanities can be an *effective* way for students to learn about values. Professor Kupperman defines a valid role for the teacher in the study of values; he responds to doubts as to the existence of moral knowledge; and he suggests sensitive means of resolving the difficult dilemma of teaching about values without "indoctrinating" students.

In the second cluster of essays, we move from the academy into the classroom. The many practicing school-based educators who participated and spoke in Phoenix and Minneapolis brought a wealth of experience and insight to our deliberations and thereby informed and improved this entire enterprise in more ways than perhaps they can imagine. We asked three of these outstanding teachers to transform their conference remarks into papers that could be included in this volume, and we believe that the results amply justify our confidence in them.

The first of these essays is the work of Patrick Welsh, teacher of English at T. C. Williams High School in Alexandria, Virginia, and a trained attorney as well, whose acquaintance we first made through a remarkable series of extended columns entitled "Tales Out of School" that he contributed to the *Washington Post*. Welsh here confronts the challenge of enlisting students in their own education in the humanities, and does so in a way that illustrates how Kupperman's two theses can be translated into concrete applications in the classroom. Welsh argues that if teaching literature is to be effective, instructors must create in students a sense of "ownership" of the subject matter, and that one of the most effective ways of doing this is by employing the texts as commentaries on the value conflicts and moral dilemmas that students encounter in their own lives. In so doing, students deepen their own interest in the works of literature and thereby acquire a better understanding of those works and of the value of literary study. Their concerns, in other words, become windows onto the texts. Mr. Welsh discusses special problems facing the high school teacher, notably the low technical skills of some students and the twin dangers of indoctrination and moral relativism.

The second essay in this section is by Claire Pelton, teacher of English at California's Los Altos High School, a faculty practitioner at the Stanford School of Education, and a veteran of the Advanced Placement program. Ms. Pelton offers some clear and time-tested counsel to humanities teachers seeking to respond to a number of challenges, but she is principally concerned here with the contemporary national education reform movement as viewed from the school classroom. She does not entirely share the gloomy appraisals of the national reports and studies, and candidly points out that some of the resulting recommendations suffer from oversight, blindness, and impracticality that might have been avoided had more practitioners participated in their preparation.

Jay Sommer, the author of the third essay in this section, occupies a special place in the hearts of many Americans (not least those of our Minneapolis conferees) who have heard his powerful, evocative, and deeply moving account of why public education is important and of how the United States is shortchanging many of its children today by providing them with an education that is not good enough. Mr. Sommer is a veteran teacher of foreign languages (until recently a faculty member at New Rochelle High School) who was the United States "National Teacher of the Year" in the year 1981–82, and who consequently became a member—the solitary teacher member—of the National Commission on Excellence in Education. In this essay, he combines some reflections on the work of the commission with a portion of his remarkable personal saga as a refugee to American shores who received here the "incredible present" of public education and later chose to try to repay his benefactors by teaching their children—and by gently but urgently exhorting their society. Sommer adds some trenchant comments on the state of foreign language instruction in American schools, a particularly valuable contribution to a volume that—we regret—is otherwise not so attentive as it should be to this crucial area of study which, along with history and literature, make up the humanities as commonly taught within our elementary and secondary schools.

The last two essays in the book offer yet a third perspective on the challenges that the humanities face. Chester E. Finn, Jr., of Vanderbilt University excavates in greater depth the origins and major directions of the contemporary national education reform movement that we began to probe above. He thereby identifies the political and policy contexts within which the challenges to the humanities will be met—if they are met. And in a graceful but hard-hitting epilogue, NEH Chairman William Bennett, who encouraged us from the outset and who keynoted the Phoenix conference, explains what the nation will lose if these challenges remain unmet. He skillfully reexamines the idea of "practicality" to show that the humanities are in important respects the most practical of all fields of study. He explains why they are indispensable for *everyone*, not only for the gifted, the fortunate, or the well-to-do. And he responds directly to the challenge posed by those who contend that we as a nation really have nothing in common with one another that has any proper bearing on what we should learn in school. As United States Secretary of Education, Dr. Bennett (whose selection for that post was announced as this volume was going to press) will be painting his ideas across a far larger canvas in the next several years, to the considerable benefit, we predict, of American schools and colleges and those enrolled in them.

When all is said and done, does this book present a unanimous view of what the challenges to the humanities are and how best to respond to them? Yes and no. Individual contributors naturally emphasize different problems and assign distinctive priorities to various solutions. In several respects—more small than large—the authors do not frame issues in quite the same way, nor do they entirely agree on how best to resolve them. Yet even if the result cannot fairly be termed unanimity, the book—and the conferences that preceded it—suggests a broad consensus about the core value of the humanities, about the perils they face, and about the importance of meeting these challenges with courage, imagination, and resolution. We agree that the general literacy of the population has been threatened by the superficial satisfactions supplied by television and other nonliterate indulgences. We agree that there are commonalities in the American experience, in our values and our beliefs, that all our children should come to understand. We agree that innumerable social forces—drugs, child abuse, and negligent parents merely begin the list—burden teachers and children in ways that reduce the incentives for formal learning and that extend the collateral tasks of the school. We agree that the case for disciplined study seems harder than ever to make and that there are fewer willing to make it, even though the costs and penalties of ignorance are greater than ever. In such a context, we agree that the case for the traditional humanities is a hard sell. Why study a foreign language, ask some, when we don't really need it? Why study history, since it is not relevant to the here and now? Why study literature when comic books, television, and computerized games supply whatever entertainment and information is necessary?

The most important challenge to the humanities, we concluded, is to persuade ourselves anew that knowledge of history and of literature has intrinsic worth. Like friendship, beauty, music, love, or any contemplative activity, such value cannot readily be quantified. The loss of such knowledge is not easily measured by standardized tests. Yet these studies, we believe, are paths to individual opportunity, and to the highest form of equality, which is that conferred by human dignity. They should not only survive but should flourish, not as the exclusive preserve of the scions of the privileged, but as the common birthright of every child in a democratic society.

Besides the debts acknowledged and thanks conveyed above, we would like to note our enduring gratitude to some of the other individuals who joined us on this voyage. As with any sizable project involving major conferences, a multiauthored volume, and complex arrangements between a federal agency and a university-based team, many people had a hand in this enterprise, and naming them does not do justice to their contributions.

Hildreth (Penny) Spencer spoke to the Phoenix conferees about the challenge of maintaining a first-rate high school social studies department in a time of teacher shortages and curricular confusion. Elizabeth Feeley spoke in Minneapolis about the remarkable efforts by the Atlanta public schools to revitalize the teaching of the humanities in a major urban system. Gabriella Canfield of the Metropolitan Museum of Art electrified the Minneapolis conferees with her dazzling lesson in the uses of art to gain greater understanding of a distant time and place. Professor Nathan Huggins of Harvard University spoke in Phoenix about the tensions of pluralism in the history of a diverse society, about the possibility of viewing American history as the saga of the land itself, and about the need to retain a common "spine" of study of political institutions and constitutional principles within a multilimbed curriculum.

To address the challenge of utilitarianism, we invited two distinguished business leaders to share their thoughts about the value of the humanities to those men and women whose careers lie predominantly outside the schools and colleges. Martin E. Segal journeyed to Phoenix for this purpose and with humor and passion spoke of the meaning of education to one who had not himself had the opportunity to complete high school; in his capacity as board chairman of the Lincoln Center for the Performing Arts, he also led an absorbing discussion of relationships between schools and cultural institutions. In Minneapolis a few weeks later, we were moved and enlightened by William S. Woodside, chairman and chief executive officer of the American Can Company, as he described some of the joint ventures that this major corporation is undertaking with the schools. Conferees also thrilled to hear Mr. Woodside's comment that in selecting senior executives he more often settles on those with strong liberal educations than on business school graduates.

The officers and staff of the National Endowment for the Humanities have, without exception, been sources of wise counsel and intellectual inspiration as well as careful guardians of the taxpayers' money. Though we must—and willingly do—assume responsibility for the product, it has been as though we were their partners in a joint venture. We would acknowledge Richard H. Ekman, director of the Division of Education Programs, who keynoted the Minneapolis conference; Carolynn Reid-Wallace, assistant director and head of the Humanities Instruction in Elementary and Secondary Education Program, who took part in the Phoenix conference and who has been our "project officer" throughout; and Stephanie Q. Katz, program officer within the Humanities Instruction Program, who attended the Minneapolis conference and served as NEH's representative there.

The publishing firm of Holmes & Meier did such a nice job with *Against Mediocrity* that we gladly accepted their invitation to return with this volume. We are especially grateful to Julie Lasky, Barbara Lyons, and Max Holmes for their care, their craftsmanship, their confidence, and their enthusiasm.

The Educational Excellence Network served as the organizational aegis for this whole project, as for the preceding one. A loosely linked group of scholars, educators, policymakers, journalists, and interested laymen, the network now numbers about six hundred members across the nation and has, in its low-profile way, become a significant force for continued improvement of American education.

Editorial, logistical, and clerical support has been supplied by many past and present staff members at the Vanderbilt Institute for Public Policy Studies. We are lastingly grateful to Erwin Hargrove, Lottie Strupp, Dottie Adams, Dot Blue, Judy Formosa, and Diane Sircy. During the first eight months of the project, Robert T. Fancher bore primary responsibility for its management, and did so with efficiency and imagination. Administrative and editorial burdens associated with conference planning and book preparation were cheerfully assumed by P. Holley Roberts, herself a student and teacher of philosophy, an unsurpassed editor of other people's work, and the original source of many of our best ideas and most felicitous phrasings. Chester Finn and Diane Ravitch are honored to be her colleagues and collaborators.

Understanding the Challenges

The Humanities and
Democracy in America

Paul Gagnon

Nearly twenty years ago, in *The Genius of American Education,* Lawrence Cremin challenged us to provide authentic education in the humanities to everybody:

> On the basis of prudence alone, no modern industrial nation can fail to afford every one of its citizens a maximum opportunity for intellectual and moral development. And beyond prudence, there is justice. No society that calls itself democratic can settle for an education that does not encourage universal acquaintance with the best that has been thought and said. This era, Arnold Toynbee has remarked, is the first since the dawn of civilization in which it is possible to provide appreciable cultural benefits for the whole of the human race. The possibility, Toynbee continues, carries with it "a moral command to execute the act of justice that is now at last within our power." Any lesser goal, it seems to me, is narrow and unlovely, and ultimately destructive of democracy.[1]

Few American educators were listening then. Few are listening now, but the right kind of talk is in the air. Several national reports call for a common core of academic subjects in the high schools, not only for college-track youngsters, but for all students, regardless of occupational destinies. For example, *High School,* the Carnegie Foundation's report, asks for two and one-half years of English, two years of foreign language, one-half year of arts, two and one-half years of history, one year of civics, two years of science, and two years of mathematics.[2] Others urge similar models, and many states are considering adopting such prescriptions.

We appear ready to rise above our "narrow and unlovely" habit of abandoning most of our students to life adjustment and vocational training. But are we? Even if we adopt the core-curriculum model, what will lie behind the official course titles, particularly in the humanities, the subjects most susceptible to dilution and fluff? There is the danger that the titles will mask the so-called education that we tend to dispense to the masses of American children prejudged to be incapable of academic learning: art and music as what turns us on; history as consumer awareness; English as "analysis" of TV ads; literature as street-talk stories. Are we ready to replace these with the best that has been created, thought, and said?

If we are, our business is first to define, then to confront, the challenges to the humanities in American education. We shall not have far to look. Cremin's notion that we can decide what is most worth teaching in history, philosophy, literature, language, and the fine arts and then prescribe it universally, is indeed under challenge in this country, and always has been. Never before have American educators decided to offer the humanities, however sloppily defined, to everyone.

At the root of this challenge lies, I believe, a narrow vision of what an education is for. This vision is realized in thousands of decisions regarding the school curriculum. In what follows, I will first discuss the role of the humanities in fulfilling the proper purposes of education. Then I will review developments in American education policy, particularly as these affect the teaching of the humanities.

The Purposes of Schooling

Even in the present rush to reform, there are few signs that Americans, educators included, believe that the humanities are good for very much. What, after all, do they contribute to our utilitarian mode of schooling? Our foremost purpose for education has always been to produce the workers and professionals the economy needs, or, put in progressive terms, to open paths for upward social mobility via occupational improvement for the individual. Sometimes, sensing trouble at home or abroad, we turn to a second reason for having schools: the nurture of good citizens, furnished with healthy attitudes, to keep our public affairs in order. The problem presented to the humanities by these two solidly practical purposes for education is that most Americans think both can be accomplished with barely a glance at the humanities, and they have been pursued that way for nearly a century.

Now, we in the humanities may object to this for several reasons. We may argue that preparation for work and for citizenship is better done when a liberal education including the humanities is part of the process. Or, echoing Cremin, we may insist that beyond work and citizenship is a third purpose for education: the private, personal cultivation of mind and feeling, the individual pursuit of moral and cultural integrity. That such words set off shivers of embarrassment in many of us is understandable: high-minded obviousness goes against the American grain. But we shall never get our educational institutions in order until we manage to keep all three purposes steadily in mind, and in balance. Our national failure to do so is the root cause of our frantic swings from fad to fad, of the chaos and emptiness of our high school curriculum, and of the unequal, undemocratic nature of our public schools.

What, then, is the place of the humanities in the pursuit of each of these three aims of education? In what follows I will take up each aim in turn, discussing the extent to which it supports the presence of the humanities in the curriculum and answering objections that have been and might be raised.

The argument based on the need to prepare students for work might not appear to carry the case for the humanities very far. Of how much direct use to most people's daily work is what they remember of history or great poems or fine arts? In most occupations, very little—at least little of the kind of usefulness that can be measured (another life-threatening problem for the humanities, on which more below). Outside of preparing teachers and kindred practitioners, very few direct applications of the humanities come to mind. It is true that not long ago a presidential commission warned of economic disaster if more Americans did not learn foreign languages and foreign ways. Ignorance, it seems, is hurting our sales pitch. But this development holds little solace for the humanities. The technical linguistic proficiency, the familiarity with foreign economics and politics, and the knowledge of what constitutes polite behavior required for business dealings with foreign countries can be acquired in ways other than through the study of the history, literature, and art of those countries. In any case, the direct usefulness of these studies to the small percentage of students likely to go abroad to work does little to justify imposing on *all* students (and on taxpayers) a twelve-grade regimen of foreign languages, history, and culture.

But direct application is not the only form of usefulness. There is evidence to suggest that the accumulation of general knowledge acquired through the study of the humanities is a crucial element in one's preparation for work. Ernest Gellner, in his book *Nations and Nationalism* (also cited below by E. D. Hirsch, Jr., and Stephan Thernstrom),[3] emphasizes the importance to an industrial society such as our own of an adaptable work force and a sophisticated medium of communication that is commonly used and understood. The flexibility of individual workers and of the work force as a whole is enhanced by "generic training," that is, universal schooling for high levels of literacy, numeracy, and communication skills. Specialized technical training can be added to this foundation as the contingencies of particular jobs demand. Studies by Hirsch and others have demonstrated that levels of literacy are directly dependent on background knowledge and familiarity with the subject matter of the text.[4] Simply put, the broadest education, incorporating literature, history, philosophy, language, and the arts, as well as mathematics and the physical, biological, and social sciences, is the best preparation for work.

Can education for citizenship provide another persuasive argument for the study of the humanities? The proponents of "worldview education" surely think so, and, to the extent that they are successful, the humanities may benefit from their emphasis on the study of other people's history and culture. But we must also ask ourselves, how realistic is it to expect students to think deeply and sensibly about *others* before having confronted *themselves* in a serious, sequential study of Western civilization and American history, literature, ideas, and arts? Preparation for world citizenship should begin with preparation for American citizenship.

Within the humanities, history and philosophy are the subjects most essential to the preparation of citizens as our eighteenth-century founders conceived of them. But history's place was usurped early in the twentieth century by the social studies, in which we are assured that the practical "lessons" of the past can be condensed and ingested without the strain of going over the whole story again! Philosophy has never been a standard subject in American schools, nor, of course, has the history of thought. We have been content to arm our future citizens with positive notions—"doing values" through case studies in problems of democracy—rather than laboring to explicate the range of ideas, originating with the ancient Hebrews and Greeks, that would enable them to make up their own minds, or at least to understand what they are talking about, when they raise the problems of democracy.

We may object that these practices represent a narrow view of citizenship, and agree with Cremin that it will be destructive of democracy. But we cannot deny that we—and Cremin—have a real fight on our hands. Many Americans in positions of authority, including those who shape our educational institutions, simply do not believe that schooling can raise the mass of people to the plane of intellectual autonomy, moral seriousness, and political sophistication thought by the eighteenth-century optimists to be essential for citizenship in a democracy. And their pessimism is reinforced by the rising complexity of public affairs, from the technicalities of interest rates and acid rain to the nuclear balance of power. Since only experts can know enough, is it not futile, they ask, to try to inform all citizens equally, perhaps even dangerous to tempt them to suppose that they know enough to influence decisions about such arcane matters?

The problem with this response is that we do indeed operate as a democratic republic. No matter how wise our experts, in our society they are constrained by decisions of political leaders who think they must limit their options to those the public can fathom. Those of us who are thankful for this arrangement, and who are more optimistic about raising the level of political debate through better schooling, must, however, be prepared to answer a good many questions before we can expect to prevail.

There are many practical questions: How many years of what kind of history would be enough? Of literature and philosophy? Where will the teachers come from? What kind of education ought they themselves to undergo? How many school districts can afford to lower the student/ teacher ratio to a point at which it becomes possible for the teacher to know the students' minds and to supervise directly their intellectual searchings?

This last question touches on one of the obstacles the humanities face, perhaps the hardest to overcome in the short run: so much of what most people, educators or not, believe about the humanities is false. It is assumed that they are the softer studies, less demanding of students than mathematics, natural sciences, and social sciences, easier to learn. In fact, the humanities are far more difficult to understand than most of the others. It is also assumed that they are easier to teach, whereas in fact they are so difficult to teach that they are rarely teachable under the present conditions prevailing in our high schools. And it is thought that in a modern, industrial society the humanities are frills. In fact, they are the most necessary of all studies in a democratic society, well ahead of the natural sciences and mathematics, the social sciences, and the practical-vocational subjects.

In presenting our case for the humanities as an indispensable part of preparation for citizenship, we need to be prepared to explain clearly what Cremin means when he warns that failing to teach the best that has been thought and said to everybody will prove "destructive of democracy." Without such explanation, we may be accused of educators' hyperbole, pushing school boards to pay for "frills," just as others garner new stoves for home economics and whirlpools for the locker room. But before we can hope to explain ourselves to others, we need to be clearer in our own minds. For we too are often beset by muddled thinking and moral uncertainty over what is meant by teaching the humanities and why and how we should engage in it.

How shall we respond to a sensible objection: surely, democracy will survive whether or not we play each semester our well-worn recording of "Eine Kleine Nachtmusik," show our slides of the Parthenon and the Mona Lisa, dust off our copies of *Macbeth*. Well, yes and no. Democracy would assuredly survive the absence of individual works we grew up with. But it cannot survive our failure to confront young people with all we can of the very best works of the past and to oblige them to wrestle, through literature, history, and philosophy, with the origins and meanings of the best, the worst, and the ordinary of human life. Where else will they meet with reality?

More educators' hyperbole, people may sniff. What is closer to reality than the predictabilities of natural science, the laws of mathematics, the data banks of the social sciences, and the vast range of practical instruction in home and manual arts supplied by vocational training? Our answer is as bold as it is simple: The *humanities* are more real. All other subjects are largely derivative. They follow upon and serve the choices we make about the worth of things. For the most part, they demand no further choice, no decisions beyond the selection of technique.

It would be naive, of course, and unfair to the natural and social sciences to assert that they have nothing of significance to teach us, nothing that could, in turn, deepen our insight into the questions dealt with in the humanities. Indeed, we ignore what they have to tell us at our peril. The entire Western experience tells us that there are invaluable things to be learned from natural and social scientists, as well as from artists, poets, prophets, philosophers, and historians.

We are, however, speaking in particular of education in a democracy, and the essence of democracy is open, constant, genuine choice, choice of values and meanings, choice of what the good human life is, and how the society, including its schools, shall order its priorities so as to make the good life possible—or to render bearable the life that is not so good. We need no historical sophistication to be struck by the plain fact that the choice of priorities by the authority in power has always shaped reality for most people, has determined the whole setting of life and death, the conditions under which artists and scientists, lawyers, cooks, farmers, carpenters, mechanics, or racketeers have done their work, or found themselves unable to do it.

We say yes to one thing, no to another, according to our order of values, our prior responses to the hardest questions of all, the only "real" questions there are: Who are we? Where have we come from? What can or should it mean to be human? Where is the good life? Where are justice, honor, love, beauty, truth? To pretend that the daily choices of a sovereign democratic people and their political servants can avoid these questions is deliberately to choose unreality, to refuse to grow up, to stay in the playpen of short-run utilitarianism. Repeatedly, throughout history, the daily, practical matters that concern men and women have been swept away in catastrophes following the real choices made by their political leaders—almost always on the assumption, right or wrong, that they were doing what their people wanted. Politics is the highest of the arts, not only because its consequences are so pervasive, but because it makes its choices on the basis of values central to all the other arts, all of the humanities.

In this light, teaching the humanities cannot be limited merely to assorted samples of Good Things, but must embrace to the fullest possible extent the entire range of the worthiest human thought and creation—for it is only in this way that students will confront the best attempts to answer the questions of value and meaning. Otherwise, they have no chance to grapple with the great questions and, indeed, no chance to know that the questions are out there at all. What strikes us in Huxley's *Brave New World* is the absence of the humanities. Other studies are quite acceptable to the dictatorship, but Mustapha Mond wants no real questions asked. He locks up the great books.

The humanities are at the heart of liberal, liberating education because they reveal the countless alternatives people have found for guiding their societal and individual lives. Western civilization itself offers an immense range of ideas and ideologies, of modes of community, personal salvation, and styles of artistic creation. Confronting all this, students are liberated from the cacophony of prevailing fashions and orthodoxies, and from the grip of present-mindedness so easily exploited by special pleaders. The dignity of free choice can proceed only out of knowledge of the alternatives possible in public and private life. Anyone who finds an unbearable paradox in the proposition that the student's freedom can emerge only out of strictly prescribed curricular patterns is not worth listening to on the subject of education.

All of this says that there is a particular body of knowledge that is more worth knowing than others, an idea that American educators have always resisted, and resist still. Rather than accept the task of choosing the best, many convince themselves that particular books, subjects, or works of art do not matter, that everything can be "humanities." Whence this astonishing inability, or unwillingness, to make distinctions? Some of these educators are themselves ill-educated, narrow specialists in Ortega's worst sense, "mass men" ignorant of their own heritage. Others see only the need to train youth for jobs, keeping them amused in the meantime. Still others have a manipulative view of preparing citizens, or frivolous, hedonistic notions of personal culture. By ignoring or trivializing the three purposes of education—or by deciding beforehand that serious study is nothing the masses want, or need, or are capable of—they can suppose that anything at all will do.

Ignorance, indifference, timidity, and rejection on the part of educators themselves are the greatest challenges the humanities face in America. Limited to a casually chosen parade of polite cultural artifacts, so-called humanities studies will surely remain "frills," and, we would have to admit, deservedly so. To do the work of liberal education, the work they alone can do, the humanities must present all of what is most significant to our ancient debate over truth, beauty, love, justice, and human nature. The main stages of that debate, the great arguments and creative works, and their settings and contexts must be known, or we shall never understand who we are, where we come from, why we think the way we do, and why others think differently. All of this requires a historical approach.

History is the basic, generative humanities discipline, upon which the coherence and usefulness of other disciplines depend. Its narrative ordering of reality, in terms of consequence and development, is essential to students' understanding of art, architecture, drama, literature, and philosophy. The retreat of history, especially Western civilization and European history, before the social studies has meant an incalculable loss to all of the humanities. Robert Fancher tells us why:

> The only ways of understanding and the only knowledge we have at the outset of adulthood are those that previous thinkers have created. Not to appropriate this knowledge as one's starting point is to undermine all efforts at improving the quality of our lives. If a generation had to start from scratch and had to experience the world in more or less primitive terms, rather than as shaped by the understanding of those who have already wrestled with the perplexities and mysteries of experience, that

generation would have to reinvent not merely the wheel but the very rudiments of civility and insight.[5]

History is also the indispensable grounding in reality for the social studies, which are prone to abstraction if taught as "themes" or "projects" or "case studies" floating out of context. Notwithstanding the trend in American education since the 1920s, social studies cannot fairly be accepted as equivalents of or substitutes for historical studies. They are not history, they will not do in place of history and, most important, they cannot do without history, particularly in the education of citizens. If the humanities are to take and to keep their rightful place in American schooling, the way must be opened by the revival of historical studies.

Not only can the study of the humanities provide the knowledge of cultural tradition required for citizenship, it can also be useful in the development of moral character. Such development was central to the notion of citizenship held by the Athenians, who found in their public leaders defects of character more often than of intelligence. For them, good character arose from a healthy well-roundedness. People who had developed all of their human possibilities to the limit—religious, aesthetic, and physical as well as intellectual—would have won dignity, would be at peace with themselves and thereby with others. They would be proud but not arrogant (since they would know the difficulty of everything and the transient nature of mastery), unafraid, unenvious. Only such autonomous, disciplined persons could make good citizens; not only would their marriage of mind and character render them capable of self-government, but—most important of all—they would understand that the ultimate purpose of any government, and of all work, was to create and to preserve the kind of society in which free and full self-realization was possible.

All of which brings us back again to our and Cremin's high-minded third purpose for education: private, personal cultivation of the individual. Jefferson called it the pursuit of happiness, the ultimate use for life and liberty. A recent statement by French educators puts it another way: "The purpose of education is not only to form qualified technicians and professionals, nor even to form citizens. The right to culture is also a right of the person—and only if we believe in the value and dignity of the person can we believe also in the necessity for democracy."[6]

If American educators were to take this seriously, and not be bashful in saying it, we could be confident of the future of the humanities in all of our schools, for all of our students. We would have added a right to schooling for culture to the more or less accepted rights to schooling for work and citizenship. But are we likely to do so? Our whole tradition says not. It is incorrectly assumed that the humanities, at least literature and history, used to be taught widely and well to most high school students and that all we need to do is to reverse the aberrations in American educational policy that caused their eclipse. But in fact the humanities have never been offered to the majority of young Americans. Far from being aberrations, the educational policies that have prevented the humanities from taking their rightful places at the center of general education have always represented and, judging from the utilitarianism of most recent reports, continue to represent the all but unchallenged norm in American schooling.

We have always rushed to the immediately useful and measurable, taking up the schools as handy (and generally submissive) instruments to fix whatever problems we see popping up. In this rush, the humanities are bound to suffer. It is so much easier to measure, to quantify, the results of education for work—using such criteria as an efficient labor force, or rising social mobility, or enough people who speak Spanish or run computers—and, having done so, to defend it in public debate and in hearings for public appropriations. Evidence of success in the other two purposes of education is more elusive. It cannot be measured in any but the most impressionistic ways. Nor can it be proved that pursuing these two purposes will "serve society" as it is, or as any particular faction wishes it to be. Preparing the citizen as a history-wise philosopher is an unpredictable business. Preparing each individual for private, personal development is even less measurable. As long as Americans prefer to pursue concrete results, the humanities will lose out.

American Educational Policy and the Humanities

A look back at American history shows that utilitarianism has dominated our discourse about culture almost from the beginning. As Richard Hofstadter points out in his great book, *Anti-Intellectualism in American Life*, the eighteenth-century founders of the republic were men of broad cosmopolitan culture, but their places were soon taken by practical men content with the Bible, gun, and plow, confident in the material progress ordained by God and nature for the New World. Between "John Quincy Adams who can write/ And Andrew Jackson who can fight," it was no contest.[7] The work of opening a continent, of industry and commerce, absorbed the imagination of the ablest men. Culture was left to the women, says Hofstadter, "establishing the masculine legend that men are not concerned with the events of the intellectual and cultural world." Intellectuals, Louis Bromfield was to say in 1952, were "over-emotional and feminine in reaction to any problem," and he preferred Eisenhower the soldier to Stevenson the "egghead"— the word Bromfield used to disparage him as remote "from the thought and the feeling of the whole of the people."[8]

Alexis de Tocqueville, observing the United States twelve decades before Bromfield, was alarmed to find that intellectual and cultural excellence was suspect. Democracy, he said, was in danger from the tyranny of the majority: The weight of mass opinion could smother ideas contrary to prevailing orthodoxies. Egalitarian envy, he feared, so much resented intellect that a democratic people could deny the minority's right to be different. Somehow democracy had to create from within itself a new kind of aristocracy, a moral, cultural, and intellectual leadership that would lift society by its own example and whose role it was "to stand apart from the tendencies of the age and to present men, when necessary, with alternative views and values."[9] Another imperative, complementary to the first, was to prepare a public willing to accept such leadership: "The first of the duties that are at this time imposed upon those who direct our affairs," said Tocqueville, "is to educate democracy."[10]

It was necessary not only to school the governing few, but to "ennoble equality" by preparing all citizens to comprehend the issues of public life. Despite its terrors, equality was here to stay. There was no going back; nobody could be shut out. As Tocqueville wrote to a friend in 1853, all political events were but secondary consequences: "The notions and sentiments dominant in a people; these are the real causes of all the rest."[11] Everyone in a democracy should understand human nature and its needs as revealed by philosophy and history, which alone, he thought, could offer people the necessary perspective on themselves and on the complexities of human affairs. For Americans, it was most necessary "not to forget" their civilizing heritage from England and Europe.[12]

To preserve democracy, Tocqueville called, as Cremin would in our time, for nothing less than an entire people's understanding of the human condition, and for a faith, based in history and religion, that human choice could render life not only endurable but dignified. For Tocqueville, the ultimate purpose of life and liberty was to allow the exercise of moral choice. He was in anguish over the moral and intellectual confusion of his day, when "the light thrown by conscience on human actions is dim, and where nothing seems to be any longer forbidden or allowed, honorable or shameful, false or true."[13]

At first Tocqueville was encouraged by the respect for religion in America, but he was not long in finding it present-minded and utilitarian, weak on those points he thought essential to citizens: a sense of the past, of the tragic, of the necessity and worth of sacrifice. Well acquainted as Americans were with personal suffering, neither their political nor their religious leaders saw much to be gained from dwelling on the past, on the tragic, or on the need to sacrifice. If American education has been mainly utilitarian, rarely concerned with the humanities and history, it is partly because it grew out of, and later sought to take the place of, that sort of American religion.

The plight of the humanities is due in no small part to the fact that they do not complement egalitarian envy nor official optimism. By definition, they are the great writings and works of art produced by extraordinary men and women in response to the great questions and in defiance of their own mortality. As the stars need the night, the humanities appear luminous to us because we know and accept the fact that we and all things are going to perish. Richard Hofstadter opens his lament over American education with words from Emerson: "Let us honestly state the facts. Our America has a bad name for superficialness. Great men, great nations, have not been boasters and buffoons, but perceivers of the terror of life, and have manned themselves to face it."[14] With few exceptions, those who shaped America's schooling from the mid-nineteenth century until now have preferred to accentuate the practical and the positive, the undeniable good that can come to ordinary people once they are freed from ancient tyrannies.

The American resistance to the traditional culture of old Europe had many roots. There was justifiable pride in having escaped the past. As Hofstadter explains,

> What was at stake was not entirely a technological or materialistic barbarianism which aimed merely to slough off all the baggage of history. Among other things, the American attitude represented a republican and egalitarian protest against monarchy and aristocracy and the callous exploitation of the people; it represented a rationalistic protest against superstition; an energetic and forward-looking protest against the passivity and pessimism of the Old World; it revealed a dynamic, vital, and originative mentality.[15]

Its negative side was a Protestant, male, and Anglo-Saxon disdain for broad reaches of traditional Western culture—for things Catholic, French, Italian, sensual, or feminine. Emerson himself said it was the lighter complexions, "the blue eyes," of Europe that came to America; the "black eyes" stayed home. Charles G. Finney, the Presbyterian evangelist, excoriated those Anglo-Saxons frivolous enough to look southward: "Byron, Scott, Shakespeare, and a host of triflers and blasphemers of God." As for classical studies, there was "no God in them."[16]

In the arts, Americans would find their own way, needing no patronage from kings, lords, or popes! Except for the English roots of constitutionalism, European history was a tale of woe that Americans had left behind. Philosophical and religious questions had been settled. In politics, the American Constitution was the last word and the world's best hope. Why should Americans not assume that the schools were needed mainly to prepare children for the practical world?

Notwithstanding the fact that late nineteenth-century America was overwhelmingly a business civilization, a good number of public and private high schools clung to a fairly traditional liberal arts curriculum. They enrolled, of course, only a small minority of the secondary school–age population. In 1890, about 360,000 students, representing 6.7 percent of all fourteen- to seventeen-year-olds, were in postelementary school, and only 3.5 percent of that age group graduated from high school. In that same year, 55 percent of all public high school students were enrolled in a foreign language course at some level, 66 percent in mathematics, 33 percent in science, 27 percent in history, and about 65 percent in English. Thus within the high school the humanities were doing fairly well, except for the fine arts. But high school was still for the few.[17] What would happen when the masses were admitted? Would the great American predilection for utilitarianism finally triumph? It would. But the issue was in doubt up to the Great War.

By 1900, there were two sharply divergent views about what high schools were for. What was to be called the school-centered view prevailed until the war: high schools were to develop the intellect of their students, including those not going on to college (a majority even at that time, contrary to our common assumption). The leading statement of this approach was the 1893 report of the National Education Association's Committee of Ten. Chaired by President Eliot of Harvard, its membership was dominated by college presidents. The committee recommended four kinds of high school curricula—classical, Latin-science, modern languages, and English—but all had a common core of four years of English, four years of a foreign language, three years of history (not yet social studies), and three years each of mathematics and science.

The statement of the Committee of Ten has a most contemporary look and could as well be reissued now. Academic training was for all who attended high school, not only for what they called the "insignificant percentage" going on to college. It proposed a larger place for art and music, and a start on foreign languages in elementary school. It demanded higher standards for normal schools and much closer involvement of university faculty members in teacher education, for it was clear to the committee that the quality of teacher preparation was inadequate to their high hopes for a seriously academic secondary education, to replace the "feeble and scrappy" courses Eliot deplored.[18]

Although the Ten hardly foresaw the day when more than 90 percent of American youth would be in high school, they did assume that more and more would be entering, so it is hard to disagree with John Latimer's view that the report was "the embodiment of the most profound, practical and democratic philosophy of education ever enunciated in America":

> It was the most profound because it cut through the shams and shibboleths of the immediate and the practical to the basic needs of the individual and of our democratic society in the dawning world of the twentieth century. It was the most practical because it set an educational pattern that could be tailored to any high school regardless of size. It was the most democratic because it made no distinction between the educational welfare of those who were going to college and those who were not.[19]

This academic mode of secondary education was not to prevail. Indeed, the committee itself was reacting against a trend toward practical, vocational training that had already begun. As enrollments rose after 1900, a newly professionalized corps of educational administrators proclaimed that to demand mastery of particular academic subjects would only ensure a high rate of dropping out. The impending triumph of the new educators was signaled in 1911 by the Committee of Nine on the Articulation of High School and College of the National Education Association (NEA). Made up of public school administrators and professors of education (there were no university members), the Nine stood the Ten on their heads. Repudiating the notion that curriculum should "fit students for college" (misrepresenting the aims of the Ten), they urged high schools to adapt themselves instead to the "general needs" of their students. The high school's business was to encourage "good citizenship and to help in the wise choice of a vocation." It should work from the individual pupil's own gifts, which were "quite as important as the development of the common elements of culture." The holding power of the schools would depend upon their ability to play upon the interests "each boy and girl has at the time."[20] To insist upon sequential study of academic subjects was to "enslave" the high school to the colleges and make them "responsible for leading tens of thousands of boys and girls away from the pursuits for which they are adapted and in which they are needed, to other pursuits for which they are not adapted and in which they are not needed."[21]

Hofstadter's judgment on the "new educators" may seem harsh: "The appearance within professional education of an influential anti-intellectualist movement is one of the most striking features of American thought."[22] But such a judgment seems wholly justified in light of the single most potent pronouncement of the twentieth century on the high schools, *The Cardinal Principles of Secondary Education*, issued in 1918 by the NEA's Commission on the Reorganization of Secondary Education and distributed by the United States Office of Education. Composed mainly of public school administrators, the commission made no mention at all of academic curriculum in its statement of seven principles that ought to determine the content of high school education: (1) health, (2) command of fundamental processes (the three Rs), (3) worthy home membership, (4) vocation, (5) citizenship, (6) worthy use of leisure, and (7) ethical character. In its view, the high school was to be the central, in time perhaps the only, socializing agent of a society in which the civilizing power of the home, church, and workplace was already weakening. The report was "breathless with the idealism of the Progressive era and the war," said Thomas James and David Tyack, but it also revealed the new educators' concern with socializing the mass of immigrant children then filling so many city schools, and with preparing different kinds of pupils for different kinds of destinies.[23]

Unhappily, "science" appeared at that very moment to be offering a foolproof way to tell the "different kinds" apart. Educators joined the craze for intelligence tests that followed the United States Army's mass testing of recruits in the First World War. Some educators took the development of the tests to mean that "mental ages" could be measured, that they were fixed, and, therefore, that great numbers of American young people were forever incapable of taking an academic program. As Hofstadter tells us, "The supposed discovery of the mental limitations of the masses only encouraged a search for methods and content in education that would suit the needs of the intellectually mediocre or unmotivated."[24]

In sum, those who shaped the new "scientific" curriculum were self-styled democratic progressives who lacked faith—or interest—in the intellectual potential of the people. Henceforth, equal access to secondary school was to mean drastically unequal education. From the 1920s onward, high schools became custodial institutions, run on the assumption that many of their clients were neither interested nor able. Masses of pupils were progressively locked into curricular tracks and "ability groups," often on the basis of outward characteristics that had little to do with individual ability or aspiration.

> The mirroring was crude; students were grouped into the broadest of categories: college bound, vocational/industrial (boys), vocational/clerical (girls), and a catch-all category often called "general." As was true

of ability grouping, the categorizations were largely defined by class, race, and sex. Boys were overwhelmingly more likely to be placed in special education and low ability groups than girls, reflecting the extent to which ability grouping was dependent upon behavioral attributes.[25]

The degree to which academic subjects were dropped or watered down between 1910 and the late 1940s reflects the dominance of the new educators. The influence of the Committee of Ten had reached its apogee in 1910. In that year, when nearly a million boys and girls attended public high schools, 90 percent of all students in grades nine to twelve were enrolled in mathematics, 84 percent in foreign languages, 82 percent in science, 71 percent in history and government, and 114 percent in English (many took two courses at once). There were only thirty-five different subjects in the entire American high school curriculum, of which twenty-seven were in the five academic fields. By 1922, twelve new academic subjects had been added, but so had twenty-one nonacademic ones. By 1934, fifteen additional academic subjects had appeared (all in English and social studies), and twenty-eight nonacademic. In 1949, academic subjects numbered fifty-nine, only two more than in 1934, but the number of nonacademic had soared to eighty-two.

Participation in the three cumulative intellectual fields fell steadily. From 90 percent in 1910, enrollment in mathematics fell to 75 percent in 1922 and 55 percent in 1949; in science, from 82 percent in 1910 to 54 percent in 1949; in foreign languages, from 84 percent in 1910 to 55 percent in 1922, 36 percent in 1934, and 22 percent in 1949. In that year, fewer students took languages than in 1934, despite a million-pupil growth in overall enrollment at the secondary level. History remained steady at 55 percent, but social studies added another 44 percent by 1949, so that the combined fields drew 99 percent; English still stood at 103 percent in 1949, but in all three cases it is impossible to tell what lay behind the course titles, so numerous had they become.[26]

The period between the wars had seen the triumph of progressive education, chronicled by Lawrence Cremin in *The Transformation of the School*.[27] It was built, as Hofstadter puts it, "upon two intellectual pillars, its use, or misuse, of science and its appeal to the educational philosophy of John Dewey." The misuse of science was largely responsible for the relegation of up to 85 percent of secondary school students to nonacademic tracks or baby versions of academic courses. The use and misuse of Dewey's ideas were partly responsible for further abandonment of the academic curriculum, including the humanities conceived of as the traditional "best."

Particularly damaging to them was the determination of Dewey's followers to minimize adult guidance of the child's academic program, to subordinate the values of traditional culture and private, reflective life to incessant social involvement in the community, and to the qualities of spontaneity and practicality. Dewey himself saw culture as "aristocratic" in its traditional form. The new age of science and democracy would not need it, and the new education would render all things and all work "cultural" by the way they were conceived. Rejecting the European past as nothing more than a tale of error and cruelty that Americans had put behind them, Dewey dismissed the study of traditional Western culture as but an "ornament and a solace, a refuge and an asylum" wholly unsuited to the unrelentingly participatory citizen, "saturated with the spirit of service." His optimistic faith in the benign character of public life in a new era of universal, scientific, and democratic education gave him no reason to suppose that people would need "asylum" in their private attainments.[28]

Dewey's view of education as "growth," without any prescribed, predetermined purpose, meant that progressives were left without guidelines based on other purposes—especially private cultivation—and on the curriculum needed to serve them. Progressive education, Hofstadter says, offered a parable on American life itself: the more confident it became of its techniques, the less clear it became about what it was all for.[29] Lawrence Cremin agrees that the major failing of the progressive educators was in curriculum making:

> Suffice it here to say that the problems were partly ideological (the view that to lay out a curriculum in advance is somehow undemocratic, or the assumption that a youngster who has trouble with history can just as well spend his time in shop) and partly political (the decision of the newly self-conscious teaching profession to separate itself from the academic scholars in the colleges and universities).[30]

From the most easily popularized ideas of John Dewey there runs a straight line to life-adjustment education, the most mindless and antidemocratic conception of schooling in our history. As Cremin notes, its proponents claimed to be Dewey's disciples, but they envisioned a world divided between masters and followers, the antithesis of Dewey's aspirations.[31]

At a conference of vocational educators in Washington in 1945, Charles Prosser, an industrial training specialist, called for a national effort to find the "right kind" of education for the 60 percent of high school–age youth who were not among the 20 percent in vocational training or among the other 20 percent going to college.[32] In 1947, the

Commission on Life Adjustment for Youth was created after a series of regional conferences to which no university academicians were invited (and no classroom teachers, it should be noted). Life-adjustment education, said the commission, was to concern itself with "physical, mental and emotional health," with "the present problems of youth as well as their preparation for future living." It stressed the importance of work experience in the community and of "personal satisfactions and achievements for each individual within the limits of his abilities."[33]

In the United States Office of Education's first manual on life-adjustment education, the 60 percent of youngsters deemed unfit for either vocational or academic work were described as from poorly paid, unskilled, or semiskilled families that offered no cultural environment; they were retarded in school, showed little interest, made low grades, scored badly on tests. Though the report claimed that these traits were "not intended to brand the group as in any sense inferior," Hofstadter calls the life-adjustment movement an antidemocratic "crusade against intellectualism":

> This verbal genuflection before "democracy" seems to have enabled them to conceal from themselves that they were, with breathtaking certainty, writing off the majority of the nation's children as being more or less uneducable. . . . What kind of education would be suitable for this unfortunate majority? Certainly not intellectual development nor cumulative knowledge, but practical training in being family members, consumers, and citizens.[34]

"The consequence of these policies," says Richard Powers, "has effectively denied the advantages of the academic curriculum to the *majority* of our young, who could benefit from it, and in practice has been highly discriminatory."[35]

Prosser himself had earlier oversimplified both Dewey's ideas and the "findings" of psychological tests. "Nothing," he claimed, "could be more certain" than that science has proven false the doctrine of general education and its fundamental theory that faculties of mind, including memory, imagination, and reason, can be strengthened by exercise.[36] There were not even general mechanical skills, according to Prosser. One learned *only* by doing, and by doing only those things that the learner recognized as immediately useful. Subjects taught in schools had to offer direct information on daily living. Even the 20 percent going to college needed few academic subjects; they could as easily (and more cheaply) be selected by a few hours of mental testing as by their performance in academic courses. The new life-adjustment curriculum could be for all—the academically fit and the unfit—the ultimate in educational democracy.

Lost in this tide was the 1948 Harvard Committee report, *General Education in a Free Society*, which, like that of the Committee of Ten in 1893, expressed the educational goals of university scholars. Like that earlier report, it sought a common, substantial, sequential academic secondary program for all, taking up at least half, and preferably two-thirds, of the high school years.[37] Its authors might have taken their principles straight from Tocqueville, beginning with his plea for a common and usable past, incorporating direct confrontation with the arts and the great books, and closing with his hope that a democratic people would be educated to all of the issues its leaders faced. But the mainstream of American education flowed on, undiverted by the Harvard report, which lacked the imprimatur of the NEA, and it was ignored by professional educators. There was no crisis to stir public attention. Those high schools that clung to some version of required general education in the 1940s and 1950s did so only in their college tracks. Otherwise, the social instrumentalists prevailed and, under new labels, prevail in most high schools today.

Not that all has been static. Fad has followed fad, each claiming quick practical results, each unrelated to the cultural evolution of the individual or to the deeper needs of the society: the Sputnik flutter, career education, "futures learning," the "greening" of the 1960s, "moral" education, "back to basics," and "global learning." All this neatly supports Tocqueville's insight that democracy would mistake change for progress or, in fact, might prefer no change at all, but revel in tumult and activity as sufficient proof of its own vitality. Although even he failed to predict in so many words that entire quasi professions would one day depend for their life's blood on promoting incessant turns of fashion, he nicely described them as addicted to "a small, distressing motion, a sort of incessant jostling of men, which annoys and disturbs the mind without exciting or elevating it," while predicting also that waves of promoters would find their reward not in the merit of their ideas but in their "seasonableness."[38]

Nothing was more seasonable than the sudden American concern for rigor that followed the Soviet Union's launching of Sputnik. But the response of the late 1950s had little to do with either the humanities or democracy. The object was to regain the technological lead by quickly producing more mathematicians and scientists.

The other great impetus for school reform in those years was provided, of course, by James B. Conant. His celebrated 1959 volume, *The American High School Today*, was simply another exercise in the familiar mode of American problem solving: for every problem there is a solution, and it is usually located in the schools. In his foreword, John W. Gardner invited readers to ask, "Precisely what can we do tomorrow morning to improve our schools?" And he was not afraid to assure them that "average schools can become good schools, and our good schools excellent, by a series of steps easily grasped by any informed American."[39]

The biggest step recommended by Conant was to close down small high schools and consolidate secondary districts. The costly side effects of creating mass high schools were disregarded in our rush down this newest path to salvation. As for the curriculum, Conant confined himself to certain distribution requirements. In social studies, he was willing to suggest three years of courses, but to prescribe only some version of American history for one year and a senior course in the problems of American government. For the third year, he was not sure. He found "widespread dissatisfaction" with world history but did not ask why. Social studies teachers, he reported, "could not think of anything" of value they might teach in a fourth year. Western civilization was not mentioned, nor any particular course content in English or literature. The more talented students should be pressed into science, mathematics, and languages.

As for the rest, Conant (who fifteen years earlier had sponsored the Harvard report) saw no objection to enrolling them in life-adjustment courses, though he did not use that terminology. Indeed, one problem Conant saw in the small high school was that only 15 to 20 percent of the students would be "academically talented" and could profit from "rewardingly advanced courses in mathematics, science and foreign languages as well as general education courses in English and social studies." The "nonacademically talented," the 80 to 85 percent, should "follow vocational goals and develop general interests."[40] And in his later book, *The Education of American Teachers*, he added that at the college level "any prescription of general education is impossible unless one knows at least approximately the vocational aspirations of the group in question."[41] These comments were indicative of the American educational mainstream: no concept of the citizen or the person apart from his level of employment, from his problem-solving slot in society.

The Sputnik scare and the expensive federal efforts to upgrade education for the academically talented left the American high school curriculum for most students untouched, unless one notes the greater ease with which life-adjustment courses could be introduced into the larger high schools created by consolidation. The decline in student enrollments in academic courses continued. Even in the "academic track," only 30 percent of high school graduates completed two years of foreign language in the year 1969–70. When one looks at all tracks, the figure for languages falls to 16 percent, and a sample of 1980 graduates suggests it is under 10 percent. Even with foreign languages left out of calculation, one study shows that only 19.5 percent of high school graduates fulfilled the minimum recommendations of the National Commission on Excellence in *A Nation at Risk,* and the 1980 sample of high schools gives a figure of 13.5 percent.[42] The self-fulfilling prophecy of those who believed the intelligence testers of the early twentieth century has been fulfilled, and worse.

The several reports issued over the past two years tell us much of what is wrong or weak in American schools, but their present-minded, utilitarian tone is not encouraging. Of them all, perhaps the most promising, surely the boldest, is *The Paideia Proposal,* put forth by Mortimer Adler and his associates in the Paideia Group. Its curricular program is the most sweeping: a French-style K–12 sequence of uniform and mainly academic courses for all children, relying heavily on the humanities—the fine arts, literature and drama, history, and foreign languages. *The Paideia Proposal* assumes, as the French have been doing since they opened their secondary schools to all in the 1960s, that neither the crises of the moment nor the influx of new clienteles should lead us to abandon academic content. On the contrary, the more technological society becomes, the more necessary is a liberal education for everyone.[43] The more diverse the population, the more necessary is the transmission by the schools of a shared national culture.

The most demanding of the changes called for by the Paideia authors is a change in teaching methods toward much more active learning—akin to Theodore Sizer's provocative recommendations in *Horace's Compromise.*[44] The humanities, they say, require genuine understanding, not mere exposure or didactic teaching. Schools, especially the high schools, must be substantially restructured and their student/teacher ratios reduced to allow more individualized coaching and more experience in Socratic seminars where students must test their ideas with teachers and peers. There should be more reading, more writing, more speaking, more direct experience in the fine arts. One cannot merely teach "about" the humanities and expect much to happen to the mind of the student. Nor will teachers whose own grasp of a subject remains at the college textbook level be able to foster the development of the necessary depth of understanding in their students. Schools organized differently, teachers and administrators markedly better prepared—even given unanimous agreement, this will take resolution and patience, qualities not often found in the American reformist mentality.

Finally, the Paideia Group's view of the relation between liberal education and democracy is elevating and challenging: At the heart of the multitrack system of public education, the authors say, "lies an abominable discrimination." Democracy demands that the level of general culture for all be raised to a point that clearly *disengages* the quality of people's education from their social origins and expected level of employment. To wait for all occupations to be equally honored is futile, but a democracy is expected to honor equally the persons who hold them.

Chester Finn and Diane Ravitch set the challenge we face:

> The important question for education policymakers—and for those spokesmen, lobbyists, and interest groups that seek to influence them—is whether the regular public schools attended by the vast majority of American youngsters are going to allow the humanities to be scorned and dismissed on the absurd ground that they are elitist, thereby ensuring that they again become the property only of those already most aware of their value and their power.[45]

Surely we can make our argument for humanities education for *all* students in good conscience. The problem is not merely to promote the humanities, to assert solely for the good of our disciplines that Americans must keep in mind all three purposes of education: for work, for public action, for private life. In democracy, the three are inextricably interdependent—the last is the ultimate justification for democracy itself. Herein lies the insight of Cremin's statement with which we began. Unless we strive to educate all of our people to their maximum potential in the humanities, democracy will not be present, it will not be possible, and in time it will not even be necessary.

NOTES

1. Lawrence Cremin, *The Genius of American Education* (New York: Random House, 1965), pp. 46, 47.

2. Ernest Boyer, *High School: A Report of the Carnegie Foundation for the Advancement of Teaching* (New York: Harper & Row, 1983), p. 117.

3. Ernest Gellner, *Nations and Nationalism* (London: Cornell University Press, 1983), pp. 19–38.

4. See E. D. Hirsch, Jr., "Literacy and Formalism," in this volume.

5. Robert T. Fancher, "English Teaching and Humane Culture," in *Against Mediocrity: The Humanities in America's High Schools*, ed. Chester E. Finn, Jr., Diane Ravitch, and Robert T. Fancher (New York: Holmes & Meier, 1984), p. 52.

6. Jacques Natanson and Antoine Prost, *La révolution scolaire* (Paris: Editions Ouvrières, 1963), p. 44.

7. Richard Hofstadter, *Anti-Intellectualism in American Life* (New York: Vintage-Knopf, 1963), p. 159.

8. Louis Bromfield, "The Triumph of the Egghead," *Freeman* 3 (December 1, 1952): 158; quoted in Hofstadter, p. 9.

9. Arthur K. Kaledin, *Tocqueville and the Democratic Imagination*, forthcoming.

10. Alexis de Tocqueville, *Democracy in America* (New York: Vintage-Knopf, 1955), vol. 1, p. 7.

11. Jack Lively, *The Social and Political Thought of Alexis de Tocqueville* (Oxford: Clarendon Press, 1965), p. 53.

12. Tocqueville, p. 327.

13. Tocqueville, p. 14.

14. Quoted in Hofstadter, p. viii.

15. Hofstadter, p. 238.

16. William C. McLoughlin, *Modern Revivalism: Charles Grandison Finney to Billy Graham* (New York: Ronald Press, 1959), pp. 118–20; quoted in Hofstadter, p. 94.

17. John F. Latimer, *What's Happened to Our High Schools?* (Washington, D.C.: Public Affairs Press, 1958), pp. 21–34.

18. Hofstadter, pp. 330, 331.

19. Latimer, p. 116.

20. Hofstadter, p. 333.

21. Hofstadter, p. 334.

22. Hofstadter, p. 323.

23. Thomas James and David Tyack, "Learning from Past Efforts to Reform the High School," *Phi Delta Kappan* 64 (1983): 400–406.

24. Hofstadter, p. 339.

25. Marvin Lazerson, Judith Block McLaughlin, Bruce McPherson, and Stephen K. Bailey, *An Education of Value* (Cambridge: Cambridge University Press), forthcoming.

26. Latimer, pp. 119ff.

27. Lawrence Cremin, *The Transformation of the School: Progressivism in American Education, 1876–1957* (New York: Alfred Knopf, 1961).

28. Cremin, *Transformation*, p. 388.

29. Cremin, *Transformation*, p. 375.

30. Cremin, *Genius*, pp. 50, 51.

31. Cremin, *Genius*, p. 46.

32. Cremin, *Transformation*, p. 334.

33. Cremin, *Transformation*, p. 336.

34. Hofstadter, p. 344.

35. Richard H. Powers, *The Dilemma of Education in a Democracy* (Chicago: Regnery Gateway, 1984), pp. 14–16.

36. The summary of Prosser's views in Hofstadter, p. 347, comes from Charles Prosser's Inglis Lecture at Harvard University in 1939.

37. *General Education in a Free Society: Report of the Harvard Committee* (Cambridge, Massachusetts: Harvard University Press, 1948), pp. 98–100.

38. Tocqueville, II, 44.

39. James Bryant Conant, *The American High School Today: A First Report to Interested Citizens* (New York: McGraw-Hill, 1959), p. xii.

40. Conant, *American*, pp. 58, 78.

41. James Bryant Conant, *The Education of American Teachers* (New York: McGraw-Hill, 1963), p. 85.

42. Karl L. Alexander and Aaron M. Pallas, "Curriculum Reform and School Performance," Report No. 347, November 1983, Center for Social Organization of Schools, Johns Hopkins University.

43. Mortimer Adler et al., *The Paideia Proposal* (New York: Macmillan, 1982).

44. Theodore R. Sizer, *Horace's Compromise: The Dilemma of the American High School* (Boston: Houghton Mifflin, 1984).

45. Chester E. Finn, Jr., and Diane Ravitch, "Conclusions and Recommendations," in *Against Mediocrity*, ed. Finn, Ravitch, and Fancher, p. 241.

Literacy and Formalism

E. D. Hirsch, Jr.

Cultural Literacy

We think of a literate person as someone who can understand serious writings addressed to the general public. The imparting of this most practical yet subtle skill is one of the major goals of humanistic education—practical because it is useful for an indefinite number of future tasks, and subtle because of the inherent complexity of reading and writing. I wish to suggest that literacy in this fundamental sense requires not just technical proficiency but also "cultural literacy." What I mean by this term may become clear in a provisional way as I describe a recent experience.

A few years ago, I was conducting some experiments at the University of Virginia to measure the effectiveness of a piece of writing when it is read by ordinary audiences.[1] We were measuring the actual effects of writing rather than mere opinions of its quality. Our readers in the experiment (who were mainly university students) performed just as we expected them to as long as we kept the topics simple and familiar. Then, one memorable day we transferred our experiments from the

47

university to a community college, and my complacency about adult literacy was forever shattered. This community college was located in Richmond, Virginia, and the irony of the location will appear in a moment. Our first experiments went well, because we began by giving the students a paper to read on the topic of friendship. When reading about friendship these young men and women showed themselves to be, on the average, just as literate as university students. The evidence showed that, based on the usual criteria of speed and accurate recall, the community college and university groups were equally skilled readers. But that evidence changed with the next piece of writing we asked them to read. It was a comparison of the characters of Ulysses S. Grant and Robert E. Lee, and the students' performance on that task was, to be blunt, illiterate. Our results showed that Grant and Lee were simply not familiar names to these young adults in the capital of the Confederacy.

Shortly after that disorienting experience, I discovered that Professor Richard Anderson of the Center for Reading Research at the University of Illinois and other researchers in psycholinguistics had reached firm conclusions about the importance of background knowledge in reading.[2] For instance, in one experiment Anderson and his colleagues discovered that an otherwise literate audience in India could not properly read a simple text about an American wedding. But, by the same token, an otherwise literate audience in America could not properly read a simple text about an Indian wedding. Why not? It wasn't a matter of vocabulary or phonics or word recognition: it was a matter of *cultural* literacy. Anderson and others showed that to read a text with understanding one needs to have the background knowledge that the author has tacitly assumed the reader to have. This tacit knowledge is fundamental to literacy. Back in the eighteenth century, when mass literacy was beginning to be a reality in Great Britain, Dr. Johnson invoked a personage whom he called "the common reader." In present-day America, the common reader needs to have cultural literacy in order to read diverse materials with understanding.

To illustrate the dependency of literacy on cultural literacy, I shall quote a recent snippet from the *Washington Post*:

> A federal appeals panel today upheld an order barring foreclosure on a Missouri farm, saying that U.S. Agriculture Secretary John R. Block has reneged on his responsibilities to some debt-ridden farmers. The appeals panel directed the USDA to create a system of processing loan deferments and of publicizing them as it said Congress had intended. The panel said that it is the responsibility of the agriculture secretary to carry out this intent "not as a private banker, but as a public broker."[3]

Imagine that item being read by persons who have been trained to read but are as culturally illiterate as were my community college students. They might possibly know words like *foreclosure,* but they would surely not understand the text as a whole. Who gave the order that the federal panel upheld? What is a federal appeals panel? Even if culturally illiterate readers bothered to look up individual words, they would not have much idea of the reality being referred to. Nor, in reading other texts, would they understand references to such things as, say, the equal protection clause or Robert E. Lee, no matter how well they could read a text on friendship. But a truly literate American does understand references to the equal protection of the laws and Robert E. Lee, and newspaper reports like the one I just quoted. As a practical matter, newspaper reporters and writers of books cannot possibly provide detailed background information on every occasion. Think, if they did, how much added information would be needed even in the short item that I quoted from the *Washington Post.* Every sentence would need a dozen sentences of explanation! And each of those sentences would need a dozen more.

Thomas Jefferson said that he would prefer newspapers without government to government without newspapers. He thought that the very concept of American democracy, depending as it does on all citizens having a vote, requires an informed citizenry and universal literacy. He thought that literate, well-informed citizens would be able, more often than not, to make decisions in their collective best interest. Under Jefferson's principles, the background information that an American citizen needs in order to be truly literate would be the information required to read with understanding serious American newspapers, magazines, and books addressed to the general literate public. This background knowledge would include not only social, linguistic, and literary conventions, but "political literacy" and "historical literacy" and also "scientific and technical literacy." These subliteracies taken together constitute what I call cultural literacy.

One reason that we as a nation have hesitated to make a collective decision about the background knowledge that Americans should have in order to be literate is that we object to such decisions being dictated to us from on high. We govern our schools through more than sixteen thousand independent school districts, each of which decides or fails to decide such matters for itself, and each of which imposes or fails to impose its decisions on students and teachers. But despite this diversity in our schools, there is an unstated body of information that is nonetheless assumed by most writers of books, magazines, training manuals, and newspapers. These writers work with an idea of what their audiences can be expected to know. They assume, they must assume, a "common reader" who knows the things that are known by other literate persons in the culture.

When I say that these writers must assume such background knowledge, I am affirming a fact about language use that sociolinguists and psycholinguists have known for twenty years: the explicit words of a text are just the tip of the iceberg in a linguistic transaction. In order to understand even the surface of a text, a reader must have the sort of background knowledge that was assumed, for example, in the *Washington Post* report that I quoted. Besides this topic-determined knowledge, the reader needs to know less explicit and less topic-defined matters, such as culturally shared attitudes, values, conventions, and connotations that the writer assumes the reader to have. The writer cannot start from ground zero, even in a children's reader designed for the first grade. The subtlety and complexity of written communication is directly dependent upon a shared background. Moreover, cultural literacy is needed not just for general-interest topics, but also for specialized and technical topics like those dealt with in textbooks and training manuals. Paradoxically, the fastest and best way for any culture to adjust to new developments in technology is for its members to be culturally literate.[4] In a rapidly changing world, narrow technological literacy may be short-lived.

To an ill-informed adult who is unaware of what literate persons are expected to know, the assumption by writers that their readers possess cultural literacy could be regarded as a conspiracy of the literate against the illiterate for the purpose of keeping them out of the club. Although newspaper reporters, writers of books, and the framers of the verbal SAT necessarily make assumptions about the things literate persons know, no one ever announces what that body of information is. So, although we Americans object to pronouncements about what we all should know, there *is* a body of information that literate people do know. And this creates a kind of silent de facto dictating from on high about the things adults should know in order to be truly literate.

Our silence about the explicit contents of cultural literacy leads to the following result, observable in the sociology of the verbal SAT. This exam is chiefly a vocabulary test, which, except for its omission of proper names and other concrete information, constitutes a test of cultural literacy.[5] Hence, when young people from deprived backgrounds ask how they can acquire the verbal abilities tested on the verbal SAT, they are told, quite correctly under present circumstances, that the only way to acquire that knowledge is through wide reading in many domains over many years. That is advice that deprived students already in high school are not in a position to take. Thus there remains a strong correlation between the verbal SAT score and socioeconomic status. Students from middle-class and upper-middle-class backgrounds get their knowledge for the verbal SAT not just from reading, but through the pores, from talk at home and social chitchat. I am the more confident that the task of disadvantaged students could be eased and given direction when I consider how tenuous and vague is much of the background knowledge that literate people actually possess. I shall illustrate that highly important point with a reminiscence.

Some decades ago there appeared in Britain a charming book called *1066 and All That.*[6] It dealt with facts of British history that had been learned by every British schoolchild, but which had become scrambled and confused in the adult mind. The book was hilarious to Britons, because their memories were not quite so vague and scrambled as the versions of history represented in the book. They knew all too well that their school knowledge had become vague with the passage of time. Of course, this forgetting of minor details didn't make them less literate than they had been as children. Background information of the sort needed for true literacy is neither detailed nor expert information, though it is usually accurate in its outlines.

For instance, to understand the *Washington Post* snippet that I quoted, literate readers would know in the backs of their minds that the American legal system allows a judgment at a lower level to be reversed at a higher level. They would know that a judge can tell the executive branch what it can or cannot do to farmers and other citizens, and they would know a lot more that is relevant. But none of their knowledge would have to be highly detailed. They wouldn't need to know, for instance, whether an appeals panel is the final level before the Supreme Court. In general, readers need to share a cloudy but still accurate sense of the *realities* that are being referred to in a piece of writing. This allows them to make the necessary associations.

The Historical Tradition of Teaching Cultural Literacy

Let me briefly place what I have been saying in a historical perspective. According to the analysis of Ernest Gellner in his fine book, *Nations and Nationalism*, only with the emergence of modern industrial nations has universal literacy become necessary or even possible.[7] In the agrarian societies that preceded the industrial states, literacy was largely monopolized by "a specialized clerical class or estate, a clerisy." This class of literate specialists represented one of several clearly delineated social strata constituting the privileged minority. The majority of the members of agrarian society were agricultural producers, living in small, almost completely self-contained communities. There, education was most often a matter of learning a skill through local, on-the-job training. With little opportunity for social advancement or mobility, literacy and cultural sophistication were unnecessary. In addition, as Gellner points out, universal literacy in an agrarian society was a practical impossibility. The stability of agrarian society lay in the maintenance of clear divisions between the privileged classes and the masses of the people, and among the strata of the privileged minority themselves. The direct contact between the clerisy and the rural townspeople that would have been required for the transmission of literacy skills ran counter to this principle of stability. It would have required either the dispersal of a large number of clerics into the countryside, thereby jeopardizing their relationship with the power-holding classes in the cities, or the movement of large numbers of townspeople into the cities, which would have been economically destabilizing. The spread of literacy and a common culture to the masses would await radical changes in the traditional structure of agrarian society.

Such radical changes accompanied the rise of the industrial state. Literacy became a necessary characteristic of the work force. Along with economic growth came the need and the opportunity for the worker to move from place to place, facilitating the "homogenization" of national culture. In the eighteenth century, as the nation-state began taking its modern form, national written languages were deliberately stabilized and were required to be taught in the schools. Throughout Europe, reading and writing in the national languages began to be taught more widely than ever before. Indeed, the modern national state could not have come into existence without standardized national written languages and compulsory schooling in literate national cultures.[8] All modern nations have depended upon this common linguistic-cultural core. With the advent of the industrial revolution and large nation states, the ability to learn new things through reading became an ever-more-desirable educational goal. Indeed, Gellner defines this ability as the central requirement of industrial society:

> Universal literacy and a high level of numerical, technical and general sophistication are among its functional prerequisites. Its members are and must be mobile, and ready to shift from one activity to another, and must possess that generic training which enables them to follow the manuals and instructions of a new activity or occupation. In the course of their work they must constantly communicate with a large number of other men, with whom they frequently have no previous association, and with whom communication must consequently be explicit, rather than relying on context. They must also be able to communicate by means of written, impersonal, context-free, to-whom-it-may-concern type mes-

sages. Hence these communications must be in the same shared and standardized linguistic medium and script.[9]

Such apparent exceptions to this principle as Switzerland and Belgium are small countries where multilingualism has been carefully counterbalanced by intensive educational systems that ensure shared knowledge and a high level of biliteracy. (Biliteracy is to be carefully distinguished from so-called bilingualism.) The effective functioning of every modern nation depends upon a national educational system that fosters a national literate culture associated with a national written language.

In short, language making and culture making are artifices that have necessarily accompanied the making of large modern nations. On this point I shall quote briefly from the distinguished Russian sociolinguist M. M. Guxman, whose comments strongly support those of Gellner:

One should not separate the formation of a literary language from the activity of normative theoreticians, from the creation of normative grammars and first dictionaries, or from the activity of language societies, academies, etc. The negative sides of this normalization in the history of individual languages are widely known. . . . The normalization of the language in 16th- and 17th-century Italy or France was of interest, undoubtedly, to a relatively narrow social stratum. . . . However, . . . the formation of a new type of literary language . . . is impossible without conscious normalization, without theoretical comprehension of the norm and codification of definite rules of pronunciation, usage, and inflection.[10]

In our country, Noah Webster's language publications, which started in 1783 and culminated in the great American *Dictionary of the English Language* of 1828, were declarations of cultural and linguistic independence that reflected our political independence and our nationhood. Webster was the George Washington of American education. He was shrewdly conscious of the connections between language making, culture making, and nation making. Because of Webster and other educators who thought as he did, schooling in America has been a repository not only of our national language, but also of our national traditions and values. The connections between language, schooling, culture, and nationhood were understood not just by Webster, but by Herman Melville and William McGuffey and many, many others. They recognized that our dependence upon the common school was even greater in this heterogeneous country than in the nations of Europe.

So much by way of a brief sketch of some relations between the rise of national languages, cultural literacy, and literacy. The patriotic instinct that prompted the teaching of shared national materials was in concord with what we now know to be the technical requirements for communication by means of national languages. But before turning to the evidence for this technical claim, I shall mention a recent educational tendency that has opposed these historical patterns of education.

The Rise of Formalism

In contrast to the early American practice of imparting nationally shared traditions along with instruction in reading and writing, we encounter today the practice of teaching literacy as a set of technical skills.[11] One must grant that in the first stages of literacy, in phonics, and so on, there is just enough truth in the idea that literacy is a set of transferable skills to make this content-neutral, basic-skills approach a respectable theory to hold. But the present state of education raises the question of the wisdom of making this change of approach. In earlier days, American educators consciously connected teaching the technical skills of phonics and spelling with the teaching of background knowledge, i.e., with the acculturative side of teaching literacy. But in our day, after fifty years of the basic-skills approach, and despite the advances we have made in reading research and educating the disadvantaged, we find a decline in SAT scores and an apparent increase in cultural fragmentation.

The notion that reading and writing are generalized skills has been an attractive theory in many countries, but especially in the United States. Such educational formalism has served the American ideal of practical efficiency. What could be more efficient than to learn a habitual skill that can be transferred to an indefinite number of future tasks? Another attraction of educational formalism has been its concord with the characteristic American ideals of diversity and pluralism. What could be more democratic and federalist than to leave the actual *contents* of teaching up to our diverse local districts? And since *any* appropriate content will serve to teach the skills of reading and writing, there is no reason to do otherwise. This theory of instruction has recently dominated not only reading and writing courses, but literature courses as well.

It should be added that the basic-skills approach has also been a safe theory to hold. Specialists in reading and writing who espouse it feel impelled to avoid commitment to any value stance other than assent to pluralism. They present themselves as technicians whose domain of expertise lies outside the realm of concern of those who worry about the values informing the content of the teaching materials.

This posture of neutral expertness is nowhere better illustrated than in the official curriculum guides of certain states (California is an example), which mention no specific contents at all.

Educational formalism is a powerful position, not because it is true, for cognitive psychology has discovered that it contains far less truth than meets the eye. It is powerful because it is highly attractive to public school teachers and administrators who must cope with the genuine political difficulties of curricular choices in our contentious and heterogeneous land. Educational formalism lends the reassurance that nothing significant is lost if we decide to omit traditional literary works that have proved controversial or difficult to teach. For the chief aim of schooling is to impart skills, and we can impart these through any appropriate materials.

This formalistic account of reading and writing instruction, with its emphasis on "how to" principles, is based on a psychological premise that educators used to call "the transfer of training" but, now that that theory is defunct, this transfer is assumed without being given any name at all. Under this formalistic approach, an acquired skill in performing a task in one domain, such as chemistry, is thought to be transferred to a skill in the methods of another domain like biology, even when the *specific* tasks do not overlap. Students are thus taught "scientific and critical thinking." This is the idea, for example, behind the doctrine that a student should be required to take a laboratory science in order to become acquainted with "scientific method." The same transfer principle is thought to hold for teaching reading in different domains, since skill in reading about sports can be transferred to other reading tasks, such as reading about a federal appeals panel. But no well-informed cognitive psychologist would today accept this formalistic theory of learning. Recent work has shown that every acquired skill is knowledge-based and task-specific and cannot be transferred to a substantially different task. This means that there is no substitute in education for the specific background information I have been calling cultural literacy.

I should not wish anyone to take these strictures against the transfer of training as favoring the utilitarian or antihumanistic impulses in American education that led to formalism in the first place. It is an irony of our current situation that arguments *against* the transfer of training were used by "progressivist" American educators to encourage a utilitarian curriculum that excluded many materials belonging to cultural literacy.[12] They successfully argued, for instance, that the study of Latin does not contribute to the skills needed by the citizen of a large, modern, industrial state. Since training is not transferred, they reasoned, the skills developed in learning Latin would not really help

American students with the skills of English. Latin should therefore be replaced by something that students would directly need.

Proponents of this view did not notice that their own theory of teaching reading and writing skills was itself based on an especially radical version of the transfer of training—the theory that skill in reading or writing about one subject will transfer as skill in reading or writing about other subjects! This baseless, content-free theory of the transfer of training underlay the whole movement of utilitarianism and formalism in education. By contrast, the more modest idea that things learned in studying Latin, such as the reality of cases and tenses, would help students learn those *very same* things about English does not involve some illicit inference about transfer. Indeed, claims for the value of a broad humanistic education need not always be as vague, general, and pious as they typically are. A broad humanistic education has a very great and direct utility in helping students to read and write. Quite aside from its other values, humanistic education has a superior utility because it teaches the *content* of a shared culture. Knowledge of that shared content is a necessary component of the skills of reading and writing within a culture.

I shall now briefly describe some of the recent research that has contravened some of the key assumptions of educational formalism.

Literacy and Background Knowledge

In the preceding section I argued that educational formalism neglects the cultural dimension of reading and writing. It draws a picture of those activities that omits the huge domain of tacit knowledge which, though never written down and quite invisible, is just as operative as the visible written word. A reading or writing task could be compared to an iceberg whose visible tip is arrangement, syntax, rhetoric, spelling, and the like, but whose much bigger submerged base is tacit cultural knowledge. By this is meant not just linguistic and topic knowledge, but also knowledge of what others know and expect about the topic, the genre, the writer, the world. Although it is hard to overestimate the importance of this tacit cultural dimension in the teaching of literacy, psychological researchers have begun to attend to it only recently. In the late 1960s, psychologists rediscovered that verbal memory was for gist rather than for form, and that the gist that was remembered depended on tacit, unspoken knowledge of the world.[13]

In 1972, Bransford, Barclay, and Franks published results of a very simple, linguistically primitive experiment whose implications were far-reaching.[14] The research turned on whether we perceive what a sentence *says,* or what it *entails* in conjunction with our extralinguistic assumptions about the world. One of the experiments used the following two sentences:

1. Three turtles rested on a floating log, and a fish swam beneath them.
2. Three turtles rested on a floating log, and a fish swam beneath it.

Half of the subjects were given sentence 1, and half sentence 2, along with appropriate control sentences. But in recognition tests, all subjects simply identified whichever sentence they were shown as the one they had previously seen. Psychologically, the two sentences were absolutely identical. That the fish were under the turtles as well as under the log was assumed to be *stated* by the sentence, even though in one case that was not so stated. Such results surprise nobody, but they remind us how far world knowledge saturates the linguistic transaction.

A variation on this principle is provided by experiments that measure the prolixity and concision of language users. Whenever there is a paucity of shared background information between interlocutors, the linguistic code itself must be made more elaborate and explicit if communication is to be secured. I presented a hypothetical case of this in my comment about how the *Washington Post* snippet would have to be written for people who lack the background knowledge assumed by the reporter. The piece would have to be many times as long as the original. More significantly, the loss in concision would also bring loss in coherence, subtlety, and the attitudinal meanings that can be conveyed by irony, humor, and allusion.

We all act on this principle instinctively in our everyday speech, and adjust what we say accordingly. The following sociolinguistic experiment was undertaken by a clever undergraduate psychology major at Harvard.[15] He goes out into the streets of Cambridge with a tape recorder hidden in his jacket. He is dressed like a native and has a copy of the *Boston Globe* under his arm. He affects a strong Boston accent when he speaks the following words to passersby: "How d'ya get to Central Square?" The length of the average reply to this question consists of just seven words.

The next day, the undergraduate goes back to the Cambridge streets in a different get-up. He prefaces his question about Central Square with the statement, "I'm from out of town." (Later on he discovers that he can get the same results just by signaling his out-of-townness by speaking with a Missouri accent.) In this second phase, the passerby typically pauses to answer the question about Central Square by saying:

"Yes, you go down those stairs into the subway. You take the train headed for Quincy, but you get off very soon, just the first stop is Central Square, and be sure you get off there. You'll know it because there's a big sign on the wall. It says 'Central Square,' and . . ."

In the same *Scientific American* article, Glucksberg and Kraus report on other experiments in which mature speakers recognize how they must adjust their prolixity to the knowledge they assume their hearers to have. The work of Basil Bernstein on "elaborated" and "restricted" codes is closely related to this theme of the dependency of communication upon relevant prior information.[16] And the theme is further confirmed in the work of Dooling and Lachman,[17] Anderson and Pichert,[18] and Hasher and Griffen.[19] A full account of the research on shared knowledge and its relation to literacy can be found in the seven chapters of the section entitled "Language, Knowledge of the World, and Inference" in *Theoretical Issues in Reading Comprehension.*[20] Although the details of this research, with a full account of current processing models, would be out of place here, perhaps enough has already been said to indicate the consistency of the results obtained, and the general agreement among psycholinguists about the crucial importance of tacitly shared background information in reading and writing. Even more embarrassing to educational formalism is the apparent dependence of *all* acquired skills on such specific background information.

The Transfer of Training

In 1946 a Dutch psychologist, Adriaan de Groot, published a voluminous book called *Het Denken van den Schaker*, later published in English in 1965 as *Thought and Choice in Chess.*[21] Although de Groot had been chiefly concerned with the thought processes that distinguished the skills of chess masters from the skills of mere experts and novices, he made a passing discovery that, while tangential to his inquiry, seemed to most later psychologists to be its most significant result. In the course of his experiments, de Groot asked his subjects to reproduce a midgame chess position that they had looked at for about six seconds. The masters performed this feat flawlessly, and the experts well, with about 70 percent accuracy, but the novices did poorly. Had the chess masters developed their memory skills for positions on the chessboard?

To test this hypothesis, de Groot performed the following experiment. He arranged the chess pieces on the board in somewhat random positions, such as would not occur in a real game. He then exposed the three groups to the positions as before. And he discovered that all the groups—masters, experts, and novices—performed equally poorly. That is, all performed as novices. The grand masters had *not* developed a general or formal memory skill for remembering chessboard arrangements. Their skill was rigorously restricted to certain types of chess positions that appeared in actual games of chess and was not transferred to other domains, even nearby domains involving chessmen and chessboards.

A similar experiment with pattern recognition skills was conducted with physicians by Norman, Jacoby, Feightner, and Campbell.[22] They, too, used subjects whose expert skills were unequally developed: practicing physicians, third-year residents, first-year residents, and second-year medical students. Four medical histories were presented to these groups. Two of the case histories were based on common diseases, but the other two were not based on any known disease. The subjects were asked in each case to set down what they remembered from the histories. As de Groot's results would suggest, the recollections of the real case histories were more fully detailed with experienced doctors, and so on, down through the groups in the predictable order, whereas with the unrealistic case histories, the performances of all groups was equally poor. This result, quite analogous to de Groot's, again showed that a skill in one domain is not transferred to a closely neighboring domain, but it may be transferred to novel situations *within* a domain. What, then, is the nature of an acquired skill?

The various real chess positions in de Groot's experiments had never been seen before by the masters who reproduced them perfectly. Hence the chess masters were not simply remembering past games that they had spent many hours with, and could therefore reproduce. They had never seen these positions before. Clearly, their superior performance was indeed in some very limited way a transferable skill, for their perfect performance was based upon their experience of past chess positions that were not exactly duplicated in de Groot's experiment. But some *aspects* of the de Groot positions undoubtedly were repeated from past experience, and this allowed the masters to reproduce the positions without overloading their short-term memory capacity. Hence the chess masters must have acquired an *intermediate* knowledge system that lies somewhere between memory of particulars, and a purely formal, transferable skill. This in-between knowledge has been given various names, depending on its function—"schema," "frame," "script"—but there is virtually unanimous agreement among present-day psychologists that this intermediate knowledge is the locus of our "skills," and that it lies at the center of educational psychology.

Schemata, then, are content-bound and domain-specific. They are tied to particular past information, to exemplary knowledge, and to model instances. The way we reconstruct meaning in reading and writing is tied to specific algorithms for specific sorts of content. This is well covered in Anderson's comprehensive essay, "The Notion of

Schemata and the Educational Enterprise."[23] Although schemata are sometimes rather vague, they allow the mind to reconstruct a domain as needed, even though only a small tip of the domain might be attended to at a given moment. Without these specific schemata, often represented by specific words and always based on the contents of past experience, we could not develop effective "skills." The very concept of a skill, when viewed in psychological terms, requires content; skills make no use of empty, transferable forms.

Thus, the educational aim that is represented by the term *cultural literacy* could be conceived psychologically as the development of the schemata of literacy. These would be the schemata shared by the literate persons of the community and consisting especially of those content-bound schemata represented by specific words, including proper names. These cultural schemata, though often quite vague, have enough available substance, based on past information and experience, to serve as available counters for meaningful reconstruction in reading and writing. Without such specific, content-bound schemata available in the backs of our minds, effective reading and writing cannot take place. It follows that our schools should encourage the development of the specific shared schemata that are necessary for genuine literacy at the present time, through the study of literature, history, language, and art, as well as math and science.

Possible Objections

I have outlined some historical and technical grounds for exposing students to a common core of information (though not necessarily a common curriculum) in the elementary and secondary schools. Indeed, the goal of cultural literacy does not imply a specific curriculum, since the information it embraces is more extensive than any curriculum could cover in detail. A lot of the information in cultural literacy is quite sketchy and superficial.

Yet if some of the material taught in the schools is not to be studied in detail, would that not be an invitation to vagueness and superficiality in teaching? This objection is well taken and should be faced openly. I have already alluded to the sketchiness of the information that people in a culture can be relied on to share. One might well take the view that to teach no information would be better than to teach sketchy, superficial material. But such a conclusion would betray too quixotic a conception of the way culture and language work. Much of our linguistic understanding is extremely hazy and superficial. As Hilary Putnam pointed out in his brilliant essay, "The Meaning of Meaning," we all operate on the principle of "the division of linguistic labor":[24] we rely on others to give us more exact or deeper knowledge of the reference of words, when and if we have need of such deeper knowledge. Indeed, most writers and speakers supply additional detail as necessary.

A more serious objection to making explicit the specific contents of cultural literacy is that our culture might be better off if its shared knowledge were left implicit and vague. To give authority to any *listing* of canonical information would be to fix the canon arbitrarily and unnecessarily, whereas when shared knowledge is allowed to develop by itself, the culture could grow flexibly and embrace all sorts of valuable elements that might be excluded if cultural literacy were explicitly defined. Again, there is truth in this objection, but it is a partial truth. In my brief historical excursus, I tried to show that large national cultures have always been conscious artifacts and cannot exist without self-conscious nurture. This fact has been known and acted on in our country from its earliest days. As recently as the teens and twenties of this century, Baker and Thorndike, the editors of our then most popular school readers, *The Everyday Classics* series, did not forbear to write,

> We have chosen what is common, established, almost proverbial; what has become indisputably "classic," what, in brief, every child in the land ought to know, because it is good and because other people know it. The educational worth of such material calls for no defense. In an age when the need of socializing and unifying our people is keenly felt, the value of a common stock of knowledge, a common set of ideals is obvious. A people is best unified by being taught in childhood the best things in its intellectual and moral heritage. Our own heritage is, like our ancestry, composite. Hebrew, Greek, Roman, English, French, and Teutonic elements are blended in our cultural past. We draw freely from all these. An introduction to the best of this is one of our ways of making good citizens.[25]

But even if my historical observations about the self-conscious culture-making element in our educational tradition should be granted, one might still object that there is much to be said against this tradition. And so there is. But the claims of the counter traditions of pluralism, antiethnocentricity, and diversity have a variable urgency, depending on the times. Recently these pluralistic counterclaims have been in the ascendency and have swung the pendulum rather far. The American public (and I as a part of it) have begun to feel that a corrective, Baker-and-Thorndike sort of impulse in the schools is overdue, and that our culture would benefit from such a corrective impulse.

Another objection to specifying the contents of cultural literacy is that no person or committee may arrogate the authority to set forth the central, canonical contents of our culture. To this I reply that the setting forth of these contents is not primarily prescriptive but descriptive. These central contents already exist in the memories of the literate public. There is remarkable agreement, for instance, that the Emancipation Proclamation belongs to the canonical core, while "bleeding Kansas" does not. We have discovered that the theoretical debate over the issue of arrogating cultural authority is a false issue, a theoretical dispute. In actual practice one finds remarkable agreement. The only people who are not parties to the large area of agreement about the canonical core are the nonliterate, the educationally and culturally disadvantaged. The doctrine of pluralism, which resists any definition of our cultural canon, is in effect a doctrine of exclusion rather than of broad inclusion, a principle for keeping nonliterate people out of the club.

Of greater merit than these pluralistic objections to the project of defining our cultural literacy is the fear of premature ossification. This is a reasonable fear but, again, an abstract one. Anyone who works even a few months inquiring into this subject discovers that large domains of cultural literacy always belong to the rather recent past and this share can never be fixed. As time goes on, only a very few temporally distant elements get deposited in our collective memory. For example, since the Dred Scott case, the only Supreme Court decision that belongs to the core of our collective memory is Brown v. Board of Education. At the periphery, the contents of cultural literacy are being continually revised and updated.

To those who fear that imparting common information in the schools might further solidify an already dominant, white Anglo-Saxon Protestant male culture, my reply is that the various movements that have been resisting such cultural dominance have been working reasonably effectively and will continue to do so. But there is something adamantine about the Three Little Pigs, Little Red Riding Hood, Betsy Ross, and George Washington. Certainly some of those mythic figures can gradually be replaced by others, and such gradual change is always occurring. But those who believe that such matters can be arranged by an ideological fiat or whim are well advised to read Edward Shils's profound recent book, Tradition.[26]

Conclusion

In conclusion I want to stress again the danger that educational formalism poses for the advancement of literacy. The real peril of educational formalism is that, although it is fundamentally wrong, and although it has proved unfruitful in the real world, it remains an extraordinarily attractive theory. Thirty-eight years after de Groot's classic results on the nontransferability of skills, results that continue to be confirmed in every domain in which they are tested, most educators still hold fast to the idea that schools should teach "the basic skills that train for life." But, in fact, the only skills that train for life are those knowledge-based activities that continue specifically to be used in life. Reading and writing, of course, continue to be used. Everyone knows they are absolutely central to productive membership in our society and to the ability to acquire new knowledge-based skills when needed. Reading and writing at the high levels required for such future flexibility are skills that are based on a large, complex system of world knowledge that I have called cultural literacy. Imparting this knowledge to our students, through the study of the humanities and the sciences, is the chief responsibility of our educational system.

We all know that our continuing failure to achieve a high level of national literacy ensures a continuing lack of subtlety in the communications that are transmitted widely by means of the national language—in speeches, books, and newspapers. Even a training manual can be much more effective and functional if it can assume a readership that is culturally literate. Moreover, we know that a low standard of literacy debases not only the level of general culture, but also the level of political discussion and of technical and economic effectiveness. It affects our ability to accommodate ourselves flexibly to new technological and political challenges. We know that a great deal is at stake in raising the level of national literacy.

But raising the level of adult literacy beyond the elementary stage is not just a matter of raising the level of linguistic skills. Adult literacy is less a system of formal skills than a system of information. What chiefly counts in higher reading competence is the amount of relevant prior knowledge that readers have. This is not a mere ideological sentiment on behalf of a shared national culture, but an empirical truth about literacy that coincides with more general findings about the importance of specific knowledge in the acquisition of all higher skills. This means that adult literacy is a problem that requires decisive leadership at least as much as it requires money. Our illiterate citizens simply do not know the essential background facts and the essential words that represent them. Our schools have not imparted these essential facts and words, because in recent times we have not been willing as a nation to decide what the essential facts and words are. Despite our national virtues of diversity and pluralism, our failure to decide upon the core content of cultural literacy has created a positive barrier to adult literacy in this country, and thus to full citizenship and full acculturation into our society. We Americans need to be decisive and explicit about the background information that a citizen should know in order to be literate in the 1980s. If we were to act decisively to define and promote cultural literacy, then the level of literacy in the nation would rise as a matter of course.

NOTES

1. For a fuller account of these experiments, see E. D. Hirsch, Jr., "Cultural Literacy," *American Scholar* 52 (Spring 1983): 159–69.

2. Richard C. Anderson, Rand J. Spiro, and William E. Montague, *Schooling and the Acquisition of Knowledge* (Hillsdale, N.J.: L. Erlbaum Associates, 1977).

3. *Washington Post,* December 29, 1983: A13.

4. Ernest Gellner, *Nations and Nationalism* (Ithaca, N. Y.: Cornell University Press, 1983), pp. 26–29, 35–38.

5. John B. Carroll, *Learning from Verbal Discourse in Educational Media: A Review of the Literature,* Final Report, Project 7-1069 (Princeton, N. J.: Educational Testing Service, 1971).

6. Walter C. Sellar and Robert J. Yeatman, *1066 and All That: A Memorable History of England, Comprising All the Parts You Can Remember, Including 103 Good Things, 5 Bad Kings and 2 Genuine Dates* (London: Methuen, 1970).

7. Gellner, pp. 19–38.

8. Francois Furet and Jacques Ozouf, *Reading and Writing: Literacy in France from Calvin to Jules Ferry* (Cambridge and New York: Cambridge University Press, 1982).

9. Gellner, p. 35.

10. M. M. Guxman, "Some General Regularities in the Formation and Development of National Languages," in *Readings in the Sociology of Language,* ed. Joshua A. Fishman (The Hague: Mouton, 1968), pp. 773–74.

11. For a discussion of the basic-skills approach to literacy and its implications for the teaching of English, see E. D. Hirsch, Jr., " 'English' and the Perils of Formalism," *American Scholar* 53 (Summer 1984): 369–79.

12. Diane Ravitch, "The Rise and Fall of Progressive Education," in *The Troubled Crusade: American Education, 1945–80* (New York: Basic Books, 1983), pp. 43–80.

13. Samuel Fillenbaum, "Memory for Gist: Some Relevant Variables," *Language and Speech* 9 (1966): 217–27; Jacqueline S. Sachs, "Recognition Memory for Syntactic and Semantic Aspects of Connected Discourse," *Perception and Psychophysics* 2 (1967): 437–42.

14. John D. Bransford, J. Richard Barclay, and Jeffrey J. Franks, "Sentence Memory: A Constructive Versus Interpretive Approach," *Cognitive Psychology* 3 (1972): 193–209.

15. Robert M. Kraus and Sam Glucksberg, "Social and Nonsocial Speech," *Scientific American* 236 (1977): 100–105.

16. Basil Bernstein, "Social Class, Language, and Socialization," in *Language and Social Context: Selected Readings*, ed. Pier Paolo Giglioli (Harmondsworth: Penguin, 1972), pp. 157–78.

17. D. James Dooling and Roy Lachman, "Effects of Comprehension on Retention of Prose," *Journal of Experimental Psychology* 88 (1971): 216–22.

18. Richard C. Anderson and James W. Pichert, "Recall of Previously Unrecallable Information Following a Shift in Perspective," *Journal of Verbal Learning and Verbal Behavior* 17 (1978): 1–12.

19. Lynn Hasher and Mary Griffen, "Reconstructive and Reproductive Processes in Memory," *Journal of Experimental Psychology: Human Learning and Memory* 4 (July 1978): 318–30.

20. Rand J. Spiro, B. C. Bruce, and W. R. Brewer, *Theoretical Issues in Reading Comprehension* (Hillsdale, N. J.: L. Erlbaum Associates, 1980), pp. 245–404.

21. Adriaan de Groot, *Thought and Choice in Chess* (The Hague: Mouton, 1965).

22. G. R. Norman, L. L. Jacoby, J. W. Feightner, and E. J. M. Campbell, "Clinical Experience and the Structure of Memory," in *Proceedings of the Eighteenth Annual Conference on Research in Medical Education* (Washington, D.C.: Association of American Medical Colleges, 1979), pp. 214–18.

23. Richard C. Anderson, "The Notion of Schemata and the Educational Enterprise," in Anderson, Spiro, and Montague, *Schooling and the Acquisition of Knowledge*, pp. 415–31.

24. Hilary Putnam, "The Meaning of Meaning," in *Mind, Language, and Reality: Philosophical Papers* (Cambridge: Cambridge University Press, 1975), II, 215–71.

25. Preface to Fannie W. Dunn, Franklin T. Baker, and Ashley H. Thorndike, *Everyday Classics*, 9 vols. (New York: Macmillan, 1917–22).

26. Edward Shils, *Tradition* (Chicago: University of Chicago Press, 1981).

The Humanities and Our Cultural Heritage

Stephan Thernstrom

The French government recently carried out a study of what sixth-grade students in the state schools had learned. One result this inquiry turned up was that only two-thirds of the youngsters could accurately date the outbreak of the French Revolution of 1789. President Mitterand declared that he was "scandalized" and "anguished" at this finding and asked for major reforms in history teaching at every level of education in order to overcome "the loss of a collective memory in the young generation."[1]

What strikes an American observer—at least this one—is not that *only* two-thirds of French youths knew that elemental fact of their national history at such a tender age, but that *as many as* two-thirds did so. I know of no comparable studies of American students. But I would be surprised if two-thirds of this country's twelve-year-olds could date the Declaration of Independence or the beginning of the Civil War. Indeed, I am not altogether sure that two-thirds of American *twelfth-graders* have that much "collective memory" anymore. A recent survey of southern California teenagers revealed an ignorance of the past—and of the present, for that matter—that was truly staggering.[2] Not one of these golden youths could identify Vladimir Ilyich Lenin, for example; one suggested tentatively that he was "the drummer with the Beatles before Ringo Starr." One student had somehow attained the junior year in college without absorbing the information that the United States and Japan had once been at war with each other. Her curiosity piqued, she asked the interviewer, "Who won?" In Peter DeVries's recent novel, *Slouching Towards Kalamazoo*, set in the late 1950s, one minor character is described as being so dim that he entered high school thinking that the French and Indian War was a contest between the French and the Indians. Perhaps that was a true sign of cultural retardation among youths of that era, as DeVries suggests, but I do not believe that it is any longer a noteworthy deviation from the norm.

The Erosion of Historical Knowledge in Our Schools

A full analysis of why American young people's grasp of their history and cultural heritage is so appallingly weak today is a task beyond the scope of a brief essay. Hence I propose only to volunteer a few impressions that may advance the discussion of what we are doing right and what wrong. I certainly do not think that the explanation is simply that the schools today have fallen away from a standard of excellence in teaching that they once enjoyed or that a revamping of what we teach and how we teach to conform to past practices will yield dramatic improvements. My own experience, and that of others with whom I have conferred, make me doubt that the schools have become markedly worse in the past generation or two, and I am quite skeptical about the nostalgia with which some commentators now view the education they purportedly received when they were young. All of which is not to say that the schools cannot be improved. But I am suspicious of some of the conventional wisdom concerning the decline and fall of American schools.

Some of the trouble has to do with features of our society that the schools by themselves can do little or nothing about. One example is the chilling fact that our children now spend twenty-five hours a week staring somnolently at a television set. When I was a boy, most of us got our weekly entertainment at the Saturday afternoon double feature. Today's youths watch the equivalent of a double feature every school day and *three* double features over the weekend. If you hold, as I do, to the belief that many important things can be learned only by reading, you can only conclude that this pattern of time use by our children poses the gravest of challenges to humanistic learning—indeed to all learning. At a time when the impulse is running strong to kick the teacher because Johnny can't read, it must be said firmly that teachers are not to blame for this enormous waste of time. Only parents can slay, or even leash, the one-eyed dragon in our midst.

Another constraint on our ability to transmit a grasp of our cultural heritage to the young lies in the realm of public understanding of the purposes of education. I have in mind the narrowly utilitarian or technocratic view that the point of schooling is to prepare students to get a good job. On this view, math, science, and, these days, computer programming are what really matter, and for the less academically inclined, mechanical drawing and shop courses; history, literature, and foreign languages, by comparison, are mere frills. The spread of this belief during a time of taxpayers' revolts and increasing uncertainty about the economic future probably accounts for the fact that history and social studies instructors made up 15 percent of all high school teachers in 1966 but less than 11 percent in 1981.[4] The decline in the number of foreign language teachers—and course enrollments—is even more severe. Cost-conscious administrators, themselves barely schooled in the humanities, find it difficult to defend the market value of the humanities when they are pressed to defend their budgetary requests.

The pressure that the public's presumed obsession with job preparation puts on school decision makers represents a serious challenge to the future of the humanities in the school curriculum. But the pressure can be countered by school practitioners and administrators, as well as by parents and other concerned citizens, who will stoutly defend the necessary role of the humanities in the education of young people. I agree with Paul Gagnon that the aim of education is not merely to equip people for good jobs, but to make them better people and better citizens, to help students to learn *how to live* as well as how to earn a living. It is difficult to say this nowadays without feeling self-conscious, but I suspect that most of us believe it. The humanities are the record of the best (and some of the worst) attempts to imagine and embody what it means to live a good life. Jane Austen's novels are not, of course, direct rivals of *Miss Manners' Guide to Excruciatingly Correct Behavior* in the 1980s, but what she has to tell us about the tension between sense and sensibility is just as relevant and a good deal wiser.

Even if one were to concede, for the sake of argument, that vocational preparation is of paramount importance, it is simplistic to think that the technical skills offered in the "hard" disciplines are necessarily much more useful in an occupational sense than the abilities acquired through the study of the "soft" humanities. The British social philosopher, Ernest Gellner, in his absorbing book, *Nations and Nationalism*, offers an analysis of modern society that undermines this widespread but naive view. He tells us that in advanced industrial societies, and even more in the emerging postindustrial society, work "does not mean moving matter":

> Work, in the main, is no longer the manipulation of things, but of meanings. It generally involves exchanging communications with other people, or manipulating the controls of a machine. . . . Most jobs, if not actually involving work "with people," involve the control of buttons or switches or levers which need to be *understood*, and are explicable . . . in some standard idiom intelligible to all comers.[5]

Such a society, Gellner says, requires "sustained, frequent and precise communication between strangers involving a sharing of explicit meaning, transmitted in a standard idiom and in writing."[6] He also asserts that:

> The level of literacy and technical competence, in a standardized medium, a common conceptual currency, which is required of members of this society if they are to be properly employable and enjoy full and effective moral citizenship, is so high that it simply *cannot* be provided by the kin or local units, such as they are. It can only be provided by something resembling a modern "national" educational system.[7]

Gellner does not spell out the curricular implications of his contention that "universal literacy and a high level of numerical, technical and general sophistication" are "functional prerequisites" of the sort of society we live in now.[8] But if E. D. Hirsch, Jr., is right (as I believe he is) that the cultural literacy required by an informed citizenry encompasses knowledge of social, linguistic, and literary conventions, as well as "political literacy," "historical literacy," and "scientific and technical literacy," then a strong case can be made for offering instruction in the humanities to all young Americans. To my mind, the analyses of Gellner and Hirsch justify extensive study of history, English, literature, and foreign languages, including the classical languages. Oliver Wendell Holmes once said that one needn't *know* Latin and Greek to be a gentleman; one need only have *forgotten* them. The same might be said of what makes a good writer, which may explain why the best British historians today seem to express themselves more fluently and gracefully than their American rivals. In sum, even if you see education as investment in human capital, as economists do, it would be well not to take too narrow a view of which particular stocks will pay the greatest dividends, and to consider the possibility that a balanced portfolio will be more profitable in the long run than a large bundle of shares in a single company.

Putting Content Back into History Courses

One indispensable element in such a balanced portfolio is a grasp of history, in particular the history of our civilization and the roots from which it developed. In 1934, the Commission on the Social Sciences of the American Historical Association (AHA) explored the question of what should be taught in secondary schools and called for greater attention to European as well as American history. It made these recommendations:

> The program of social science instruction should provide for a more detailed study of the evolution of Western civilization, emphasis being placed on changing modes of production and distribution, on the succession of social systems, ways of life and ethical conceptions, on the development of democratic ideals and practices, on the accumulation and spread of knowledge and learning, on the advance of science, technology, and invention, on abiding traditions of the unity of Western culture and its growing integration in world culture.

This served for a generation or so as the rationale for most high school social science instruction, as well as for college "Western Civ" courses, once enormously popular but now largely extinct. Today, half a century later, is it a defensible statement of the proper focus of history teaching in the schools? Save perhaps for the emphasis on "abiding traditions of the unity of Western culture," I believe it is. An understanding of contemporary American society in all its aspects— economic, social, political, cultural, and scientific—requires knowledge of the events and processes that brought them into existence, and the history of Western civilization is the record of these interrelated processes of development.

What, then, should be the essential elements of a course in Western civilization? There are many ways to organize such a course, and the suggestions that follow are not meant to be rigid prescriptions, but examples of different ways of giving students a working framework of historical knowledge. By "working framework" I mean a coherent outline, in the dual sense that it gives meaningful shape to the procession of names, dates, places, and events of history, but is not by any means complete in its details.

One strategy is to build a course in Western civilization around one or two of the emphases cited in the AHA recommendation. For example, a course that emphasized an understanding of European economic history—of "the changing modes of production and distribution"— would examine the causes and consequences of the shift from village-based agriculture and industry to a town-based merchant economy, and then to industrialization and the accompanying urbanization. The voyages of the early explorers are part of this story, too, as are the opening of new trade routes and subsequent colonization.

Similarly, a course focusing on the "succession of social systems, ways of life and ethical conceptions" might begin with a comparison of the pre-Roman kinship systems of northern Europe and the pre-Athenian culture of the Mediterranean region. It might also include a consideration of the nature of citizenship in the Greek *polis* and in the Roman empire; the feudal system of the Middle Ages and the interplay among the country, the courts, and the religious communities; the Reformation and the ensuing proliferation of religious denominations; and the social effects of industrialization and the activities of social reformers.

A course with a civics focus might trace the origins of democratic ideals in the assemblies of the Greek *polis*, in the Roman conception of law, in the revolt against traditional authority during the Enlightenment, and in the writings of Rousseau, Locke, Paine, and others. It would also concentrate on the events that led to the replacement of absolute monarchies with constitutional monarchies (England), with democratic republics (the United States and France), and with other forms of government (Russia).

To trace the accumulation and spread of knowledge, one would need to look again to Greece and its academies for the sources of the liberal arts. In addition, attention ought to be paid to the widespread use of the Latin language across Europe, the establishment of libraries, the rediscovery of classical texts during the Renaissance, the rise of the secular university, and the invention of the printing press. Such a course might also incorporate elements of the story of "the advance of science, technology, and invention," such as the discoveries and theories of Copernicus, Galileo, and Newton, the beginnings of experimental science, and the origins of modern medicine in the work of Pasteur, Harvey, and others. Alternatively, the history of science and technology might be studied in conjunction with an emphasis on changes in social conditions. The impetus for invention and the advances in medical technique brought about by war, the tension between science and the church, and the interplay among science, technology, and industrialization are examples of topics that might be included in such a course.

There are other defensible emphases and combinations, but it should be stressed that the goal of *any* course in European history—or American history, for that matter—is to give the student an understanding of the American society of which he or she is part: what its main features are and how they came to be, and, derivatively, a way of understanding himself or herself as a member of that society. Such an understanding is essential, it seems to me, before the study of other cultures can be of much benefit. I do not hold that non-Western cultures are unworthy of attention; far from it. But at the secondary level a knowledge of the underpinnings of one's own society must take priority.

The teaching of the historical discipline, then, is centrally concerned with the transmission of certain essentials of our cultural heritage. Or so it would seem. In fact, most of the history that is taught in schools today is labeled "social studies," and too often it fails to convey a sense of the broad movement of Western civilization and of the interrelatedness of its constituent elements. Many teachers, curriculum planners, and textbook writers, reacting against what they perceive to be mindless chronology or "elitist" and "ethnocentric" assumptions, appear to have lost sight of the main goal in their rush to devise novel approaches to "understanding contemporary society" and such like.

The teaching of history through the "inquiry" method, now much in fashion among avant-garde educators, is an example. This is the view that the central aim of instruction is to teach students "how to think like a historian." Factual control of the subject is downplayed, or at least taken for granted; the focus is on the process of historical inquiry, techniques of investigation, and modes of analysis. This is a radical departure from the straight "gangbuster" history I was taught long ago: "Just the facts, ma'am, nothing but the facts." We were given no idea why those particular facts were the important ones, nor any sense that there were competing interpretations of important historical problems. Nothing was problematic at all, except how good our memories were and how hard we worked to assimilate the textbook. At an early age, I knew just how Woodrow Wilson felt after taking a graduate exam in colonial history at Johns Hopkins in 1884. He told a friend that he went into it "crammed with one or two hundred dates and one or two thousand minute particulars of the quarrels of nobody knows who with an obscure governor for nobody knows what. Just think of all that energy wasted! The only comfort is that this mass of information won't long burden me. I shall forget it with great ease."

That history is rarely taught that way anymore is altogether to the good. It was not even faithful to the nature of the discipline. Historians do not merely ferret out the facts and let them speak for themselves. They select relevant facts from countless numbers of irrelevant ones and build them into interpretive structures. Some attention to the shifting winds of historical opinion can engage the minds of young students and give them the exciting sense that in studying history they are constructing their own distinctive view of the world. But in the current emphasis upon "doing history," the elevation of process over content has severe drawbacks as well. It is quite impossible to grasp the nature of historical reasoning without a secure command of a large body of factual material. The most intelligent and imaginative of students cannot appreciate the complex historiography concerning the coming of the American Civil War without knowing what the Kansas-Nebraska Act was, when and why it was passed, and what its repercussions were. People must crawl before they can run in marathons; what suits a graduate student or excites a scholar is not necessarily what an adolescent most needs to learn. The first objective, though assuredly not the only objective, of a good history course is to communicate the factual outlines of the subject, to provide students with enough pieces of the puzzle to be able to begin thinking about the varying ways historians have fitted them together.

If learning to "think like a historian" is really the chief aim, it might seem that the study of any time or place will be equally valuable, so long as there are surviving records to work with. History, in this view, is a game whose rules can be learned with materials drawn from any past culture; what matters are the rules, the canons of evidence, and modes of analysis. Physics, chemistry, and perhaps even economics may be games in this sense, but history is not. It is a particularizing science, in the sense that the interpretive process is brought to bear on a specific sequence of events. The process of making "the facts" intelligible by fitting them into an explanatory narrative does not invoke general laws like those found in physics or chemistry; rather, it requires a sense of how the subtle intertwining of an enormous number of contextual variables may have produced this unique chain of events. The teacher of history is not dealing with interchangeable atoms as a physicist does. The study of early Mayan civilization may impart valuable skills, but it does not yield the same historical knowledge as the study of World War I.

If the study of the Mayas and the study of World War I are not interchangeable, we must then ask the hard question: On what basis should we choose between them when we are planning a high school curriculum in history? Both surely merit attention from historians, but the former is demonstrably less important for high school students in the United States. While the civilization produced by the Mayas may continue to be visible to some small degree in the American Southwest and in Latin America, its relevance for the understanding of self and society of young Americans today is minuscule compared to the momentous implications of the Great War. The forces that brought that war about and the legacy it left, notably the new regimes it ushered in in Russia, Germany, and eastern Europe, are part of our living cultural heritage in a way that Mayan civilization is not. It is essential for our young people to know why Lenin and Hitler came to power; it is not essential—though it is certainly desirable—for them to know why Mayan civilization disappeared.

The Excesses of Social History

I have misgivings about another tendency shaping the treatment of history in the schools: the rapid shift of emphasis away from political and constitutional subjects toward issues of social history. It is ironic for me to express such reservations, since my own scholarship has all been of this genre, and I have often repeated E. H. Carr's dictum that "the more sociological history becomes, and the more historical sociology becomes, the better for both."[9] But it is possible to be an advocate and practitioner of the "new history" and still see a need for balance. In many schools today, the pendulum has swung too far in the direction I once sought to push it. What, then, is the proper balance?

It is no longer adequate to organize an American history course around the old "presidential synthesis," making the succession of national administrations the primary focus. The analogous point must be made about European history approached exclusively as a story of kings, battles, treaties, and the epic deeds of great statesmen. The concerns of historians today are broader than that. They examine not only past politics, but patterns of economic growth, shifts in the social structure and the composition of the population, family patterns, religious beliefs and practices, and the relations between high culture and popular culture. They also are sensitive to the fact that most surviving historical documents were produced by members of elites, and they have made imaginative efforts to reconstruct "the history of the inarticulate" and to write "grass roots social history"—history "from the bottom up." These newer emphases are often more engaging—and rightly so—to beginning students than the stuff of the traditional introductory course. It is indefensible to examine the career of George Washington in detail without some consideration of the lives of the several dozen slaves whose labor supported him.

Just how much attention to devote to George Washington, however, and how much to his slaves, is not easy to decide. Although I have never heard anyone so bold—and so foolish—as to make this standard explicit, lurking beneath some discussions is the assumption that a simple head count will resolve the problem. Since females have formed about half of the population in all societies, it can be argued that they represent "one-half of our history" (a favorite phrase of feminist historians) and should be given equal time. The difficulty with this logic is that it follows equally that, since 48 percent of the American population at the time of the first United States Census in 1790 was less than sixteen years old, almost half the attention of a unit on American history in the 1780s and 1790s should be devoted to children. So we have half the time going to children, another quarter to adult females, and 5 percent to adult male slaves (the remaining 15 percent of slaves get in as children or women). Precious few moments remain for a consideration of the achievements of the Philadelphia Convention, the battle over ratification, and the difficulties of setting up a new national government. But no matter. The fifty-five men at Philadelphia, after all, were but .000014 percent of the population. No neat formula will tell us what weight we should actually place upon the forging of the United States Constitution, but one need not succumb to the uncritical Constitution-worshiping that Charles Beard decried to claim that its being the work of a tiny group of prosperous white males is less important than the popular assent it commanded during the ratification struggle, the impact it had on republican opinion throughout Europe, and its shaping influence upon American life ever since.

E Pluribus Unum

The variety of grass roots history that has undoubtedly exerted the greatest influence in the schools in the past fifteen years or so has been that concerned with the search for ethnic roots, the product of our ethnic revival of the late sixties and seventies. This is an enormously complex issue that arouses passionate emotions, and it is impossible to provide a properly nuanced appraisal in a few pages. But it is another case, I suggest, of a pendulum that has swung from one extreme position too far toward another.

In my days as a schoolboy, ethnicity was a dirty secret. All Americans were alike. The standard textbook we used, David Muzzey's *American History*, began its discussion of the population of the United States by saying, "leaving aside the Negro and Indian population," and continued to leave them aside thereafter. The Irish, the Italians, the Poles, the Jews, and other immigrants were only alluded to as exemplars of the melting-pot myth, people who had fled to the land of opportunity and had quickly become "plain Americans" indistinguishable from their neighbors.

All that changed during the cultural upheaval of the 1960s. The civil rights revolution culminated in the demand for black power, echoed by calls for red power, brown power, and yellow power. Then came "the rise of the unmeltable ethnics," the mobilization—or apparent mobilization—of various white European groups hoping to claim their share of entitlements on the grounds of their origins. The situation of each of these aroused ethnic groups differed, and so did the character of their movements, despite some efforts by leaders to insist that they were unified by a common desire to put an end to WASP cultural domination. It was perhaps not coincidental, though, that all took root and flourished in the midst of the most unpopular war in American history, a war that was so agonizing and divisive that it created widespread doubt that the United States was indeed the "last best hope" of freedom in the world and seemed to discredit the very conception that Americans have a common history in which they can take pride. For many, celebrating one's non-American origins became a means of dissociating oneself from a military adventure that was difficult to square with American ideals.

It is doubtful that the ethnic revival was the deep and enduring shift in national self-understanding that many took it to be. Its impact is already fading, as may be seen from the rapid withering away of the grandly named Ethnic Millions for Political Action Committee, which even at its peak numbered its supporters in the mere thousands. But at least one major national institution was deeply and lastingly affected, it appears, and that was the schools. The change is most easily documented in the history texts our children are assigned. Frances Fitz-Gerald's *America Revised* and Nathan Glazer and Reed Ueda's *Ethnic Groups in History Textbooks* vividly reveal how the older textbook image of a unified and successful American society has given way to one of a divided and fragmented America made up of permanently unmelted and victimized ethnics and their WASP oppressors.[10] The United States was no longer a melting pot; instead, it was a stewpot or salad bowl, with a multitude of separate and immiscible ingredients.

I have attacked this simplistic and misguided view at length elsewhere and will not restate the entire critique here.[11] Suffice it to say that I am in full agreement with a fine recent essay by John Keegan, who notes that Americans have had enormous difficulty grasping the problems of multiethnic Lebanon because American society has not been divided into distinct and murderously antagonistic groups in the way that Lebanon has. Instead, as Keegan argues:

> The supreme triumph of the American people is to have produced the largest homogeneous cultural unit on earth. Neither China nor Russia, comparable though each is in extent and population, can claim that the official language of the state is understood from border to border or that the values that obtain among the governing and intellectual class of the capital are the raw material of public life in the remotest province. Both

countries are the cultural inferiors of the United States in that respect. But the "melting pot" ethos that has long directed the outlook of the United States is . . . a drawback when the country seeks to exercise its power in regions that do not resemble it.[12]

America is superficially much like Lebanon, the Soviet Union, India, and Yugoslavia in having an ethnically diverse population. What proponents of the ethnic revival, including many teachers and textbook writers, have neglected is the deeper reality—the overwhelmingly strong blending and melting influences that have absorbed dozens and dozens of distinct groups and made them into one people, processes of integration and absorption that have operated more feebly or not at all in most other countries.

Of course, we all want teachers to be sensitive to the variegated ethnic backgrounds of their pupils—as well as to the class, regional, religious, and any other social characteristics that distinguish them. The schools I attended can be faulted for insensitivity on this count. But the current fashion of asking students "who they are" and encouraging them to explore their ethnic roots can also be carried too far. Too often, it is assumed that we all are or should be ethnics, and that an awareness of our distinctive origins is more important than a sense of our common identity as Americans. Enlightened liberal teachers who shudder at the idea of "putting Jesus back in the classroom" engage in ethnic consciousness-raising that is just as intrusive and dangerous. As the example of Lebanon reveals so clearly, ethnic awareness is not necessarily benign and colorful. It can be enormously destructive if cultivated to the point at which a sense of the ties that bind a nation together is lost. It is not the job of the schools to cultivate the ethnic identity of its students; that task, like the task of religious instruction, belongs in the private sphere. It is one of the jobs of the schools, and a vital one, to convey an understanding of how the United States managed successfully to incorporate such an incredible array of diverse peoples from every corner of the globe. Central to that story are characteristically American ideals of religious tolerance, individual freedom, cultural openness, economic opportunity, and democratic, participatory government.

Such an emphasis upon the absorption of peoples need not and should not be a story of unrelieved sweetness and light. American history—I would say, the history of all ethnically complex societies—is rife with bias and bigotry. Virtually every immigrant group was ill-treated at times. Furthermore, not all of us descend from voluntary immigrants: the ancestors of some of us came here against their will, in chains; and others are the offspring of people who were here before the

Europeans landed and who were stripped of their land by the invaders. Every student should understand that the experiences of enslaved or conquered peoples were different from and far more painful than those of newcomers who crossed the ocean in search of greater opportunity. That their histories are no longer neglected as they were in my school-days is unquestionably a great advance, and the foregoing critical ob-servations are not intended to suggest that it is time to bring back David Muzzey.

It is time, though, for the schools to pay more heed to the Unum in the motto on the seal of the United States—E Pluribus Unum. When it was adopted in 1782, the phrase referred to the forging of a single nation out of the original thirteen colonies, but it has since come to refer as well to the binding together of so many diverse peoples into one. For all of our differences we have long had a common national history and a common national identity, a feeling for what Abraham Lincoln called "the mystic cords of memory" that bind successive gen-erations of Americans together. Millions of newcomers who arrived after much of that history had already been made were nonetheless able to identify with it and appropriate it as their own. We all should know something of our roots. But it is parochial to conceive of our roots in a narrowly genealogical sense. We have other, thicker and deeper roots that have made us what we are, and it requires a grasp of the full sweep of the history of American civilization, and indeed of the history of other societies that shaped our cultural heritage, to understand fully who we are today and how we came to be that way.

NOTES

1. *American Historical Association: Perspectives* (February 1984): 4.

2. The survey was conducted by Benjamin J. Stein and reported in "Val-ley Girls View the World," *Public Opinion* (August/September 1983): 18–19. The examples were cited by Kenneth Seib, "Point of View: How the Laws of Acadynamics Work to Prevent Change," *The Chronicle of Higher Education* (January 25, 1984): 72.

3. U.S. Bureau of the Census, *Social Indicators III* (Washington, D.C.: U.S. Government Printing Office, 1980), p. 560.

4. *Digest of Education Statistics, 1982*, p. 55, cited by Kathleen Neils Conzen and Irene D. Neu, "The State of the Job Crisis in the Historical Profes-sion," *OAH Newsletter* (February 1984): 12.

5. Ernest Gellner, *Nations and Nationalism* (Ithaca, N.Y.: Cornell Univer-sity Press, 1983), pp. 32–33.

6. Gellner, p. 34.

7. Gellner, p. 34.

8. Gellner, p. 35.

9. E. H. Carr, *What Is History?* (New York: Alfred Knopf, 1962), p. 84.

10. Frances FitzGerald, *America Revised: History Schoolbooks in the Twentieth Century* (Boston: Little, Brown, 1979); Nathan Glazer and Reed Ueda, *Ethnic Groups in History Textbooks* (Washington, D.C.: Ethics and Public Policy Center, 1983).

11. Stephan Thernstrom, "Ethnic Groups in American History," in *Ethnic Relations in America*, ed. Lance Liebman (Englewood Cliffs, N.J.: Prentice-Hall, 1982), pp. 3–27.

12. John Keegan, "Shedding Light on Lebanon," *The Atlantic* 253 (April 1984): 46.

From History to
Social Studies:
Dilemmas and Problems

Diane Ravitch

When I attended public school in Texas in the 1950s, I took the standard three-year social studies sequence, which included a year of world history in the ninth grade, a year of American history in the eleventh grade, and senior-year civics. I had a superb ninth-grade teacher, but the course was impossible; it covered too much material and gave students a smattering of events, dates, and cultures, picked up hastily in a forced march across thousands of years and all continents. The eleventh-grade American history course was worse: the teacher used every incident in American history to support her own cranky political bias. When I reached college, I realized just how poorly educated I was in history; I felt hopelessly inadequate when I compared myself to fellow students who had attended private schools. Many of them seemed to have a wide-ranging knowledge of ancient history, medieval history, and modern European history that was utterly beyond my grasp. What was more, their knowledge of history was enhanced by an exposure to art and literature that my school had never even attempted.

My strength, I mistakenly believed, derived from my keen interest in current events. So in college I majored in political science, a decision that I now believe to have been a grievous error because I simply compounded the flaws of my high school education. The issues that seemed so urgent in the late 1950s are today of merely antiquarian interest. Why should anyone care about Quemoy and Matsu anymore, those offshore islands that Kennedy and Nixon argued about in 1960, except as a footnote to contemporary Asian history? Does Sputnik really matter now except as a milestone in the history of technology? Why should anyone recall the confrontation between Governor Faubus of Arkansas and President Eisenhower in 1958 except as an incident in the history of racial relations in America? Almost everything that once seemed surpassingly important has now faded, to be remembered only by historians, keepers of the human record.

I eventually turned to the full-time study of history when I realized that I could not understand the present without studying the past. My continued interest in contemporary issues made me a historian; there was simply no other intelligent way to understand the origins of our present institutions, problems, and ideas. As a latecomer to the study of history, I am—like all converts—a zealous advocate; I believe in its importance and value, and I would like to see it strengthened as a subject in the schools. It is from this perspective that I began to inquire into the condition of history in the schools and how it got that way. As of mid-1984, however, this was nearly impossible to appraise. Education data collection is today so inadequate that no one can accurately say how history is taught, how well it is taught, what is taught, or what is learned. Most states have figures on course enrollments, and some national surveys have tallied the percentage of children who are enrolled in courses entitled "history," but these figures are highly suspect. Because of the enormous variety of practice extant in the nation's classrooms, there is not necessarily any identity of content among courses bearing the same label.

Furthermore, we have no reliable measures of achievement or mastery for the field of history; the makers of standardized tests long ago abandoned the attempt to assess historical or literary knowledge and instead devote their entire attention to abstract verbal and mathematical skills. We can't really say definitively whether high school graduates today know more or less than their counterparts of ten, twenty, or thirty years ago. Because we live in a time of cultural fragmentation, the idea of testing large numbers of students for their knowledge of history seems outrageous. It was not surprising, for example, that many of the national reports of 1983 cited test scores in mathematics, science, and verbal skills, but their bills of particulars omitted any mention of the humanities. We have no objective data to tell us how we are doing, because we lack consensus on the minimum knowledge that we expect of all students. We do not agree on what literature is important, nor do we agree on what history should be taught to all American youngsters.

We know that many states require high school students to study at least one year of United States history, but we do not know what lurks behind the course label. National data tell us that 65 percent of high school graduates in 1982 took at least three years of social studies, but it is almost certain that few of these credits were taken in history, since most districts require only one year of United States history.[1] A survey published by the Organization of American Historians (OAH) in 1975 revealed that in at least five states—New York, Indiana, Iowa, Oklahoma, and Oregon—virtually no training in history was required for high school history teachers.[2] In New York City, the history teacher's license was abolished in 1946, and at present it is not necessary to have studied history in order to be licensed as a high school social studies teacher.[3]

If one were to judge by the accumulation of anecdotal reports—a notoriously unreliable source of evidence—many college professors think that freshmen know little about American history, European history, or any other history. One frequently hears complaints about students who know next to nothing about events that occurred before the twentieth century, or who are ignorant of the Bible, Shakespeare, the Greek myths, or other material that was once common knowledge. As a Berkeley professor put it to me a few years ago, "They have no furniture in their minds. You can assume nothing in the way of prior knowledge. Skills, yes; but not knowledge."

While it is not possible to know definitively how history is faring in the schools today, there is reason to fear that it is losing its integrity as well as its identity as a field of study under the umbrella called "social studies." The field of social studies, in the view of a number of its leaders, is in deep trouble. Bob L. Taylor and John D. Haas claimed in 1973 that "secondary school social studies curricula are in a state of 'curriculum anarchy'; which is to say that local curriculum patterns are more varied than at any other time in this century. No longer is it possible to describe a typical state, regional, or national pattern of social studies curriculum. Furthermore, it appears each junior or senior high school in a given school district is 'doing its own thing.'"[4] A 1977 study by Richard E. Gross of Stanford University found that the field was characterized by increased fragmentation and dilution of programs; by a growth of electives and minicourses; by a rapid proliferation of social science courses; by a drop in required courses; and by a tendency toward curricular anarchy.[5] In keeping with these trends, other reviews noted the pronounced absence of agreement about the content of the field.

While the field of social studies was having an identity crisis, history as a subject was struggling for survival. The 1975 study by the Organization of American Historians reported a significant dilution and fragmentation in the teaching of secondary school history.[6] In New Mexico, the trend was toward ethnocultural courses; in Hawaii, toward integrating history into a social science framework focused on problem solving, decision making, and social action; in Minnesota, teachers were encouraged to shift away from historical study toward an emphasis on concepts that transcend "any given historical situation." The OAH representative in California predicted that history would yield time to such "relevant" topics as multicultural studies, ethnic studies, consumer affairs, and ecology. Similar reports about the deteriorating position of history within the social studies curriculum came from Vermont, Rhode Island, Connecticut, New York, Maryland, Wisconsin, Missouri, Nebraska, North Carolina, Oklahoma, West Virginia, Illinois, and Iowa. The OAH report confirmed what many had long feared: history in public high schools has been seriously eroded, absorbed within the amorphous field of the social studies.

The OAH survey, like the Gross study, was conducted in the mid-1970s and reflected the curricular fragmentation of that time. A survey carried out in the mid-1980s would doubtless show that many states, cities, and school districts have substantially increased their graduation requirements. Yet even a cursory review of the actions taken in the early 1980s would reveal that history continues to be left out in the cold and that social studies requirements have been increased without reference to history. Even the tough-minded National Commission on Excellence in Education failed to mention history as a necessary subject of study for all American students. Thanks to the hazy and unfocused nature of the social studies, students may meet the enlarged requirements by taking more courses in current events, drug education, sex education, environmental education, citizenship education, values education, law studies, economics, psychology, or other nonhistorical studies.

How did history fall to this sorry state? A review of the "history of history" suggests that certain ideological and political trends caused history to lose its rightful place in the public high school curriculum. History entered the public school curriculum as a regular subject of study before the Civil War, but it did not become well established until the end of the nineteenth century, as secondary school enrollments grew. History, English, modern foreign languages, and science entered the curriculum as modern subjects, in contrast to the classical curriculum of mathematics and ancient languages.[7] Most public schools offered one or more history courses, such as ancient history, medieval history, English history, modern European history, and United States history. The schools of the nineteenth century also offered courses that were predecessors of the social sciences: courses, for example, in civil government, political economy, and moral philosophy. By 1895, 70 percent of the nation's universities and colleges required a course in United States history for admission, and more than a quarter required the study of Greece and/or Rome.[8]

In order to understand the fate of history over the years, it is necessary to examine the rationale for its inclusion in the curriculum. Why study history? It was argued, first, that history offers valuable moral lessons by demonstrating the kind of personal and national behavior that should be admired or abhorred; second, that history enhances personal culture by revealing the great achievements and ideas of the past; third, that history inspires patriotism; fourth, that history trains good citizens by defining civic virtue; fifth, that history reinforces religious ideals; and sixth, that history strengthens and disciplines the mind.

Some of these rationales were profoundly damaging to the integrity of the subject. Promoting history as an instrument for the teaching of morals, religion, and patriotism undermined respect for history by treating it as a form of propaganda. It distorted the most essential value in history, which is the search for truth. The subject was even more severely injured by the proponents of mental discipline, who believed that rote memorization of the textbook strengthened the mind; this method must have destroyed student interest in the content of history, and it certainly reared up legions of people who hated historical study (though they might better have directed their ire against the tyrannical method by which it was taught).

Between 1893 and 1918, three major reports were issued on the public school curriculum; these are important not only because they influenced practice, in some cases quite substantially, but also because they vividly portray the ideas that were dominant or gaining ascendancy among leaders of the education profession. Everyone interested in history as a secondary school subject should read them, because by reading between the lines, it is possible to discover the answer to the question: What happened to history?

The first major report on the curriculum appeared in 1893, the product of a group called the Committee of Ten. During the late nineteenth century, it had begun to seem to many educators that the high school curriculum was growing in uncontrolled fashion, without rational plan. In response to this sentiment, the Committee of Ten was created by the National Education Association (NEA) as the first national commission on the high school curriculum. It was composed of distinguished educators, including five college presidents. Its chairman, Harvard's President Charles Eliot, was widely known as a proponent of the elective system and the modern subjects. The Committee established nine subject-matter groups to make recommendations on content and methodology. One of the most important issues that the Committee of Ten was asked to address was whether there should be different curricula for children who were going to college and those who were not. The committee, and all of its subject-matter consultants, agreed that all children should receive a broad and liberal education, regardless of their future occupation or when their education was likely to end.[9]

The report of the history advisors was remarkable. This group, which included both academic scholars (one was a young Princeton professor named Woodrow Wilson) and school officials, attacked the rote-memorization method of teaching history. Memorizing facts, they said, was "the most difficult and the least important outcome of historical study." The group commented, "When the facts are chosen with as little discrimination as in many school textbooks, when they are mere lists of lifeless dates, details of military movements, or unexplained genealogies, they are repellant." To know such facts, they held, was like "a curious character in Ohio" who was said to remember what he had eaten for dinner every day for the past thirty years. The committee insisted that it would rather see history eliminated than to see it taught "the old fashioned way," through painful and pointless memorization.[10]

The committee argued that when history and its allied branches were instead taught in a manner that teaches judgment and thinking, and when they were taught in conjunction with such studies as literature, geography, art, and languages, they "serve to broaden and cultivate the mind. . . . They counteract a narrow and provincial spirit. . . . They prepare the pupil in an eminent degree for enlightened and intellectual enjoyment in after years . . . and they assist him to exercise a salutary influence upon the affairs of his country." The "newer methods" endorsed by the committee included inquiry, comparative studies, informal presentations by students, individualized work, field trips, debates, and audiovisual aids; in addition, the committee advocated better textbooks, better-trained teachers, and better-equipped libraries.[11]

The committee recommended an eight-year course in history, beginning in the fifth and sixth grades with biography and mythology. American history and government would be taught in the seventh grade; Greek and Roman history, in the eighth grade; French history (as an illustration of European history in general), in the ninth grade; English history (because of its contribution to American institutions), in the tenth grade; American history, in the eleventh grade; and intensive study of a special historical topic, in the twelfth grade.

The history committee insisted that its recommendations were not intended for the college-bound. On the contrary, they said, "We believe that the colleges can take care of themselves; our interest is in the school children who have no expectation of going to college, the larger number of whom will not enter even a high school." They argued that there should not be separate courses for the college-bound and others. Under such a system, they said, those who would get the most education later on would be the only ones to get any training in history in the schools. Such a distinction, "especially in schools provided by public taxation, is bad for all classes of pupils. It is the duty of the schools to furnish a well grounded and complete education for the child," regardless of his later destination.[12]

The specific influence of this report is hard to estimate, but it did encourage good relations between professional historians and the school establishment, and it was important in curbing rote-memory methods. A few years later, the NEA invited the American Historical Association to create yet another committee, this time devoted entirely to the subject of the history curriculum and college entrance requirements. This group, called the Committee of Seven, wrote a document that affected the teaching of history for many years. Like the Committee of Ten's history conference, the Committee of Seven was deeply critical of the rote system of history teaching. It endorsed the use of varied methods to stimulate the interest and participation of pupils. It criticized the typical textbook as "mental pabulum" and urged the introduction of supplementary materials. It recommended the inclusion of biographies, primary source materials, and innovative techniques. It conceived of history not only in terms of political institutions and states but also as the study of the social and economic fabric of human activity. It recommended a four-year course in history for the secondary school: first year, ancient history to A.D. 800; second year, medieval and modern European history; third year, English history; fourth year, American history and civil government. The committee made these recommendations not because this particular sequence would prepare students for college, but because the members believed that historical study was the very best sort of general education for all children. The curriculum, they insisted, "must be prepared with the purpose of developing boys and girls into young men and women, not with the purpose of fitting them to meet entrance examinations. . . ." They believed that history was "peculiarly appropriate in a secondary course, which is fashioned with the thought of preparing boys and girls for the duties of daily life and intelligent citizenship. . . ."[13]

The committee complained that there were too many people teaching history who lacked appropriate training: "In one good school, for example, history a short time ago was turned over to the professor of athletics, not because he knew history, but apparently in order to fill up his time. In another school a teacher was seen at work who evidently did not have the first qualifications for the task; when the examiner inquired why this teacher was asked to teach history when she knew no history, the answer was that she did not know anything else."[14] The committee expressed the belief that history teachers should have a firm knowledge of their subject, should have command of professional skills and methods, should have the enthusiasm to inspire students' interest in the struggles and conflicts of the past, and should themselves be lifelong students of history as well as teachers.

The Committee of Seven believed that the best way to understand the problems of the present was through study of the past; that students would best understand their duties as citizens by studying the origins and evolution of political institutions, not only in their own society but in other societies and other times; that the ability to change society for the better depends on knowledge of our institutions and our ideals in their historical setting. Further, they believed that historical study teaches students to think, cultivates their judgment, and encourages accuracy of thought.

Part of this curricular evolution is the change in the rationale that was offered for the study of history. The Committee of Seven's rationale was that history, honestly taught, yielded valuable benefits. Study of the past, they believed, would create intelligent, thinking, responsible citizens, men and women who shared that "broad and tolerant spirit which is bred by the study of past times and conditions."[15] They were convinced that the study of history was valuable both intrinsically and extrinsically. They believed that history was a synthesizing subject that belonged at the center of the curriculum because it gave meaning and coherence to everything else that was studied.

The report of the Committee of Seven in 1899 set a national pattern for the history curriculum. By 1915, the overwhelming majority of high schools offered courses in ancient history, medieval and modern European history, English history, and American history. Furthermore, in most high schools, American and ancient history became required subjects. A historical survey of history teaching in 1935 held that the history departments of the nation's high schools "attempted to swallow the report of the Committee of Seven 'hook, line, and sinker.' " The so-called four-block plan was widely adopted, and there was an increase in both the number of history courses offered and the number of history courses required of all students. Further strengthening the influence of the Committee of Seven report, textbook publishers used the report as a model for their history series.[16] This situation, following the committee's report, was a far cry from 1893, when history was still struggling to gain legitimacy as a proper subject of study in the high school.

If the story of the history curriculum ended in 1915, there would now be good news about the status of history. The overwhelming majority of high schools, we would discover, would offer at least three years of history, including ancient history, European history, and American history, and nearly half would offer English history.[17] It would be necessary only to recall the reports of several other numerically named committees—the Committee of Eight, the Committee of Fifteen, and the Committee of Five, among others, and to note the emphasis on biography, mythology, legends, and hero tales in the elementary grades. The same approach, brought up to date in the 1980s, would certainly include histories of non-Western societies. But 1915, alas, was the high-water mark for traditional, narrative, chronological history in the schools.

Nascent social and political trends were by then making their mark on the public school curriculum, deeply affecting the teaching of history. In the 1890s, history had been deemed a modern subject, but only a few years later, during the first decade of the twentieth century, educational progressives began to treat it as part of the "traditional" curriculum. The traditional curriculum became a target for progressives, who sought to modernize the schools and to make them responsive to the needs and problems of contemporary life. In the opening decades of the twentieth century, progressivism emerged as a dynamic movement in American life, committed to society's reform and betterment. Many of the nation's ills were associated with the vast hordes of poor immigrants who crowded into the cities. The schools were given the primary responsibility for Americanizing immigrant children. Not only were they to function as academic institutions, teaching English to their charges, but to assume a custodial role, preparing the newcomers to be good citizens, training them for the job market, and introducing them to the ordinary necessities of daily life, such as nutrition and hygiene.

To meet some of these needs, new courses entered the high school curriculum, such as training for specific trades, sewing, cooking, and commercial studies. As high schools added practical courses, curricular differentiation became common. In many schools, there was a manual training course of study, a vocational course, a commercial course—and, for the academic elite, a college preparatory course. A "course of study" was a carefully sequenced series of individual courses, lasting two, three, or four years; in schools where curricular differentiation was fully developed, in keeping with the latest pedagogical thinking, the students' selection of a course of study was often tantamount to the choice of a vocation. The admonitions of the Committee of Ten and the Committee of Seven on behalf of liberal education for all children were scorned by progressives as an attempt to force everyone into a narrow academic curriculum. The reformers insisted that an academic curriculum was inappropriate for children who intended to go to work, and that there must be different programs for the small minority who were college-bound and the vast majority who were job-bound.

Vocational education became popular in the early decades of the twentieth century as part of a broad reform movement to make the work of the schools more practical. Since the nation's economy was shifting from an agricultural to an industrial base, progressive educators believed that the schools had to readjust their programs and goals in order to keep in step with the demands of the new era. Furthermore, vocational education seemed to be an appropriate response to the problems of educating the slow learners in the school population, many of whom were from illiterate immigrant families. American industry needed skilled workers, and the schools accepted the responsibility of preparing adolescents for the world of work; vocational education seemed the logical solution. Reformers could find little of value for working-class children or poor children in the traditional academic curriculum. They insisted that academic studies like history, literature, science, and mathematics failed to meet the needs both of modern society and of most students. Except for the small minority who were college-bound, most children needed more job training, more preparation for specific occupations. Those who were not college-bound, said the reformers, had no need for academic studies; instead, they needed the skills to participate in the new industrial age as efficient workers, farmers, and homemakers.

Progressive educators became accustomed to thinking of the schools in terms of their social function and to asserting that the work of the schools must meet the test of social efficiency. In education, social efficiency meant that every subject, every program, every study must be judged by whether it was socially useful. Did it meet the needs of society? To the new profession of curriculum makers and policymakers, the prospect of shaping society was doubtless far more exciting than merely teaching literature or history or science. In contrast, the traditional curriculum seemed anachronistic: What point was there in teaching history, science, literature, mathematics, and foreign language to children who would never go to college? How was society served by wasting their time in such manifestly "useless" and impractical studies? Although not all school officials or teachers agreed (and many strongly disagreed), educational leaders in national organizations and in major schools of education repeatedly asserted that the traditional curriculum was intended only for the children of the elite and was inappropriate to schools in a democracy. Teaching children to think and imparting to them knowledge about science and culture clearly did not make the grade with those who made social utility their touchstone.

By the time of World War I, social efficiency was widely accepted as the chief goal of education, and this consensus emerged full-blown in the third major report on the secondary curriculum, prepared by the National Education Association's Commission on the Reorganization of Secondary Education. Published in 1918, the report of this group was known as *The Cardinal Principles of Secondary Education*, and it is generally considered the single most important document in the history of American education. It proclaimed a utilitarian credo that deeply influenced the nation's schools for decades to come. The main objectives of a high school education, according to the commission, were these: "1. Health. 2. Command of fundamental processes. 3. Worthy home-membership. 4. Vocation. 5. Citizenship. 6. Worthy use of leisure. 7. Ethical character."[18] In contrast to the Committee of Ten and the Committee of Seven, the *Cardinal Principles* strongly endorsed differentiated curricula, based on such future vocational interests as agricultural, business, clerical, industrial, fine arts, and household arts. The report gave welcome support to proponents of vocational education, curricular tracking, and useful subjects and to those who believed that academic studies were only for the college-bound elite; it disappointed those who wanted all children to have a liberal education.

Like the earlier Committee of Ten, the commission established subject-matter committees, which wrote individual reports. But this time there was no committee on history. Instead, there was the Committee on Social Studies, whose report appeared in 1916. The committee defined the social studies as "those whose subject matter relates directly to the organization and development of human society, and to man as a member of social groups." The major purpose of modern education, said the committee, is "social efficiency." By their very nature, the social studies "afford peculiar opportunities for the training of the individual as a member of society. Whatever their value from the point of view of personal culture, unless they contribute directly to the cultivation of social efficiency on the part of the pupil they fail in their most important function."[19] By this standard of utility and relevance, there was scant justification for the study of ancient civilizations or premodern societies. From the outset, the field of social studies was associated with social action, social history, contemporary issues, and social efficiency.

The "constant and conscious purpose" of social studies, said the committee, was "the cultivation of good citizenship." Unlike history, which had no obvious social utility, the social studies promised to address issues of immediate concern: "Facts, conditions, theories, and activities that do not contribute rather directly to the appreciation of methods of human betterment have no claim," said the Committee on Social Studies, thereby cutting the ground from under ancient and medieval history and attaching greater value to current events than to history. But history was not to be jettisoned altogether. The principle enunciated by the committee for deciding what history to teach was this: "The selection of a topic in history and the amount of attention given to it should depend . . . chiefly upon the degree to which such topic can be related to the present life interests of the pupil, or can be used by him in his present processes of growth." The committee was blunt in stating that the widely adopted four-year history sequence set out by the Committee of Seven less than twenty years earlier was "more or less discredited," based as it was on "the traditions of the historian and the requirements of the college."[20] Appeal to pupils' interests, not transmission of knowledge, was to determine the content of history courses.

The *Cardinal Principles* and the report of the Committee on the Social Studies accurately enunciated the new canon of professional educators: the public schools were to be society's instruments for guiding the rising generation into socially useful roles. Those who objected that the primary responsibility of the schools was to democratize and redistribute knowledge, and that they accomplished this by expanding children's intellectual power, by transmitting the accumulated wisdom of the past, and by enabling young people to make their own decisions about how to be socially useful, were likely to be dismissed as reactionaries, out of touch with the times and with the findings of modern pedagogical science.

The acceptance of social efficiency as the touchstone of the high school curriculum proved disastrous to the study of history. What claim could be advanced for the utility of history? Knowing history didn't make anyone a better worker; it didn't improve anyone's health; it was not nearly so useful for citizenship training as a course in civics. When judged by the stern measure of direct utility, history had no claim except its utility for meeting college entrance requirements; without these, there was scant defense for history's study. Professional historians might have argued that the study of history teaches children how to think, how to reach judgments, how to see their own lives and contemporary issues in context, but they seemed content to abandon curricular decisions to the pedagogues who scorned these claims. Nor could history meet the immediate needs of young people, in the sense that it did not tell adolescents how to behave on a date, how to be popular with the crowd, or how to get a job. In the new era of social efficiency and pupil interests, the year-long course in ancient history began to disappear from American schools, and before long the four-year history sequence was telescoped to three, then to two, and, in many places, to only a single year of American history.

In the decades that followed the 1916 report of the Committee on the Social Studies, the emphasis in the social studies curriculum shifted decisively toward current events, relevant issues, and pupil-centered programs. The introduction of such courses was not, in itself, a bad thing. A modern, dynamic society needs schools in which students study the vital problems of the day and learn how to participate in the democratic process. But the time for the new subjects was taken away from history. Except for American history, which was thought to be useful as preparation for citizenship, the place of historical studies shrank in the schools. Even in the elementary schools, where earlier generations had studied biography and mythology as basic historical materials, the emphasis shifted to study of the neighborhood, the community, and preliterate peoples, a trend encouraged by the report's recommendation of courses in "community civics."

Of course, the report of the Committee on Social Studies in 1916 was not responsible for the erosion of the position of history; the report merely reflected the ideas, values, and attitudes of the emerging education profession. Unfortunately, these ideas, values, and attitudes were not congenial to the study of history for its own sake, nor even to the study of history as a means to improve the intelligence of the younger generation. The ideology expressed in the 1916 report was hostile to a study that had no demonstrable claim, no practical value, that offered so little promise of immediate social betterment.

Subsequent efforts to reexamine the social studies curriculum did little to restore the once-lofty position of history, because the ideology of social efficiency maintained its dominance. When the American Historical Association created a commission to analyze the social studies in the midst of the Great Depression, the commission declared that the most important purpose of the social studies was to produce "rich and many-sided personalities."[21] Whatever the other courses in the social studies may have been capable of doing by way of promoting personal development, it is difficult to imagine anyone claiming that the study of history produces "rich and many-sided personalities."

Even the innovative curricula produced after Sputnik, known collectively as "the new social studies," failed to restore history in the secondary schools. This was not because the case for history was weak, but because the case that should have been made was never made at all. The approach of the "new history" of the 1960s proceeded on the assumption that children should be taught to think like historians and to learn the historical method, just as students of science were learning to think like scientists and learning the scientific method. The problems with this approach were many: First, few children then or now actually know enough history or have enough context to make it worthwhile or possible for them to conduct a genuine historical investigation. Second, historians themselves do not agree on the definition of a single "historical method." Third, learning the process of how to write history is appropriate to graduate students but not to students in school, and it is certainly far less interesting than learning the actual stuff of history.

For history ever to regain its rightful place in the schools, educators must accord value to the study of history both for its own sake and for its value as a generator of individual and social intelligence. History has a right to exist as an autonomous discipline; it should be taught by people who have studied history, just as science and mathematics should be taught by persons who have studied those subjects. The other social studies also have their unique contributions to make, but their contribution should not be made by stealing time from history or by burying the study of history in nonhistorical approaches.

In 1932, Henry Johnson of Teachers College, Columbia University, wrote a delightful review of the teaching of history throughout the ages, somewhat misleadingly called *An Introduction to the History of the Social Sciences*. Johnson quoted a sixteenth-century Spanish scholar, Juan Luis Vives, to explain why it is valuable to study history. "Where there is history," wrote Vives, "children have transferred to them the advantages of old men; where history is absent, old men are as children." Without history, according to Vives, "no one would know anything about his father or ancestors; no one could know his own rights or those of another or how to maintain them; no one would know how his ancestors came to the country he inhabits." Vives pointed out that everything "has changed and is changing every day," except "the essential nature of human beings." Johnson referred to seventeenth-century French oratorians, who believed that study of history cultivated judgment and stimulated right conduct. He cited their view that "history is a grand mirror in which we see ourselves. . . . The secret of knowing and judging ourselves rightly is to see ourselves in others, and history can make us the contemporaries of all centuries in all countries."[22]

History will never be restored as a subject of value unless it is detached from the vulgar utilitarianism that originally swamped it. History should not be expected to teach patriotism, morals, values clarification, or decision making. Properly taught, history teaches the pursuit of truth and understanding; it establishes a context of human life in a particular time and place, relating art, literature, philosophy, law, architecture, language, government, economics, and social life; it portrays the great achievements and the terrible disasters of the human race; it awakens youngsters to the universality of the human experience as well as to the magnificence and the brutality of which humans are capable. Properly taught, history encourages the development of intelligence, civility, and a sense of perspective. It endows its students with a broad knowledge of other times, other cultures, other places. It leaves its students with cultural resources on which they may draw for the rest of their lives. These are values and virtues that are gained through the study of history. Beyond these, history needs no further justification.

NOTES

1. National Center for Education Statistics, Bulletin 83-223, "How Well Do High School Graduates of Today Meet the Curriculum Standards of the National Commission on Excellence?" (Washington, D.C.: U.S. Department of Education, September 1983).

2. Richard S. Kirkendall, "The Status of History in the Schools," *Journal of American History* 62 (1975): 557–70.

3. Telephone conversation, Office of Social Studies Director, New York City Board of Education, June 1984.

4. Bob L. Taylor and John D. Haas, *New Directions: Social Studies Curriculum for the '70s* (Boulder, Co.: Center for Education in the Social Sciences, University of Colorado, and Social Science Education Consortium, 1973).

5. Richard E. Gross, "The Status of the Social Studies in the Public Schools of the United States: Facts and Impressions of a National Survey," *Social Education* 41 (March 1977): 194–200, 205.

6. Kirkendall, pp. 563–64.

7. Edward A. Krug, *The Shaping of the American High School, 1880–1920* (Madison, Wis.: University of Wisconsin Press, 1964), pp. 4, 29; Rolla M. Tryon, *The Social Sciences as School Subjects* (New York: Charles Scribner's Sons, 1935), pp. 100–117.

8. Tryon, p. 142.

9. National Educational Association, *Report of the Committee on Sec-*

ondary School Studies (Washington, D.C.: U.S. Government Printing Office, 1893), hereafter cited as Committee of Ten Report.

10. Committee of Ten Report, p. 168.

11. Committee of Ten Report, p. 167.

12. Committee of Ten Report, pp. 167–68.

13. Committee of Seven, *The Study of History in Schools: Report to the American Historical Association* (New York: Macmillan, 1899), pp. 120, 122; hereafter cited as Committee of Seven Report.

14. Committee of Seven Report, p. 113.

15. Committee of Seven Report, p. 17.

16. Tryon, pp. 177, 187–89.

17. Tryon, p. 182.

18. Commission on the Reorganization of Secondary Education, *Cardinal Principles of Secondary Education* (Washington, D.C.: U.S. Government Printing Office, 1918), Bulletin 35.

19. Committee on Social Studies of the Commission on the Reorganization of Secondary Education of the National Education Association, *The Social Studies in Secondary Education* (Washington, D.C.: U.S. Government Printing Office, 1916), Bulletin No. 28: p. 9.

20. Committee on the Social Studies Report, pp. 9, 40, 44; Krug, p. 354.

21. American Historical Association, *A Charter for the Social Sciences in the Schools* (New York: Charles Scribner's Sons, 1932).

22. Henry Johnson, *An Introduction to the History of the Social Sciences* (New York: Charles Scribner's Sons, 1932), pp. 3, 21, 29, 30.

The Social Sciences and
the Humanities

Joseph Adelson

I strongly suspect that many social scientists, perhaps all of them, think of the humanities as a mode of secular uplift. The humanities! Ah, yes, the humanities! Very nice, very good for all of us, very important for the young, keeps them from being barbarians, don't you know. I have observed that my more rigorous colleagues, in appraising applicants for our graduate program, find it quite acceptable if the candidate's record shows some exposure to the humanities; but they become quite uneasy if there is too much of it, as though that might bespeak a certain mental or emotional weakness. Needless to say, I have never heard that uneasiness expressed about applicants whose records show a heavy concentration in science. Several years ago, I was offered a fellowship at the National Humanities Center, and on telling these colleagues about it, the common reaction was a sort of uncertain grin, followed by vague murmurs of very vague approval, mixed with some disbelief, much as though I had announced I was leaving to attend a school of divinity. Oh, how interesting, is what they said; Is he having a midlife crisis? is what they were wondering.

To put it another way, the common attitude among social scientists, even friendly ones, is condescending. The humanities are all right in their place, but our ultimate allegiance is to science, and if you should forget that, you will quickly be reminded. Through the wonders of serendipity, on the same day I wrote that sentence, I came across an illustrative letter in the *Wall Street Journal*. In the course of an editorial on the "yellow rain" controversy, the *Journal* had been dismissive of the credentials of some of its opponents and had termed anthropology and sociology "sort of second-cousins to science." There was a quick response from the president of the American Anthropological Association, reminding the editors quite firmly that the field *was* a science, that it had been recognized as such by the American Association for the Advancement of Science (AAAS) as far back as 1882, and that the National Science Foundation had given it two hundred grants the year before. The letter concludes: "Some of us are admittedly kissin' cousins to the humanities, but the discipline of anthropology is firmly based in the biological and social sciences." An equivalent response would no doubt be given by the president of any other social science association. It is quite obvious why. The sciences are prestigious, indeed awesome; they are powerful both intellectually and in worldly influence; and as that letter tells us by indirection, they have the money, so much so that their leftovers are sufficient to keep many social scientists fed.

There is of course another reason for distancing the humanities, in that during the nineteenth century most of the social sciences evolved from humanistic disciplines—psychology from moral philosophy, political science from political philosophy, sociology in part from history. There is another derivation, from the sciences: psychology from physiology, the other social sciences not so much from particular disciplines as from the general growth of quantitative and empirical methods during that century. It was indeed the collision of scientific and humanistic modes of thinking that was central to the thought of many of the early masters of social science. The great example is the great work by William James, the *Principles of Psychology*; but much the same is true, though perhaps less obviously, in Freud's earliest and most seminal psychoanalytic writings; and some of the same tensions can be seen elsewhere, as in Durkheim's *Suicide*, which merges statistical and historical analysis.

It is interesting to note that both James and Freud in time turned away from their scientific origins. James began as a physician, drifted into physiological psychology, then into larger psychological questions, ultimately to philosophy. Freud's early training was in science, then in medicine; his earliest efforts at psychology were highly physicalistic; he moved gradually toward a more psychological approach and ultimately toward humanistic questions—indeed, the fullest range of those, to history, religion, literature, the arts, theology, philosophy. In both cases we sense, reading their lives, that the movement to the humanities was either accomplished or occasioned by impatience with the constraints of conventional science—think of the ever-amiable James poking fun at the tedium and ultimate irrelevance of German psychophysical research; or think of Freud's ill-concealed disdain toward those who would limit analytic training to physicians, thus depriving psychoanalysis of that animation brought to it by, above all, the humanities.

There is one more career that may be instructive to us, in that it shows much the same evolution and many of the same tensions. Henry Murray is for all intents and purposes the inventor of modern personality psychology, a feat he accomplished during the 1930s. Murray, too, began in the natural sciences, initially as a physician and embryologist, then had a genuinely transforming encounter with Carl Jung, which persuaded him to turn to psychoanalysis and psychology. Eventually, he gave himself over almost fully to humanistic studies, above all to a series of works on Herman Melville. Once again, we note the evolution from the natural sciences to the social sciences to the humanities. And in Murray's case, too, we note how a restless mind finds it cannot be peacefully contained by the limits set by conventional science and seeks to rise above them. (It is of some interest to note here that one of Murray's most important psychological papers is on the myth of Icarus.) Murray's disaffection was quite open, indeed outspoken, so much so as to have played a role in alienating his colleagues and leading to an unconscionable delay in his being awarded tenure. He makes his complaint most forcefully in a controversial paper written just about fifty years ago—still quite applicable today—that examines the state of research, theory, and teaching in psychology. After reviewing sardonically a series of topics of interest to some hypothetical psychologist, all of these picayune or irrelevant, he concludes, "Academic psychology has contributed practically nothing to the knowledge of human nature. It has not only failed to bring light to the great, hauntingly recurrent problems, but it has no intention, one is shocked to realize, of attempting to investigate them."

What Murray is saying is that he, and social scientists like him, are problem-driven, whereas most others are method-driven, or perhaps method-limited. Murray's first question is, What are the important—or interesting—problems? Only after that is determined does he ask the second: Is there a way to study them, and if not, can we invent a way? The more common approach, Murray might tell us, is to work within a tradition dominated by certain tried-and-true methods, and to seek new discoveries within that tradition. In looking for new problems, one first

scans, perhaps unconsciously, the range of acceptable or perhaps toler-
able techniques and then exercises a silent, reflexive veto over those
approaches that are felt to be beyond the parameters. There is a well-
known joke about this, about the drunk who is found looking for his car
keys under the lamp post, not because he lost them there, but because
that is where the light is. I have told that joke myself, because tempera-
mentally I share Murray's inclinations; yet I now believe that Murray
vastly understated the problems involved in studying the great, hauntingly recurrent questions. Since Murray's time, a great many people
have been doing it, or trying to, and we have begun to understand how
extraordinarily difficult it can be.

The movement we see in these three towering figures—James,
Freud, and Murray—from the sciences to the humanities, is the reverse
of what we have seen in the social sciences as a whole. Although most
of these fields began closely allied with the humanities, they moved—
perhaps it is better to say that they were moved, gravitationally—
toward the quantitative, or toward experimentation, so that they seem
to be dominated by science, or the scientific ethos, or—quite commonly—by scientism. If the social sciences are in their "foreign policy," so to speak, awed and at times obsequious toward the sciences,
while patronizing toward the humanities, those attitudes are amplified
on the domestic front. Most of the social sciences have been marked—
some continue to be—by bitter schisms between scientific or quantitative approaches on one side and nonquantitative approaches on the
other, these being termed variously idiographic, clinical, or interpretive. There may be exceptions here and there, but so far as I can tell, the
quantitative approach is dominant over the long run, though of course
it remains arguable whether that is due to merit or simply to the temper
of the times.

That long run can take a long time, and until hegemony is attained,
conflicts can be fought out with a fratricidal intensity, so much so that
it can be hard to convey to an outsider the lunatic rages that can sometimes overcome the participants. The outsider is liable to find these
disputes strange indeed, filled with arguments about matters entirely
incorporeal, not necessarily about divergent findings as about differences in research strategy, or the proper way to give credence to different classes of evidence. When I was in graduate school I had one
teacher, a very famous man given to violent opinions, who absolutely
hated psychoanalysis. During the course of a graduate seminar, one of
his students rather saucily pointed out to him a passage from the writings of an analyst who had many years before anticipated a theoretical
breakthrough lately proposed by our teacher. He responded that it
would make no difference if *everything* psychoanalysis propounded

should turn out to be true; it would still be false because it had not been earned honestly, that is, discovered through the proper procedures. In his view—and I think he was dead wrong in believing this, but so he believed—psychoanalysis employed largely solipsistic methods, which *eo ipso* were not the rational methods required by science.

I am quite aware that this example is an extreme one, yet I think it tells us something about the nature of the schisms within the social sciences. They have to do with profoundly different epistemologies. Sir Isaiah Berlin, possibly the leading humanistic thinker of our time, has traced the conflict between the sciences and humanities back as far as the eighteenth century, where we see the final triumph of an attitude toward knowledge deeply rooted in Western thought. Berlin tells us that this attitude, or tradition, in its many forms, rests on three basic assumptions: (1) every genuine question has one true answer and one only, all others being false; (2) the methods leading to correct solutions are in essence identical, and rational in nature; and (3) the solutions achieved are "universally, eternally and immutably" true for all times, places, and men.

A lustrous vision, yet also, alas, a Lorelei for those wanting to believe that the social sciences already have or will sometime soon provide such questions, methods, and solutions. Many of those lured to shipwreck have been social scientists themselves, so often possessed of illusions of an imminent "breakthrough" that will allow lawlike generalizations meeting Berlin's criteria. To be sure, steady disconfirmation has produced some tempering of our millenial zeal, has even produced heretics who no longer believe that the social sciences can ever become "scientific." But this skepticism has not yet shaken the serene convictions of most of us inside the compound that yes, yes, we *are* sciences, albeit young and undeveloped. For the moment our own belief has persuaded our fellow citizens and provides much of the rationale for teaching the social sciences in the secondary schools. Let me turn to that curriculum and to some of the assumptions sustaining it.

It seems fairly clear that in the competition for time and attention in the high school curriculum, the humanities have suffered losses during the last two decades or so, the winner much of the time being one or another of the social sciences, or what purports to be social science—that is, courses in self-improvement or mental hygiene or family harmony and the like, or courses that draw heavily on the jargon or data of the social science disciplines, most commonly a watered-down psychology or sociology.

When we ponder these changes, we lament what has been lost— that knowledge of history or literature or languages or the classics or political theory, which we believe to make up an important part of what it is to be educated. That emphasis, on what is being lost, is quite understandable—it startles us when we observe how little of our cultural legacy is being passed on. But there is another side to the matter one finds rarely addressed: the character and quality of that which replaces what is no longer taught. We tell ourselves that while we might prefer our youngsters to be taught literature and history, the psychology and sociology they are getting instead are, after all, quite satisfactory in their own way, and probably more interesting to most students. The question is, Are they in fact satisfactory?

I believe not. The social sciences are in my view far weaker than is commonly realized. They are especially weak in those areas likely to be of interest to a general audience, most frequently taught in high school courses, and for that matter in introductory undergraduate courses. I will argue that these deficiencies are extensive enough and deep enough to warrant a reconsideration of the place of the social sciences in the curriculum. Let me first set limits and offer some clarifications.

What I will say does not apply, obviously, to all of the social sciences; but on the other hand, it is meant to apply to those with which I am acquainted: such fields and topics as clinical psychology and psychiatry, many parts of child and adolescent psychology, personality theory and research, and portions of social psychology and sociology. Furthermore, the more deeply one penetrates into the literature of a given topic, the more one is likely to entertain doubts—I mean grave doubts—about the adequacy of our knowledge. Let me stress that I do not have in mind exalted standards, the stringent criteria a philosopher of science might bring to bear in judging the strength of a discipline. I have in mind weaknesses that would be plain to any educated citizen, instructed in its languages and techniques. Finally, the problems I will be discussing are not in my view due to incompetence or to lack of talent or insight or diligence. Almost all social scientists actively engaged in research are intelligent, most are resourceful, and many are brilliant, quite the equal in capacity, *mutatis mutandis*, of scholars and scientists in other disciplines.

The difficulties lie deeper. They derive from the fact that human nature and social existence are stubbornly, irreducibly complex, so that the problems of studying them are maddeningly refractory, often insoluble, except in a long run that seems never to arrive. Easy problems turn out to be hard; hard problems turn out to be close to impossible. Problems that were thought to be long solved turn out never to have been solved at all. I sometimes believe that the myth of Sisyphus was written with a social scientist in mind.

As an example, consider what would seem to be an easy problem:

Some years ago I was asked whether educating secondary school students to the hazards of drug use would prove to be effective. I said that I did not know but would try to find out. I discovered that there was a substantial literature, many studies having already been done. I also discovered that the question remained unanswered. Some of the time drug education reduced drug use; some of the time it made no perceptible difference; some of the time it increased use. So far as I could tell, there was no relationship between type of outcome and the apparent quality of the research—that is, the more carefully controlled studies did not seem to produce different types of results from others. This was some years ago, as I said, and it may well be that a pattern has begun to emerge. A mystery—no doubt soluble, given enough time and effort, but bear in mind that the question posed could not have been more straightforward, nor the design necessary to answer it easier to implement.

It is not an odd or anomalous example; to the contrary, one can find dozens—no, hundreds—of other questions where research findings point in no particular direction. After much earnest and ingenious effort, we still have no clear idea as to whether and when and how viewing television violence induces aggressive behavior. Nor do we know whether or when or how early experience affects the development of personality; nor whether and when and how emotional disorders are consequent to trauma; nor just why it is that boys are more able in mathematical and girls in verbal skills. These four examples come from the top of my head, without searching memory. Just why is our level of achievement so low? Here are three reasons.

Thinness

It is not usually recognized by the general public—or, for that matter, by specialists in adjoining areas—how skimpy our knowledge really is on many important topics. Several years ago I edited a handbook of adolescent psychology, designed to be a definitive reference work, aimed at scholars and graduate students. The most unsettling effect of this task was to make me aware of how little is known on some very vital matters. For example, two distinguished experts separately refused my request to prepare a chapter on female adolescent psychology, on the grounds that there was too little solid information at hand to warrant it. I had the same experience in casting about for a treatment of adolescent family relations: here again, those I consulted argued that while there was a great deal of writing on the topic, it was on the whole anecdotal, little of it informed empirically. I discovered we have only recently begun to study the effect of part-time work on the lives of adolescents, despite its being a major social and economic phenomenon. We know little about normal personality development, not much about the growth of adolescent thinking. And so on.

Now one may suspect that for various reasons adolescence is an underfunded and understudied topic within developmental psychology, just as developmental studies in general are underfunded compared with many others. Be that as it may, there are a great many other topics within the social sciences where we have the sense of knowing much more than in fact we do. There are many reasons. We quite naturally tend to study what is or seems easiest to study, or what seems feasible. As a result, we have many more studies of children's thinking, a fairly accessible topic, than of children's personality, which offers formidable difficulties; for the same reasons, we have more studies of children's thinking on mathematical and scientific tasks than on how they deal with problems in such areas as literature and history. We also tend to study what is being funded, and funding is often a response to political pressures or to the crises of the moment. Or we study what it is fashionable to study, which may or may not prove to be of enduring value—examine any ten-year-old journal in the social sciences. The reasons are many, and the usual result is a relative surfeit of work on some topics and a remarkable barrenness elsewhere.

Unless one is deeply expert in a topic, and beyond that, given to a certain mordancy in the appraisal of others, one is not apt to become fully aware of these deficiencies. There is that tendency to strive for closure, to achieve narrative consistency and completeness, so that we find ourselves, unwittingly, filling in what we do not know by reference to what seems plausible, or intuitively correct, or the current conventional wisdom. We find ourselves offering our students (or the press) a portrait of our knowledge that unwittingly covers over its limitations. It is not unusual to find our assumptions not merely shaken, but entirely overturned by the appearance of one or two new studies, a state of affairs we would likely not find were our data base more substantial to begin with.

Complexity

Even in areas where we have an apparent abundance of evidence, we soon find that it adds up to much less than we thought; it merely instructs us that the topic is far more convoluted than we imagined. The deeper we penetrate, the more information we amass, the more confused and uncertain we become. Consider that question the clinical psychologist is so often asked: Does psychotherapy work? As it happens, we have had a vast number of studies carried out on the question—over a thousand, in fact. Through a statistical *tour de force* called meta-analysis, this plethora of investigations has now been reduced and analyzed, so that we may conclude that it does indeed work. Yet having discovered this much, over the years and painfully, we now find that we can say little more. We do not know whether any given form of therapy is more effective than any other, or which therapists do good work and which do not—that is, whether it is the training that counts, or the theory, or the personality, or the experience, or the mode of treatment, or whatever. We cannot tell with any degree of confidence which patients are likely to get better, and which are not.

Now one may reply that even these questions have been posed too broadly, that if one were to ask more focused questions about psychotherapy and its effects, one might well come up with satisfying answers. Yet here is what one finds in a quick survey of two recent volumes of *Psychological Bulletin,* a magisterial journal specializing in literature reviews. There are six articles in very specific areas of psychotherapy. Here is a sampling: an article on desensitization procedures in the treatment of childhood disorders—sixty-six studies are reviewed. The conclusion is that "clear evidence for the effectiveness of any variant of desensitization with children is limited. . . ." There is another on the effect of therapists' interpersonal skills. It reviews ninety-one studies and concludes that "the efficacy of popular interpersonal skills models has not been demonstrated." Finally, there is a review on a very narrow topic indeed, the effects of disconfirmed client role expectations in psychotherapy. There were seventy-two researches available for review, the idea tested being that it will have a negative effect on the therapy if something happens that the patient did not look forward to. The conclusion: "The empirical studies are evenly divided in supporting this hypothesis." During the two-year period surveyed, in no instance do we find unequivocal support for any given hypothesis or expectation.

Bias

A third source of weakness is the unrecognized influence of ideology, such that the results achieved confirm the sentiments or attitudes or presuppositions of the investigator. One senses that although the problem is recognized, its full dimensions are not. For one thing, social scientists are extremely homogeneous in politics and social outlook; for another it is infra dig to raise that kind of objection to any line of research, except when the position being criticized has acquired pariah status, as in studies of race and intelligence. Yet whether or not social scientists are ready to face up to it, unrecognized ideological bias exercises a corrosive effect on the probity of the work. There is a strong and persistent bias against nativist explanations with respect to personality, psychopathology, competence, and so on. There is a strong tendency to write glowingly of those groups that share the modernist-liberal outlook common to most social scientists, and to patronize those groups that do not; studies of the "authoritarian personality" are one example, studies of "radical youth" are another. Research on sex differences has recently become so politicized that one cannot accept findings before giving them the most careful scrutiny. And much the same is true of many topics within such domains as sexuality, child care, marital conflict, and the like.

These weaknesses—and others—are most evident in those areas likely to be of widespread general interest—the family, politics, morality, and so on; and it is also worth noting that many of these topics are also the concern of the humanities.

The social sciences are attractive to us through the promise—sometimes made openly, sometimes merely implied—that they will provide a scientific answer to age-old questions the humanities have handled through mere assertion, or by Jesuitical disputation, or by a stubborn reliance on tradition. For example, how can we decide about right and wrong, without relying entirely on the dogmatic asseverations to be found in most Western religions or becoming lost in the linguistic tangles of analytic philosophy? How do we choose, let us say, between a doctrine treating morality as a commitment to the social order and one that stresses a universally valid sense of inner conscience? How appealing it would be to learn that there is a scientific theory, supported by hard empirical findings, meeting those difficult positivist criteria specified by Isaiah Berlin, which will bring us to the solution of those presumably insoluble questions!

The example given is by no means hypothetical. Our most widely known theory of moral psychology, proposed and elaborated by Lawrence Kohlberg, makes just that claim. By analyzing the responses to a rather limited set of moral dilemmas (involving distributive justice) he is able, Kohlberg says, to establish a level of moral maturity and place the respondent on a six-step scale ranging from a brutish *Macht-ist-Recht* primitivism at the bottom to a sort of Kantian nimbus of principled morality at the top. This is not the place to examine the system and its claims in detail; nevertheless it should be said that most other scholars of moral psychology hold it to be deeply flawed technically and empirically, and most moral philosophers interested in psychological questions view it as both naive and mistaken. Even those writers who honor Kohlberg's effort or find some merit in parts of his work see the system as grandiose and simpleminded, promising more than it can possibly deliver and delivering a highly reduced version of the realm of moral experience. Yet these grave reservations have not so far hindered a general acceptance of Kohlberg's system as a pathbreaking discovery. It is treated in a variety of college-level texts as though it were among the established truths of contemporary psychology. Why should that be? Because its very deficiency, its reductiveness, is taken to be, mistakenly, the concision characteristic of the natural sciences. It is a six-rung ladder of virtue, easily remembered, easily understood, yet with enough apparent complexity to suggest that the social sciences are fully up to the large, eternal questions.

If that is the moral theory we provide for undergraduates, it is not hard to imagine the further reductiveness required to accommodate the high school student's far more limited background. Inevitably, the stages of moral development would become fixed truths, hence facts to be memorized, like the table of elements or the Watson-Crick model of DNA. What is most troubling is that the conversion of a humanistic issue to a "scientific" one will almost certainly inhibit the discussion of those moral questions we would address more fruitfully in the study of history, philosophy, and literature—such questions of moral relativism and absolutism, or the relation between moral belief and moral action, or the nature of free will in moral choice.

The case of moral psychology is in no way unique. To the contrary, it is difficult to think of instances where social science—particularly through its quantitatively derived findings—genuinely enhances our grasp of the humanities, or of those haunting, recurrent issues Henry Murray wrote about. Up to this point the social sciences have been most fruitful as a new and alternative mode of humanistic discovery and interpretation. In psychology, Freud is the most obvious example, but our other great thinkers—James, Piaget, even Skinner—will survive not through their scientific findings but as humanistic visionaries.

If they were taught in that fashion, one would have few qualms about the social sciences in the secondary schools. Yet the social sciences are taught in entirely different ways and for entirely different reasons—because they are topical, or because students find them personally relevant. One teacher told me that the social science curriculum could not be displaced because students found the courses enjoyable and because they believed, however erroneously, that they were learning matters of great value to them. If that is so, and I fear it is, so be it; but we ought to recognize that what is taught most of the time is a gussied-up version of the human-interest social science we find in newspapers, mindcult magazines, and TV docudramas. These bring us breathless news about solutions to "important social problems" provided by "recent studies." There is a good chance that the account provided will be of that new journalistic genre called faction, that is, not quite fiction yet not quite hard fact either—rather, a mélange of studies with varying and unknown degrees of reliability, varying and unknown degrees of validity, varying and unknown degrees of generalizability. If the social sciences were taught honestly, with their defects fully visible, as an example of the pain and patience required to secure a few truths, then and only then would they merit a place in the schools.

Even then, they could not provide that amplitude of knowledge and mind we gain from the humanities taught earnestly and well. It cannot be put better than it was by John Stuart Mill, a century and a half ago, in the great essay on civilization. Discussing the study of history, he wrote that it must occupy an important place in education "partly because it is the record of all the great things which have been achieved by mankind, and partly because when philosophically studied it gives a certain largeness of conception to the student, and familiarizes him with the action of great causes. . . . Nowhere else will the infinite varieties of human nature be so vividly brought home to him, and anything cramped or one-sided in his own standard of it so effectually corrected, and nowhere else will he behold so strongly exemplified the astonishing pliability of our nature, and the vast effects which may under good guidance be produced upon it by honest endeavour."

That would be true as well for other humanistic disciplines, certainly literature and philosophy, the exacting study of which can stimulate other largeness of conception and offer other exposures to the variety and pliability of the human spirit. How much we have lost through the eclipse of the humanities is evident each time we read, say, the documents of the American Revolution, above all the Federalist Papers, and remember that the writers were on the whole ordinary citizens of the educated class, their collective genius formed by the classics and literature and philosophy; or in reading the letters of William James, and finding much the same command of language and ideas among so many of his correspondents, not themselves great men, but educated to the standard of the times. Regaining that standard is almost certainly beyond our means, yet some effort must be made in the schools to restore some of the common culture. Otherwise, the citizen becomes, as Mill said in another compelling essay, "a poor, maimed, lopsided fragment of humanity."

The Natural Sciences and the Humanities

Bernard R. Gifford

As a professional educator trained in the sciences and devoted to the humanities, I have often stood in the midst of debates between humanists and scientists over which policies would result in real and effective school reform. These encounters have rarely been real debates, in the sense that they rarely have produced a set of shared assumptions about what constitutes a well-balanced curriculum. The scientists characteristically advocate more courses in science and mathematics for precollegiate students. The humanists express similar sentiments in favor of more study of the humanities. More often than not, where agreements have been reached, they have been the result of a search for accommodation, not the product of mutual understanding.

Similar "debates" are taking place all over the country as more and more school districts consider restructuring their schools' curricula in light of the various education reports and commission recommendations. These debates tend to pose a serious challenge to the humanities, for advocates of courses in English, history, language, and art all too often find themselves on the defensive in the face of pressure to shift more emphasis to math and science courses. The situation is treated as a zero-sum game: the schools have finite resources, and enhancement of the math and science curriculum poses the threat that the necessary resources will come from a reduction of resources to the humanities curriculum.

The debates arise over legitimate questions: Why not reduce a three-year course of study in French to two years and add a year of computer programming instruction? Why not replace the social studies unit on European history with a unit on elementary statistics? After all, isn't it better to encourage scientifically and mathematically inclined youngsters to develop their talents than to require them to study the languages or histories of countries they will probably never visit except as tourists?

The humanists have a reply to such questions: in defense of keeping the traditional humanities courses in the curriculum, they cite the benefits of humanities study, the central role these subjects play in developing creativity and moral maturity, and the insight they provide into ways of life foreign to our own. But too often humanists sense that they are fighting a losing battle. Worse, it is a puzzling battle, for often they find that they do not agree with their colleagues on the other side of the debate on the issue of what counts as a good reason for justifying the inclusion of a course in the curriculum. From the point of view of the humanists, the "other side" places too much value on technical training and job preparation and not enough on contemplative and reflective activities. On the other hand, advocates of scientific and mathematical education believe that studying the humanities is a good thing, but it ought not take priority over the responsibility of the school to instruct students in what they see as the more useful knowledge provided by mathematics and the sciences. Amid a climate of public opinion that demands verification of the productivity of the educational process, the case for the humanities seems difficult to make against the manifest benefits of additional science and math education.

How should such debates be adjudicated? Must humanists always feel threatened? There are no easy solutions, but in this essay I wish to argue that any proposal to tip the balance of the school curriculum in favor of math and science, if grounded in a belief in the superiority of scientific knowledge over that provided by the study of the humanities, is a proposal based on an error. Moreover, this regrettably widespread belief is a historical product with its roots in European intellectual history. Assuming here the role of an amateur historian, I propose to uncover those roots in order to establish the reasons for the split between the sciences and the humanities and to show why many of the beliefs that serve to justify the continuation of this split are false, the more so when applied to the school curriculum.

Studying the humanities provides access to knowledge of a quite different sort than that acquired through learning the latest formulas of physics or mastering the elements of numerical analysis. It can provide insight into the human condition in all its variety and complexity. Other contributors to this volume have explained why this insight is an essential part of a youngster's education. It will be my task to support their efforts by putting the competing claims of scientific knowledge into the proper perspective.

The Two Cultures

The issues underlying this debate are scarcely new. More than a quarter of a century ago, in May 1959, C. P. Snow delivered the Rede Lecture at Cambridge University and took as his title and theme "The Two Cultures and the Scientific Revolution."[1] Snow's celebrated thesis, simply expressed, was that there existed a gulf of mutual incomprehension between natural scientists and humanists. In summarizing that lecture, Snow says:

> In our society (that is, advanced western society) we have lost even the pretence of a common culture. Persons educated with the greatest intensity we know can no longer communicate with each other on the plane of their major intellectual concern. This is serious for our creative, intellectual and, above all, our normal life. It is leading us to interpret the past wrongly, to misjudge the present, and to deny our hopes of the future. It is making it difficult or impossible for us to take good action.
>
> I gave the most pointed example of this lack of communication in the shape of two groups of people, representing what I have christened "the two cultures." One of these contained the scientists, whose weight, achievement and influence did not need stressing. The other contained the literary intellectuals. . . . Literary intellectuals represent, vocalise, and to some extent shape and predict the mood of the non-scientific culture: they do not make the decisions, but their words seep into the minds of those who do. Between these two groups—the scientists and the literary intellectuals—there is little communication and, instead of fellow-feeling, something like hostility.[2]

Snow admitted that the gulf separating the two cultures was more pronounced in Britain than in the United States, but the lack of communication presented no less serious a problem in this country. Indeed, in the United States today, the gulf that Snow described continues to separate scientists and humanists. It is growing and will not easily be narrowed. Many people know little of science. As

Stephen R. Graubard, editor of *Daedalus*, notes in a recent special edition on scientific literacy, "To say that science is a mystery for great numbers—that it appears to be largely inaccessible even to men and women who believe themselves educated—that this condition is scarcely improving, is now commonly accepted."[3]

Others, well versed in the sciences, are estranged from the humanities and, as a result, are blind to the power of humanistic learning and understanding needed to illuminate the dark corners of our civilization. During the late 1960s, for example, when the social fabric of our country, especially in the nation's urban centers, was being torn by racial, political and intergenerational conflicts, the dean of M.I.T.'s College of Engineering proclaimed: "I doubt if there is such a thing as an urban crisis, but if there were, M.I.T. would lick it in the same way we handled the Second World War."[4] Of course there was, and still is, an urban crisis. M.I.T., through a myriad of research efforts, did try to "lick it." The crisis—both then and now—resisted approaches used by those who ignore the importance of blending scientific technique with humane intelligence.

The separation of the two cultures has not prevented some mutually enlightening contacts. Communication has been maintained by some on both sides of the gulf who insist upon seeking truth in all its forms. The complex problems of contemporary society require both technical proficiency and culturally informed judgment. The key to any adequate response to these problems is the active involvement of individuals and groups who possess both kinds of knowledge. The schools can play a central role in making this knowledge available to all. Snow himself recognized the importance of education for bridging the gulf between the two cultures:

> There is, of course, no complete solution. In the conditions of our age, or any age which we can foresee, Renaissance man is not possible. But we can do something. The chief means open to us is education—education mainly in primary and secondary schools, but also in colleges and universities. There is no excuse for letting another generation be as vastly ignorant, or as devoid of understanding and sympathy, as we are ourselves.[5]

As one whose formal academic training is in the sciences and as an administrator and faculty member at a research university, I have thought often about Snow's observations and their larger implications for curriculum planning and development. It is clear that the current trend of encouraging students to specialize ever earlier in their education runs counter to the objective of providing a sound education in the humanities *and* in the sciences. If permitted to continue unchecked, this trend alone promises to turn C. P. Snow's gulf into a deep and permanent chasm across which no bridge of mutual understanding can be constructed and maintained.

Narrowing the gap will require other changes in the way we educate our young people, and I will have more to say about some of these later. First, however, I hope to convince those who do not believe that the humanities are just as deserving as the natural sciences of a place in the school curriculum. Such doubters typically believe that anything worth knowing can be discovered via the methods characteristic of the natural sciences. A look into the history of the split between the sciences and the humanities will demonstrate the falsity of this belief. Different kinds of objects of knowledge require different methods for their investigation. Inquiry guided by questions like, What constitutes a life worth living? cannot be conducted as though we were, for example, investigating the electrical properties of metals. The good life is an entirely different sort of thing.

I believe that both the humanist and the natural or physical scientist are seeking true knowledge. In the following account, I will try to show that it is wrong to regard each side of the gulf as one of two adequate and complete ways of seeing the world—one pursuing truth in a quantifiable way, the other in a qualitative way. Alone, each side represents an incomplete view of the world. Each approach to the truth is not only valid, but a much-needed complement to the other. This insight offers guidance for considering ways in which the rift between the two cultures can be bridged in the schoolroom, both through the content of the curriculum and through methods of instruction, so that our students can have the opportunity to develop a comprehensive and critical vision of the world.

In the next several sections, I trace the beginnings of the rift between the two cultures through an examination of the history of literature and science. These sections conclude with an argument for the importance to a democratic society of both scientific knowledge and knowledge gained through the humanities. The final section returns to the American school of the late twentieth century and the implications of my investigations for the curriculum. First, however, accompany this amateur historian on a brief sojourn into the past.

Sincerity and the Pursuit of Truth

The work of the distinguished literary critic, Lionel Trilling, offers a clue to the origins of the rift between the two cultures. In *Sincerity and Authenticity*, Trilling writes,

Now and then it is possible to observe the moral life in process of revising itself, perhaps by reducing the emphasis it formerly placed upon one or another of its elements, perhaps by inventing and adding to itself a new element, some mode of conduct or of feeling which hitherto it had not regarded as essential to virtue. . . . At a certain point in its history the moral life of Europe added to itself a new element, the state of quality of the self which we call sincerity. . . . It refers primarily to a congruence between avowal and actual feeling.[6]

Trilling is primarily concerned with the treatment of sincerity in European literature. He finds Shakespeare's *Hamlet* to be especially concerned with this theme. Of particular interest to him is Polonius's famous advice to his son Laertes: "This above all: to thine own self be true/ And it doth follow, as the night the day,/ Thou canst not then be false to any man." The statement surprises us, says Trilling, for "our impulse to make its sense consistent with our general view of Polonius is defeated by the way the lines sound, by their lucid moral lyricism. This persuades us that Polonius has had a moment of self-transcendence, of grace and truth."[7]

Concern with being true to one's self in order to avoid being false to any man marked the emergence of the conception of the individual. Trilling's claim, "At a certain point in history men became individuals," sounds strange to the modern ear. Trilling acknowledges this fact:

Taken in isolation, the statement is absurd. How was a man different from an individual? A person born before a certain date, a man—had he not eyes? had he not hands, organs, dimensions, senses, affections, passions? . . . But certain things he did not have or do until he became an individual. He did not have an awareness of what one historian . . . calls internal space. He did not . . . imagine himself in more than one role, standing outside or above his own personality; he did not suppose that he might be an object of interest to his fellow . . . simply because as an individual he was of consequence. It is when he becomes an individual that a man lives more and more in private rooms.[8]

The appearance of a new literary genre, the autobiography, is for Trilling indicative of the new sense of the "sincere self": "The subject of an autobiography is just such a self, bent on revealing himself in all his truth, bent, that is to say, on demonstrating his sincerity."[9]

As the virtue of sincerity became increasingly self-evident and self-perpetuating, systematic flattery, demonstrative self-abasement, and even compulsive buffoonery—behaviors that had been expected and acceptable—began to be the objects of scorn and disdain. Acts rooted in dissimulation, feigning, and pretense were condemned by persons whose conception of proper conduct was informed by this new element in the moral life, as were acts of empty piety and routine ritual.

The mark of the sincere life, the revelation of one's true self, finds another parallel in the new scientific consciousness emerging in the same period. This parallel aspect is science's orientation toward discovering the truth about some object of knowledge through an examination of the thing itself, rather than through secondhand reports about the object. In order to understand the significance of the emergence of this new scientific consciousness, we must take note of some salient features of the social setting from which it arose.

In Transition: Sixteenth-Century Europe

While it was never literarally true that European society before the sixteenth century was divided into those who ruled, those who prayed, and those who labored, these three functions were assigned to particular classes, and these classes occupied definite places in a rather rigid, hierarchial social order. First were the nobility, almost always a hereditary caste, whose privileged position rested on the belief that they were morally responsible for supplying authority and order to those beneath them in the social structure. Second were the clergy, the dominant intellectual voice and spiritual authority. Third were the masses of the people, largely engaged in agriculture, living at the level of bare subsistence, without the means to choose their occupations or to move very far from their places of birth.

Until the sixteenth century, the majority of the princes who functioned as the heads of states were illiterate. Literacy and learning were concentrated in the clergy. One important aspect of the church's role as intellectual authority was the preservation of many of the classics of Greek and Roman learning, which in many cases were incorporated into official Christian dogma. Chief among these are the works of Aristotle and Ptolemy, whose writings on natural philosophy were taken as authoritative accounts of the place of the earth in the universe.

Aristotle, whose attempt to organize all knowledge into a systematic and coherent system remains unparalleled in the Christian era, developed a theory of the universe that governed the theoretical formulations of astronomers into the sixteenth century. His universe was self-contained and self-sufficient—a sphere, whose outer surface was the orbit of the stars. Outside that sphere there was nothing, a void. Inside was a series of nesting spheres whose center was the earth. These spheres marked the orbits of the heavenly bodies that moved around the earth.

Building on the theories of Aristotle, Ptolemy developed a theory that fairly accurately accounted for the motions of the sun and the moon, and the regularities as well as irregularities of the seven known planets. In the *Almagest* (A.D. 240), Ptolemy presented a systematic mathematical account of all of the celestial motions, and this remained the basic astronomy text for nearly thirteen centuries. The conception of compounded circular orbits within an earth-centered universe dominated every theory of planetary motion until the work of Copernicus (1473–1543), whose *De Revolutionibus Orbium Caelestium* (1543) removed the earth from the center of the universe, treating it as just another planet revolving about the sun.

As Thomas Kuhn notes in *The Copernican Revolution*,[10] Copernicus did not rush to embrace his own findings. Had he sought to press for recognition of the validity of his views, he would have found little support, for he was not only presenting a new astronomical theory, he was also an *individual* challenging a church dogma whose validity was seen to rest on centuries of affirmation by the learned members of the religious community. There was as yet no other community of learning to which to appeal for recognition.

With the accumulation of more evidence for the validity of the new astronomy, including the work of Kepler (1571–1630) and Galileo (1564–1642), it became increasingly clear to thinking people that a theory of astronomy based on observation was preferable, even superior, to one based on traditional authority. This change of thinking accompanied the breakdown of the church's monopoly on learning. The church's authority to act as the sole arbiter of truth began to be challenged by a new community of scholars—both scientists and humanists. That these scholars often had deep loyalties and strong connections to the ecclesiastical establishment made their challenge that much more momentous. As a result of this challenge, the power and influence of traditional authority on the intellectual temper and style of Western civilization were lastingly altered in the direction of greater respect for the truth-seeking powers of the individual intellect. To explore how this came to be, we need to note several concurrent changes in European social and cultural life.

By the end of the fifteenth century, it was evident that the stability of the castelike social structure could no longer be taken for granted. Relationships among the church, the nobility, and the masses, which had remained relatively stable from the period following the disintegration of the Roman Empire to medieval times, were coming under new pressures. One important development was the rise of commerce and trade, resulting in increasing economic and political influence of the merchants and a corresponding growth of the towns and cities that served as centers of trade. New opportunities for commercial interaction among and between the various classes and the development of new professions hastened the disintegration of the traditional barriers between the classes through enhanced social mobility.

Of all the events that resulted in a redistribution of the traditional functions of the clerical class, perhaps none made so dramatic an impact as the technological marvel of the fifteenth century—the invention of the printing press. It made possible the transcription and transmission of knowledge across class lines and institutions. It facilitated a new way of knowing, a tutorless knowledge, thus making education more democratic and more personal. It enabled people to read the Bible for themselves, to gain intimate knowledge of antiquity, to take part, if only vicariously, in religious debates over practices and intellectual foundations. It also enabled nonclerics to pass on their thoughts about the present and the future. Above all, the printing press stimulated the growth of a secular reading public and promoted the secularization of scholarship. All of these changes threatened the traditional intellectual authority of the church. Historian Hugh Thomas observes:

> Printing posed a challenge to the 'propaganda by sight' upon which preachers had relied for so long. In Victor Hugo's *Notre-Dame de Paris* a scholar deep in meditation in his study gazes first at the first printed book which has come to his hands, and then at the cathedral visible through a window: 'This will kill that,' he says. Printing also raised a fundamental question about the need for an institutionalized Church: if all could understand the Bible what need was there of a middleman, so to speak, between God and man, in the form of a priest?[11]

The Authority of the Individual: Erasmus, Bacon, and Descartes

In the figure of Desiderium Erasmus we find the convergence of the main elements of our discussion thus far: the value of sincerity, the secularization of learning, and the increased importance of individual moral authority. Copies of Erasmus's books, written in Latin, were widely circulated all over Europe and were read by princes, clergy, and laity. Included among his works is *Enchiridion Militis Christiani*, published in 1503 and commonly referred to as *The Manual of the Christian Knight*. Erasmus wrote *Enchiridion* to teach laymen how to practice true Christian piety. While asserting that knowledge, especially moral knowledge, comes from the Bible, Erasmus also argued that the study of classical poets, rhetoricians, and philosophers supplies an important complement to the study of traditional religious texts. He also emphasized that penances, fasts, and good works, hitherto considered the marks of a good Christian, were all to no avail if they were done without a sincere spirit of Christian charity. There was no salvation in simple adherence to prescribed ritual. Merely acting out the required ceremonies—fasting, making pilgrimages, lighting candles to the saints, and praying for indulgences—did not make a good Christian. These good works might be necessary, but they were not sufficient.

A subsequent work by Erasmus, *The Praise of Folly* (1511), is concerned with insincerity and is a direct attack on the vices and pretenses of morally impoverished but behaviorally correct members of the clergy and the nobility. He also continued to be particularly harsh in criticizing the emphasis placed on formal obedience to church law. The omission of pious practices, Erasmus argued, might be regarded as unimportant in the sight of Heaven if the sincere intention of the individual Christian was in accordance with the spirit of the gospel.

If sincere intention, not overt behavior, was to be the true mark of moral and spiritual worthiness, the only person who could know for certain whether one was in a state of spiritual health was oneself. One could test and improve the adequacy of one's sincere faith by serious study of the scriptures and other traditional texts—study now accessible to the layman. Of course, the opening up of the possibility of individual religious study did not spell the demise of the church, but it was part of the emergence of a new, secular community of learning that recognized the moral and intellectual authority of the individual.

Scientists, too, were part of this new community of learning. Much as Erasmus had emphasized sincerity as the criterion of acceptable moral character, scientists were concerned with criteria for acceptable scientific claims. The sincerity of the individual investigator was one requirement, but scientists found that what most often blocked the advance of scientific knowledge were uncritical habits of mind, resulting in claims that were not based on the actual findings of experiment and observation, but that represented what the investigator wished or supposed to be the case about the object under investigation. Consequently, some scientists wrote works on the proper and improper conduct of scientific investigation, offering guidelines for the correct use of the intellect and warning against common sources of error.

Among those writers, perhaps the most celebrated was Francis Bacon (1561–1626). In a series of three works—*Advancement of Learning* (1603), *New Atlantis* (1618), and *Novum Organum, or True Suggestions for the Interpretation of Nature* (1620)—Bacon presented a general survey of the state of scientific learning in many different areas, indicating which were well developed, which in need of improvement, and which entirely unexplored. He also explained his theories for the proper use of reason, relying on the following principle: "Those . . .

who aspire not to guess and divine but to discover and know; . . . to examine and dissect the nature of this very world itself; must go to facts themselves for everything."[12] One of Bacon's targets was the method of deduction, based on Aristotle's theory of the syllogism and one of the scholastics' favorite means for discovering the joint implications of a set of statements. Such methods, Bacon noted, were good for little else but "disputations and contentions" and had no application to the newly developing methods of experimental science, where knowledge was not deducible from speculative metaphysics but derived from the scientist's own observations.[13]

In place of deduction, Bacon advocated his own refinements of the method of induction. The scholastics had employed a conception of induction, *enumeratio simplex*, to explain how we learn from repetition of instances. According to this conception, "we generalise on the basis of chance observation and, if we encounter no contrary instance, we pronounce it valid."[14] For Bacon, this conception of induction was nothing more than "overhasty generalisation of everyday experience." An inductive method generative of scientific knowledge of nature must proceed step by step, he contended, through carefully planned experiment and observation. The scientist must avoid making generalizations about a natural phenomenon until he has contrived to observe that phenomenon under as many different conditions as possible. Bacon also prescribed a discipline for the self-purification of the mind from the power of "idols," or unconscious prejudices and distorting influences, including uncritical acceptance of the evidence of the senses and misleading conventions of language.

Bacon was not alone in his determination to critically examine and purify the processes by which an inquirer gained access to knowledge. René Descartes (1596–1650), the French mathematician, found the classic works of antiquity deficient in their intellectual foundations. He compared them to palaces built on sand and mud. What the ancients had written might be true, he said, but without a demonstrated solid base in absolute certainty, the ancient classics had no claim to be counted as science. In his *Discourse on the Method of Rightly Conducting the Reason and Seeking Truth in the Sciences* (1637), Descartes outlined the method by which he believed it was possible to ascertain true knowledge. The "method for rightly conducting the reason" can be summarized in the four rules by which Descartes bound himself in his own investigations:

> The *first* was never to accept anything as true when I did not recognize it clearly to be so, that is to say, to carefully avoid precipitation and prejudice, and to include in my opinions nothing beyond that which

should present itself so clearly and so distinctly to my mind that I might have no occasion to doubt it.

The *second*, to divide each of the difficulties which I should examine into as many portions as were possible, and as should be required for its better solution.

The *third*, to conduct my thought in order, by beginning with the simplest objects, and those most easy to know, so as to mount little by little, as if by steps, to the most complex knowledge, and even assuming an order among those which do not naturally precede one another.

The *last*, to make everywhere enumerations so complete, and surveys so wide that I should be sure of omitting nothing.[15]

The recognition of clearly and distinctly indubitable opinions was the work of the faculty of mind that Decartes termed "intuition."

Both Descartes and Bacon attempted to deal with the problem of how to ensure that the individual scientist used reliable procedures, including reasoning processes, in generating new knowledge. The picture that emerges of the ideal investigator is an individual with "an unclouded and attentive mind," alert to the dangers of untested opinions and misleading language, conducting carefully designed experiments, and recording the results and conclusions to be drawn from them in unambiguous language for the edification of other members of the scientific community. This picture has remained the dominant popular conception of the scientist to our own day.

The conception of the sincere autobiographer—the scientist's counterpart in the realm of human nature—has not, however, enjoyed as successful and durable a career. Trilling explains that "sincerity" was found to be deficient as a moral category and was in time replaced by "authenticity." Understanding the reasons for this development will illuminate the alienation of the investigation of nature from the exploration of human nature.

From Sincerity to Authenticity

Complications in the development of the notion of sincerity began to appear soon after its introduction into the moral vocabulary of the sixteenth century. The contrast between Shakespeare's sincere Horatio, on the one hand, and Hamlet, insincere in his feigned madness, on the other, represents one step in the exploration of sincerity. Alceste, the protagonist of Molière's play, *Le Misanthrope*, represents another. The play is ultimately about the opposition between society and the sincere man: society finds the sincere man ridiculous; the sincere man renounces society in protest of its subversion of sincerity.

A further development of the theme of the shaping influence of society is found in Diderot's Le Neveu de Rameau, or Rameau's Nephew, written between 1761 and 1774. The young man of the title is an excellent example of the adaptations necessary for survival in the high society of late eighteenth-century France. Trilling offers a summary portrait of this extraordinary character: Out of concern for self-preservation,

> he is preoccupied, we might say obsessed, with society and with the desire for place and power in society. . . . Reduced to a bare subsistence as a parasite at the tables of the rich, he directs all his ingenuity towards perfecting the devices of systematic flattery, yet he cannot succeed even in this miserable mode of life. . . . He is the victim of an irresistible impulse to offend those with whom he seeks to ingratiate himself.[16]

On one interpretation of this work, the Nephew has succumbed to the temptations of luxurious living and is striving, by flattery and guile, to insinuate himself into the company of the rich. On such an interpretation, he is to be judged for his insincerity and the base behavior to which it leads. But Trilling warns us against too hasty a judgment. Diderot's purpose, he contends, is much more complex:

> Whatever is to be said in condemnation of the self-seeking duplicity of society, of the great financiers, their wives and their little actresses and singers, and of the courtiers, and the King himself, one person, the Nephew, transcends the moral categories and the judgement they dictate. Diderot the deuteragonist is at pains to treat him with discriminating condescension and to rebuke him for a deficiency of moral commitment, but we know that Diderot the author of the dialogue gives us full licence to take the Nephew to our hearts and minds, where he figures not only as an actual person but also as an aspect of humanity itself, as the liberty that we wish to believe is inherent in the human spirit, in its energy of effort, expectation, and desire, in its consciousness of itself and its limitless contradictions.[17]

The character of the young man cannot be summarily dismissed as insincere. His insincerity represents a universal trait, an adaptation demanded by society's rules for survival. The Nephew thus transcends judgment according to the criterion of sincerity. The reader's identification with and acceptance of the young Rameau is a response of recognition—the young Rameau is a modern man, caught in the struggle to remain true to his inmost self, the self beneath the masks and poses. The struggle is not, however, for the purpose of presenting one's true self to the world; it is directed to the end of personal identity and autonomy. One strives to be authentic.

The theme of autonomy and authenticity is a characteristic mark of contemporary literature, says Trilling. The fundamental belief in the limitless possibilities of the human spirit is, I believe, the point on which humanists came into sharpest opposition to science and its claims for the unlimited power of the scientific method to explain and predict human behavior.

Mechanism and Autonomy

Belief in the eventual illumination of *all* phenomena, including the inner life of the individual, through scientific investigation was a natural enough extrapolation from the astounding success of the physical sciences. As early as the time of Bacon and Descartes, thoughtful men dreamed of a comprehensive science provided with reliable methods for acquiring true and certain knowledge, a trustworthy arbiter of disputes and a powerful tool for the betterment of life. One product of this way of thinking was a mechanistic worldview, given impetus with the success of Newton's theory of natural laws that govern the movement and interaction of physical objects. Mechanists believed that all human actions result from the interaction of physical objects. They also believed that all interactions of physical objects can be predicted by the laws of Newton's physics. It follows from these two beliefs that all action is susceptible to explanation and prediction on the basis of the laws of physics. The analytic forms of such human sciences as history, economics, psychology, and sociology owe something to the mechanistic worldview of those who tried to turn the dream of universal science into reality. But, as Joseph Adelson observes, the project of applying the methods of the natural sciences to the study of human beings has met with mixed success.

The reason that the human sciences have not enjoyed complete success is, I believe, explainable by a crucial if little-recognized difference between knowledge of physical objects and knowledge of human nature. When inquiry is directed toward uncovering the nature of the thing itself, the scientific method of forming and testing hypotheses through carefully controlled experiment works well for an object whose chief point of interest lies in its fixed nature. Questions such as, Why do metals melt at different temperatures? or, How do plants make chlorophyll? are questions about aspects of metals and plants that are not restricted to unique conditions. Although the observations by means of which these questions are answered include observations under a variety of circumstances, the focus of attention is on the regularities that emerge in the course of the observations.

But when inquiry is directed by such questions as, Is this act that I am about to perform a good act? or, Am I living a worthwhile life? (questions of everyday, practical interest), a method based on abstraction from particular circumstances does not work well at all. Knowledge of what constitutes appropriate action in a particular situation is acquired through the interaction between one's knowledge of what has on previous similar occasions counted as appropriate action and one's own experience of making those choices. Such knowledge does not consist of generalizations about choices and behavior that apply regardless of circumstances, but, rather, it consists in informed judgment of when and how to take into account both the novel and the typical aspects of a situation that calls for decision and action.

The overwhelming success of scientific inquiry led some to believe that all knowledge worth having was knowledge of a thing's fixed nature. With respect to human nature, they believed that one day we would have good reason to believe that a human being, like a chemical element, had a fixed nature and that knowledge about human nature would be accessible to the methods of inquiry used in the physical and biological sciences. But the insight, however clearly or vaguely articulated, that knowledge about human nature is not the same sort of knowledge as that about the movement of the planets is precisely the point on which nineteenth-century humanists rejected the universalistic claims of scientific knowledge. The mechanist worldview, with its belief in the universal applicability of physical laws and its emphasis on prediction and control, was anathema to anyone whose conception of human nature was based on the autonomy of individual choices.

The extent to which the heirs of the traditional humanist culture removed themselves from contact with science is evidenced by the failure of the Western intellectual community to come to terms with the industrial revolution. C. P. Snow cites this failure in his own attempt to account for the continued separation of the "two cultures."[18] In the mid-nineteenth century, he tells us, in neither Britain nor the United States did intellectuals, including the scientific community, recognize the importance for the continuing success of the industrial movement of university training for specialists in applied science. And if industry was not welcome in the academy, neither did humanists venture to explore the human effects of industrialization. The development of a rift between science and technology on the one hand, and the academic humanist culture on the other, was unmistakable.

To Snow's eyes, the detachment, ignorance, and lack of interest with which nineteenth-century intellectuals treated the industrial revolution was still to be found in the 1960s and 1970s in the attitude of much of the general public toward the "scientific revolution," his term for the large-scale application of scientific knowledge to large-scale industry, which has developed out of the industrial revolution.[19] As a consequence, Snow said, most people, including scholars of the humanities, pure scientists, and the average worker, were almost wholly ignorant of the science and technology on which industry relies. The situation today is not significantly different. To borrow Hirsch's terminology, our society has a very low "technological literacy." But similarly lacking is widespread familiarity with thoughtful reflection on the impact of science and technology, both its beneficial and harmful effects, on the lives of human beings. This kind of reflection is the domain of the humanities.

The low level of technological literacy and the absence of shared insight into the human benefits and costs of technology pose twin challenges to the ideal of a truly democratic polity. As more and more public policy decisions require an understanding of scientific and technical processes beyond the level of instruction currently afforded by television and popular magazines, the arena in which democratic decision making can take place will shrink. We are in danger of tyranny by expertise unless we make a determined effort to raise the general level of public understanding. The complexity of the issues demanding attention is staggering. Consider only a few: genetic engineering, acid rain, toxic waste pollution, and defense technology. The task will require dedication and determined effort, and the schools must play a central role. But along with instruction in basic scientific and technological processes, we must not overlook our responsibility to provide our future decision makers with an education that also makes real the dignity of the individual human being, the need for community, and the value of tradition. These values are an important part of the informed decision making appropriate to the demanding task of maintaining a high-technology society committed to democracy.

Implications for the Classroom

Because the rift between the sciences and the humanities has grown into such a serious one with such far-reaching consequences, it is imperative that educators, especially classroom teachers and curriculum developers, take the lead in building bridges that will give students access to and facility with knowledge on both sides of that rift. This is equally important for all students, regardless of career objective. We have a responsibility to make certain that the same assumptions that led us to require that no portion of our system become the exclusive domain of any single group are also applied to the struggle between the sciences and the humanities. For example, ordinary citizens serve on juries to guarantee fairness in the legal system and to guard against tyranny by expertise. Similarly, our governmental system demands that a civilian be commander in chief of the armed services, again to ensure that the wider view will at all times be considered. As citizens, we are familiar with and understand the system of checks and balances within the government. Should we fail to provide the polity with the knowledge its members need—knowledge drawn from both the sciences and the humanities—this system will surely break down.

Of importance to all students is the understanding that the search for truth is in *everyone's domain*, and that each person has a responsibility to seek the truth, regardless of his or her individual vantage point. This makes building bridges across the rift especially important because, to a great extent, the degree to which we can show students various modes of truth-seeking is the degree to which we will be able to involve them in their own pursuits of truth. This process must commence with kindergarten and continue through high school. As students become increasingly familiar with the processes and the products of knowledge on both sides of the rift, they can simultaneously become active users of data and develop into people who respect multiple viewpoints because they understand what those viewpoints represent.

The fact that our society is becoming increasingly technical means that we must provide our students with the broadest-based education that we can. If the only constant is change, then those who are narrowly educated in a single tradition, lacking even an understanding of how that tradition developed, are doomed to obsolescence the moment that the next crop of students learns of newer developments. We must not only provide our science students with an understanding of the history of science, of the development of scientific thought, of the interaction between science and society throughout history, but we must also infuse them with a sense of responsibility to themselves to grow into well-rounded individuals, able to understand themselves and to be conversant with multiple viewpoints. If their perspective is drawn principally from the scientific side of the rift, we must make certain that their vantage point also permits interaction with the humanities, including languages, art, music, and history. Such experiences are a necessary basis for the scientist's sense of responsibility for the implications of his or her research. An integrated education that balances the sciences and the humanities serves to enrich the soul and permits scientists to understand better the complexity of life in the social sphere. Tolstoi gave us all a warning when he said, "Science is meaningless because it gives no answer to our question, the only question important for us: 'What shall we do and how shall we live?' "[20] We must give our future scientists the wherewithal to respond to Tolstoi's question.

Carrying out this ambitious task within the limits of the school curriculum and school year will require innovations in the content of courses and in the ways they are taught. We may have to surrender that narrow conception of the humanities and the sciences that assumes that teaching the one has no relation to teaching the other. I do not ask that disciplinary boundaries be blurred or ignored; rather, I urge that knowledge generated within a discipline be used to enhance learning in other fields.

The point can easily be illustrated: It is a fairly simple matter to include some history of science and technology in a history course. Consider so elemental a matter as the development of urban culture; we would have no cities as we know them without elevators, and no elevators without a knowledge of the laws of physics. Similarly, history can be incorporated into mathematics classes. Students should learn that Descartes invented the coordinate geometry, and Newton the calculus, in order to solve particular methodological problems in their scientific investigations. In literature courses, students ought to read the writings of scientists, who, after all, include some of our greatest humanists. Watson and Crick's *The Double Helix*, an exciting account of their investigations into the structure of DNA, is one example of many excellent texts that might be used. Lewis Thomas's *Lives of a Cell* and the writings of Stephen Jay Gould both combine the best of scientific knowledge with a humanistic perspective. Writing ought likewise to be an important part of science classes. Learning to make concise, step-by-step outlines of procedures is an analytic skill useful in many contexts. Science can also enhance other humanities and art classes: introduction to the principles of the geometry of perspective, the chemistry and physics of color, and the physics of musical instruments are some obvious examples.

The success of such a curriculum hinges on the proper preparation of students, beginning in the earliest grades, where teachers must be able to nurture beginning skills and knowledge of science and math, as well as language, history, and art, in ways that suggest the complementarity of all knowledge. Without a doubt, in order to narrow the gap between Snow's two cultures, we will also have to change the ways we recruit and train teachers. Students cannot be expected to acquire true cultural literacy, in all its dimensions, unless we give them as models teachers who are themselves broadly literate. Schools of education have a responsibility to see that their teacher training programs do not encourage narrow specialization to the neglect of general knowledge.

Finally, those in decision-making positions need to be wary of the temptation to succumb to prevailing pressures to enlarge the science and math curriculum at the expense of literature, history, and language courses. Their solemn obligation is to ensure that American education remains carefully balanced. We cannot expect our young people to make well-informed decisions about career specializations until we have given them knowledge of the alternatives and a chance to explore their talents. It is up to us to make sure that they have the best chance to make the right choices.

This is a tall order. There is already too much to do in school and too little time in which to do it. But when we examine carefully what is at stake, I think that we will all be more willing to work together. By working together, drawing on knowledge from our own various disciplines, the perspectives of our own vantage points, and wisdom drawn from our own experiences, we will not only make the job of bridging the rift easier, we will teach our children by example. There is no better teacher than that and no more effective lesson than one that exhibits a congruence of message and method. We in the schools cannot make the two cultures one. But we can and should take as our solemn responsibility the preparation of every young person to receive the best that both have to offer, and to enrich the lives of all of tomorrow's adults with the valuable knowledge, ideas, and possibilities contained in each.

NOTES

1. See C. P. Snow, *The Two Cultures: And a Second Look* (Cambridge: Cambridge University Press, 1963). This volume contains the Rede Lecture and Snow's response to a rather vigorous, even vituperative, rebuttal of his thesis by F. R. Leavis, published in *Two Cultures? The Significance of C. P. Snow* (London: Chatto & Windus, 1962).

2. Snow, pp. 60–61.

3. Stephen R. Graubard, Preface, "Scientific Literacy," *Daedalus* 112, no. 2 (Spring 1983): v.

4. "Reaching Beyond the Rational," *Time*, April 23, 1973: 49–52.

5. Snow, p. 61.

6. Lionel Trilling, *Sincerity and Authenticity* (Cambridge, Mass.: Harvard University Press, 1972), pp. 1–2.

7. Trilling, p. 3.

8. Trilling, p. 24.

9. Trilling, p. 25.

10. Thomas S. Kuhn, *The Copernican Revolution: Planetary Astronomy in the Development of Western Thought* (Cambridge, Mass.: Harvard University Press, 1957), pp. 132–84.

11. Hugh Thomas, *A History of the World* (New York: Harper & Row, 1979), p. 249.

12. Francis Bacon, *The Great Instauration,* in *The English Philosophers from Bacon to Mill,* ed. Edwin A. Burtt (New York: Random House, 1939), p. 19.

13. Quoted in Catherine D. Bowen, *Francis Bacon: The Temper of a Man* (Boston: Little, Brown, 1963), p. 35.

14. This quotation and the one immediately following are from Hans-Georg Gadamer's discussion of Bacon in *Truth and Method* (New York: Seabury Press, 1975), p. 312.

15. René Descartes, *A Discourse on Method,* trans. John Veitch (New York: Dutton, 1975), pp. 15–16.

16. Trilling, pp. 28–29.

17. Trilling, p. 32.

18. Snow, pp. 22–25.

19. Snow, pp. 29–33.

20. Quoted in *From Max Weber: Essays in Sociology,* ed. H. H. Gerth and C. Wright Mills (New York: Oxford University Press, 1979), p. 143.

The Teaching of Values

Joel J. Kupperman

My topic is the interrelation between the study of the humanities, especially literature and history, and teaching of values. The dual thesis, that the study of the humanities should include attention to values, and that indeed the humanities can provide important insights into values, is controversial. There certainly are intelligent people who would dispute it, either because they believe that any education that is not value-neutral is an undesirable form of indoctrination, or because they question whether there is anything that qualifies as knowledge about values to be learned, or because they doubt that anything of importance about values is likely to be learned by studying the humanities. Dogmatism is out of place in relation to a topic like this, and so is a straight line of argument that ignores what is to be said on the other side. In what follows I will create a case for my dual thesis, but at each of the two steps I also will take time to inquire why an intelligent person might feel drawn to an opposite view.

Studying the Humanities Requires Attention to Values

The thesis that the study of the humanities should include attention to values needs some qualification. First, I am not advocating the sort of excessive moralizing that characterized the attention given to values a hundred years ago. Some of our predecessors were always looking for the moral of the story and were too anxious to make judgments of right and wrong that would assign blame.

Second, by "attention to values" I mean more than concern with strictly moral issues. The study of values covers much more ground than that contained within morality.[1] We tend to classify as "moral" those choices in which a person has a serious possibility of doing drastic and visible harm to others. But some value judgments concern the desirability of ways or patterns of life, or of goals and ideals. Important as these are, they are not normally classified as moral judgments: we do not normally, for example, consider it a moral issue whether one takes popularity, wealth, or a sense of personal achievement as the primary goal of one's life, even though the choice can make a huge difference to the quality of that life.

One reason for emphasizing this point at the outset is that although there are connections between the study of the humanities and morality, they are less numerous and less rich than the connections between the study of the humanities and questions of value that lie outside of morality. In particular, a great deal of literature (to anticipate part of the argument that will follow) provides a sense of how ways or styles of life work out: one gets a better sense of the details or texture of a certain kind of life, or of what it can lead to. And while it is true that thoughtful people of any age can encounter difficult moral questions and gain moral insight, adolescence is, par excellence, a time of orienting oneself in the central goals and purposes of one's life. Thus the study of the humanities can have a peculiarly strong relevance to the value questions that adolescents ask.

Thus my first thesis, as qualified, is as follows:

Thesis 1: *The study of the humanities should at some points (but not constantly) include attention to and thought about values; the values thought about should include those involved in the direction of personal life as well as in moral behavior.*

The argument for Thesis 1 will be developed more fully in the discussion of examples. It rests on the claim that both history and literature are more meaningful, and come alive, if they are taught in terms of choices. History certainly must be presented in terms of sequences of events and their chronology; but it is most meaningful if it is presented also by means of discussion of human choices, which includes consideration of why people did what they did and what their alternatives were. Similarly, the study of literature should be not just an admiring look at great works, but should also include consideration of alternatives, with respect to both form and content. Clearly, drama and fiction can become especially meaningful if students focus on the choices made by fictional characters, what they thought they were doing, and what their alternatives were. But especially in the case of poetry, consideration of alternatives can also include reflection on why one word or phrase was used rather than an alternative. Indeed, discussion of alternatives of form can open the way to an appreciation of the different literary genres and how these have changed over time.

We cannot satisfactorily understand the actions of figures in history, of fictional personages, and of writers without some sense of why a reasonable person might have chosen such an action. This understanding in turn requires examination of the choice in order to determine which values were involved and what there is to be said for them. In short, we cannot approach history and literature without becoming aware of other people's values and testing them against our own.

The best way to support Thesis 1 is by means of examples. In the study of history one repeatedly encounters individuals and groups who enter into unusual and risky projects because of a strong sense of how life ought to be lived. One example would be the Puritans who settled New England. Students can gain only the most superficial picture of these people if they are described merely as having left England because of their religious views. A sharper image emerges when the life of the New England Puritans is portrayed as reflecting an ideal that centered on the relation of the individual to a thoroughly integrated community governed by respect for a certain kind of religion. Students can be led to see that the style of life of the Puritans involved a trade-off: on one hand there was a heightened sense of community, which many students will find painfully lacking in their own lives; on the other hand, in such a tightly integrated community, it would have been difficult or dangerous to be very different from the others. Discussion of the values involved in the life of the New England Puritans cannot be confined to a simplistic demand that students choose, yes or no, whether they would want such a life style. (Probably very few of us would elect it.) Rather, students begin to understand the Puritans when they begin to appreciate how a large number of people, some of them highly intelligent, could feel that both religion and a sense of community provide values that should be at the center of life.

When students turn to the nineteenth century, they encounter one of the most dramatic developments in American history: the abolition of slavery, which had been preceded by decades of debate about the institution. It is impossible to understand this period without some appreciation of the moral fervor of the abolitionists, who certainly thought that moral ideals were compromised in a country that permitted slavery. It is significant also that the abolitionists were a minority, even in the North, and must to some degree have regarded themselves as reformers rather than as having the ability to recall others to an already shared consensus. Episodes like this raise very interesting questions. There is evidence to suggest that not all Southern slaveholders were Simon Legrees, and that some must have been, in their relations with their families, neighbors, etc., fairly likable and decent people. But there would be general agreement today that they were doing something that was morally very wrong, and that they were blind to this. Are there any practices or policies about which most or all of us are complacent that our descendents will find equally horrifying?

Thus the history teacher knows, and the students can readily be helped to learn, that the historical record is not simply a collection of facts of the order, "This happened, then that happened." To understand it is to understand people playing their roles, and to understand why they acted as they did. One cannot comprehend the abolitionists, or some of the people who in the thirties advocated preparing for war against Hitler, or for that matter some of those who at that time opposed preparing for any war, without appreciating the way in which values were at work. These people cannot be taken seriously in the way they deserve unless we realize that the values that governed their choices were ones that could have a genuine appeal for intelligent people.

Some widely read literary works provide other examples in support of Thesis 1. Jonathan Bennett's provocative essay, "The Conscience of Huckleberry Finn," centers on the episode in *Huckleberry Finn* in which Huck knows that he ought to turn in the escaped slave, Jim, but cannot bring himself to do so.[2] Bennett's point is that Huck's conscience in fact is telling him to do something that we would generally agree is wrong, and that it is only by acting against his conscience that Huck succeeds in acting correctly. This comes back to a point about moral dogmas; there is no reason for students to regard morality (at any point in history, including the present) as a closed system in which everything is known and nothing new could be learned. It also suggests, of course, that any study of the novel that does not include some sensitivity to the moral issues that confront Huck Finn is seriously lacking.

Dostoyevsky's *Crime and Punishment* offers another example. Very obviously, the novel is a variant of "crime does not pay," but the moral issues embedded in the story are not meant to be easy. If I were teaching the novel, I would make the case for Raskolnikov's original decision to commit a crime not look ludicrously weak. There were reasons both for thinking that the money to be stolen would indeed have done more good in Raskolnikov's hands than in the hands of the old pawnbroker, and for regarding the society in which Raskolnikov lived as a manifestly unjust one in which the very poor often did not have a fair chance. Dostoyevsky takes pains throughout the novel to illustrate this last point. The teaching strategy that I am suggesting is in a sense risky; it would be very unfortunate if a student finally concluded that Raskolnikov's original choice had been correct. But it is impossible to read the novel with anything like a clear head and come to that conclusion.

Other examples that appear later will also support Thesis 1. But the ones already provided should suffice to convey a sense that in the study of literature and history questions of value are obtrusive and cannot be ignored without ignoring part of the fabric of what is being studied. To many people this seems obvious. To others it does not seem obvious at all, and in fact the whole idea seems threatening. Why would someone find it threatening to include study of values as an integral part of study of the humanities? Let me suggest that there are two especial reasons for this. When these have been examined, we can see why they might appeal to intelligent and reflective people, but we also will be able to see that in fact they do not count against Thesis 1.

The first reason is a worry about the possibility of what amounts to indoctrination of students. This worry takes two forms. First, there is the sense that indoctrination simply is improper, at least within public schools. Secondly, there is the estimate that it has either no effect or has negative effects: either students laugh it off, or they react against it. I will respond to these two concerns separately.

Anyone who holds that indoctrination is improper must be asked, "Of what kind of indoctrination are you speaking?" It would be absurd to miss the opportunity, if one exists, to indoctrinate children with the idea that it is wrong to murder, to steal, or to inflict needless pain on other humans or on animals. It is possible that, in some cases, traditional methods of indoctrination are not the best ways of getting these points across; but, one way or another, they must get across. We are all in trouble if the majority of the population does not accept the views in question. It is hard to argue that the teacher's taking sides on these issues is improper; after all, theft and murder are against the law and certainly are not permitted in the classroom, as is the case also for infliction on others of needless pain.

Most of this, though, is learned in the primary school years. Some of the issues of value that can and should be discussed in secondary schools are of a more complicated character and admit of disagreement among intelligent, decent people. Some do not: it would be wrong for a teacher, in presenting *Huckleberry Finn*, to remain studiously neutral on the subject of slavery. But we can all think of issues—capital pun-

ishment and abortion come to mind as examples—on which there are
people on both sides who are intelligent and decent and have strong
moral convictions. Clearly it would be wrong to try to indoctrinate
students with regard to such issues; and there is much to be said for
teachers' going so far as to keep their own views on such issues out of
sight in the classroom.

My judgment of propriety here comes out of the experience of
having for a number of years taught a freshman course in the philosophy of religion. Students in the course read parts of the Bible as well as
religious texts from India and Japan; they read the classical proofs of
the existence of God as well as counterarguments produced by skeptics
and atheists. Many of my students have strong religious convictions,
attached to a wide variety of positions. My principle is to present sym-
pathetically every one of the conflicting positions that are discussed, so
that it can be seen how an intelligent person might feel drawn to such a
view, and to keep my own religious opinions out of play and out of
sight. Anything else would violate my sense of the importance of students' thinking through their own responses to the issues without undue influence from the teacher.

This teaching strategy can be applied to the presentation of most
values issues in high school humanities courses. A teacher can be reti-
cent about personal views while at the same time stressing the fact that
there are real issues of value, that intelligent people differ about them,
and that they cannot all be right. For example: either God exists or God
does not; but to say that there is a fact of the matter is not to say that
what it is will be so luminously apparent to human reason that all
intelligent people would have to agree. This does justice both to the
personal and cognitive importance of major value questions while
avoiding anything that could be considered indoctrination.

Thus my response to the concern that indoctrination is improper is
to meet it halfway. Some indoctrination is improper, in that it is improper to impose one's opinions on students who are trying to think
through their own ideas about important topics about which reasonable
people can differ. It is not improper, on the other hand, to indoctrinate
students with the view that torture is wrong. Torture is unlikely to
come up as an issue in the study of the humanities, but somewhat
comparable issues will. It is impossible to study American history in
the nineteenth century without recognizing that a great many Americans, including many abolitionists, believed in racial discrimination.
(That so many abolitionists held appalling views as to what should be
done with blacks once they were freed illustrates the general truth that
someone who tries to see history as a record of heroes and villains will
usually find that the heroes are less heroic and the villains less villain-

ous than one might have hoped.) It is impossible to understand the civil rights movement of the 1960s without understanding that it was still the case that a great many Americans believed in racial discrimination and that there were moral issues that made this an urgent problem. Surely it would not be improper for a teacher to indoctrinate students, in case any of them had doubts, with the idea that racial discrimination is immoral. This is a piece of moral teaching that is in fact part of the law of the land.

The second worry about moral indoctrination—that it will backfire—is legitimate. It is based on widespread experience of just this happening. But this experience has to be viewed in context. Indoctrination is most likely to backfire when it is heavy-handed and continuous, when no reasons for the position indoctrinated are evident, and when the indoctrination is perceived as constricting rather than enlarging the student's possibilities. Perhaps the bottom line here is that no teaching technique works if it is clumsy and antagonizes students. But I believe that moral issues can be well taught. The moral indoctrination that I am suggesting might be appropriate on the secondary school level would be occasional rather than so frequent as to appear heavily moralistic. The moral claim that racial discrimination is wrong should not be presented in the secondary school as an arbitrary dictum on the part of the teacher. There is no reason why secondary school students, of whatever level of ability, cannot be led to see the reasons against the behavior involved in racial discrimination. It is possible for them imaginatively to put themselves in the place of the victims and to have some sense of how it might feel. Moral claims can be presented positively, in terms of goods the students have already learned to value— the attraction of sisterhood and brotherhood and the satisfaction of the needs of victims—rather than negatively, in terms of forbidden naughtiness. They can be presented in ways that appeal to students' imaginations, and they can be argued for: this rational presentation amounting, in fact, to very effective indoctrination.

The second reason why someone might oppose Thesis 1 is this: Thesis 1 in effect not only claims that issues of values are an integral part of the study of the humanities, but also assumes that they are a cognitive part. It assumes, that is, that students can *learn* something about values as an integral part of learning about the humanities.

The objection that there is nothing that can be learned about values is itself of historical interest. Throughout recorded history, except for a period running roughly from the late 1930s through the late 1960s, the strong consensus among philosophers has been that there is such a thing as ethical knowledge. But during the thirty years in question it was widely held, under the influence of Austrian and British logical positivists, that claims about values had no literal meaning, could not be objectively correct or incorrect, and at most represented or expressed the attitudes of the people who made them. Two of the most prominent philosophers who held this position were A. J. Ayer in England and Charles Stevenson in America. Views like theirs were widely taught in American philosophy departments, and their influence outside of philosophy led to a good deal of talk about "value-free" social science and history.

There still are philosophers who hold such views, but they have become a distinct minority, and most of their colleagues now consider the Ayer-Stevenson position in ethics to be extremely implausible. What accounts for this reversal? Part of the answer rests in the counter-intuitive character of what Ayer and Stevenson had to say. Their work had the brilliance of one-sidedness; and they were bringing out a side of value judgments that their immediate predecessors, who neglected any account of the relation between ethical judgments and attitudes or moral action, had left out. What they themselves left out had eventually to be noticed.

The main reason for the reversal, though, is this: Logical positivists believed that there is a stark contrast between science and all other putative knowledge of the real world. They thought of scientific theories as primarily predictive devices in relation to the data provided by observation or experiment. Scientific data, in the logical positivist account, were in themselves neutral among theories, thus standing in sharp contrast with the heavily interpreted and theory-biased experiences sometimes cited in support of ethical or religious views. Virtually no reputable philosopher of science now accepts such an account, and it is hard to believe that many ever will. Thus the view of science that provided the basis for logical positivism now looks extremely naive. Several figures spearheaded the recent attack on positivism. One book in particular stands out: T. S. Kuhn's *The Structure of Scientific Revolutions*, first published in 1962 and quite possibly the most influential book of the last quarter-century.

Under the influence of thinkers like Kuhn it has become orthodoxy to say that in fact there is no such thing as the "neutral given," that is, no theory-neutral observation data; scientific data are permeated by the point of view represented by the theory held by those who design experiments and conduct observations. Nor is it as clear as it used to be that scientific theories are decisively refuted or confirmed, at least immediately, by the results of experiments. Kuhn quotes the great physicist Max Planck: "A new scientific truth does not triumph by convincing its opponents and making them see the light, but rather because its opponents eventually die, and a new generation grows up that is familiar with it."³ The current understanding of science will not support the logical positivists' distinction between scientific knowledge on the one hand and other forms of putative knowledge, including ethics, on the other.

It would be foolish to claim that ethical knowledge and scientific knowledge are exactly parallel in every respect. But two similarities should be mentioned. One is that in both ethics and science we can distinguish between issues about which reasonable people can differ and issues that we can regard as essentially settled. If a student believes that the world is flat, a responsible science teacher will in effect take steps to indoctrinate the student with a different view. Reasonable physicists differ about whether light can be considered to be waves, particles, or some difficult-to-understand compromise between the two. It would be irresponsible and unprofessional for a physics teacher to impose on students her or his own views on that issue.

To avoid possible misunderstanding on this point, let me stress that neither in the sciences nor in ethics is agreement the test of what is correct. Important truths can be contested, and, conversely, everyone can agree with what is actually incorrect. We are all fallible. But, in general, we are in a much stronger position to regard a question as settled satisfactorily if all competent scientists (in the case of science), or all responsible and thoughtful members of the community (in the case of ethics), agree on it. There are especially grave risks in any policy that allows individuals to impose on children views that are not supported by a consensus of competent judges.

The second similarity is that in both ethics and the sciences we are able (with some limited confidence) to decide who are the competent judges. We are able to distinguish people who are in good positions to be confident of certain claims from people who are not in such positions. An important factor in making that distinction is the personal experience of the one making the claim. For example, in the early nineteenth century, anyone could have known that slavery was immoral; but few were in as good a position to make that claim as Fanny Kemble, the English actress who married a Southern slaveowner and lived on his plantation before ultimately divorcing him. Someone who has witnessed the misery produced by a certain practice, and has shown herself to be a balanced and mature judge of circumstances, is in a better position to judge the morality of that practice than someone with no acquaintance with its effects. Also, in the sciences, someone who is familiar with experimental results and current theory can be in a position confidently to make scientific judgments—a position that cannot fully be matched by the average person.

This second similarity lends positive support to the claim that there is knowledge about values, for if ethics were just a matter of feeling and attitude, and if no ethical claim were correct, it would make no sense to speak of some people as being in a good position to make an ethical judgment and others as being in a poor position. Because of arguments like this, it has come to seem dogmatic and simplistic to deny that there is ethical knowledge and that it is possible to learn something about values.[4] And, as we have seen, the main justification for such a denial was a philosophical theory that has been shown not to do justice to the complexity either of the sciences or of ethics.

Learning about Values through Studying the Humanities

The argument up to this point has been that value questions are an integral part of what is to be found in the study of history and literature. I have argued that to take up these questions does not necessarily constitute improper (or ineffective) indoctrination, and that there is no reason to assume that there is nothing about values that could be learned when the questions are taken up. Even if all of this is accepted, it still leaves open the possibility that in fact *not much* about values *will* be learned as part of the study of the humanities. Someone could say, that is, something like this: "Of course issues of values come up in the study of history and literature; students should discuss them because they are an integral part of the subject matter. Perhaps indeed understanding why the New England Puritans or the abolitionists thought as they did, or Huck Finn decided as he did, will enrich the understanding of the historical events or the novel. But what will be enriched will be primarily the insight into history or literature; if students learn anything significant about values this will be fortuitous."

This position must be taken seriously. In opposition to it, I will argue for the following:

Thesis 2: *At least some parts of study of the humanities provide an effective mechanism for students to gain important insights into values.*

Before I argue for this, we should see why intelligent people might very well be inclined to deny it.

A great many witty things have been said about the use of historical knowledge: for example, the saying that those who do not know history are condemned to repeat it. On the other side it often is pointed out that a little knowledge of history can lead to fixations on patterns of events that are unlikely to be repeated: the French preparing for World War II with the Maginot Line, and American preparation since 1946 for

Pearl Harbor, are sometimes cited in this regard. It can be argued that the variety of kinds of behavior to be found in history is so great that it offers at best slender guidance as to how one should respond to present difficulties. The value judgments, such as that slavery was wrong, that suggest themselves in the reading of history are by and large ones that now are not difficult to make. An intelligent student is unlikely to have the experience of suddenly seeing, as a result of the study of history, something about values that she or he otherwise would not have seen. So the argument runs.

All of this may seem even more clear-cut in the case of literature. What, after all, is there about values to be found in short lyric poems? Novels and plays might seem to provide more promising territory. But the history of attempts to link literature, even of these genres, with value judgments can look pretty dismal. The moral of the story persistently looks banal, even if the story is a very good one indeed. Thus the lesson of many of the classic Greek plays, if one tries to put it in words, often seems little more complicated than "Pride comes before a fall"; and surely one does not need to see an entire play to get that message. It is widely agreed, also, that to write a novel or a play in order to get across a point about values is a recipe for aesthetic disaster.

We should bear in mind all this in relation to what follows. My position, briefly, is this. The argument that students are unlikely to gain much direct insight into values from the study of *history* seems to me well founded. I will argue, though, that there are important indirect connections between knowledge of history (and of literature) and values, and that these can be seen if we consider the role of cultural tradition in the development of values. First, however, I will argue that the study of *literature* can provide an effective mechanism for students to learn about values.

The argument that follows is not original with me, in that it includes elements borrowed from a number of thinkers. It claims two connections between the study of literature and values, as follows:

1. The study of literature can strengthen students' sense of detail and of character structure, which is crucial to intelligent consideration of many issues of values.
2. The study of literature can directly stimulate awareness of the correctness of certain value claims.

Just as the study of history is trivialized if it is presented as a matter of "This happened, and then that happened," so also the study of literature is trivialized if it is presented as "Here is something pretty, and there is a Great Work." American adolescents tend not to venerate monuments. Of course cultural monuments should be visited in the study of literature, but they will seem much more meaningful if the tour group does more than merely stand and gape. Great literature indeed comes alive for students only if it is seen as problematic, rooted in responses to a cultural context or a set of problems, and if it can be seen as representing a contingent choice among alternatives. In drama many of these alternatives are within the play: One can ask why Hamlet did not kill King Claudius when he had the chance, or why Cordelia did not try a little at the crucial moment to butter up her father, old King Lear. (Was it that she was her father's daughter, stubborn and wanting to have the emotional relationship on her own terms?) In any play or novel, to ask why someone behaved as she or he did is usually to see characters as having a distinctive unity in their lives. Usually, that is, answers to questions like these have at least something to do with what it is for a person (fictional or real) to act "in character."

The ethical relevance of a sense of character structure is this: Both in literature and in life, one choice leads to the next, and there can be unexpected consequences. Study of the role of character in fiction and drama can promote an awareness that one makes more than momentary choices, in that one chooses policies and personality characteristics that can carry over into most or all of a lifetime, and that some choices thus have an internal logic that leads to other choices. There are, indeed, works of literature that pursue the logic of choices that initially seem very attractive: for example, Brecht's play, *The Good Woman of Setzuan*, pursues the logic of being a thoroughly giving person; Dostoyevsky's *Crime and Punishment* pursues the logic of being a criminal *Ubermensch*; and Arthur Miller's *Death of a Salesman* pursues the logic of a life built around being "well liked." Values can be understood much better if they are seen not just in relation to isolated choices, but as integral parts of patterns of life.

In all kinds of literature there also are linguistic alternatives; and the sharpest, most effective teaching of English literature that I have witnessed centered on details of language (chiefly in poetry and short prose passages). One can learn a great deal about a poem or a piece of prose by asking why a certain word was used rather than another. This is an exercise that illuminates literature, and it can illuminate it in ways that allow students to recognize in detail how words are used to describe different characters and the lives they choose.

The relevance of this eye for detail to value judgments is as follows: Adolescents are often engaged in deciding the kind of life they will lead. Arguably the broad outlines of a life do not by themselves tell us its value; we need to look more closely at details. In his book *The Myth of Sisyphus*, the French novelist and philosopher Camus sketches a number of ways of life that he thinks could have high value. These illustrations are not "models." Not only is a "certain vocation" required, but Camus also makes it clear that a style of life can result in much lower value for one person than for another.[5] There are lives that are like those fancy-looking watches and pens that are hawked for absurdly low prices in the corners of the world. At first glance they are worth a great deal. It is when one inquires into the details—how the various parts fit together, and how they function in a variety of situations—that one has a better sense of their value. What at first looks as if it is of high quality is not necessarily so. Adolescents can benefit greatly by bringing a sense of detail to their thinking about their future lives. To be fooled about value may mean to choose a life that will either be deeply disappointing or will drain one of dignity and sense of purpose. Of course one can always rechoose, but our culture is full of people who in their forties and fifties are rechoosing, in anguish and with great difficulty, what was chosen badly earlier. Most of them would agree that it is far better to choose well early in life.

Sensitivity to detail that is promoted by the study of literature can prepare students not only for life choices, but also for those smaller-scale, highly dramatic, other-regarding choices that we normally place under the heading of morality. The role of sensitivity in moral choice has been pointed out by a number of philosophers and is a major theme in the Confucian tradition in China. R. M. Hare in his recent book, *Moral Thinking*, elaborates this as a logical point about moral judgment. No one is compelled to make moral judgments; as Hare points out, it is always possible to eschew moral language and to talk simply of what one likes or dislikes. To use moral language is to commit oneself to a logic in which the best-founded judgment is one made in the light of all relevant facts. Hare argues, to my mind convincingly, that the facts relevant to a moral judgment include not only the outward-seeming states of all those persons affected by an action, but also what it is like to be any of them. To be in an ideally good position to make a moral judgment would require complete sensitivity to what it is like to be any of those persons affected by the choice in question. Hare argues from this that someone who is in an ideally good position to make a moral judgment would have to give equal weight to everyone's interests, and hence that it is logically true that a valid morality must be altruistic.[6]

But not everyone agrees with Hare. The importance of sensitivity in moral judgment remains a much debated topic both among philosophers and among psychologists of moral education. Take, for example, the disagreements between Lawrence Kohlberg and Carol Gilligan. Kohlberg regards the grasp and application of highly general principles as the apogee of moral development. In this view he has an acknowledged debt to the philosophy of Kant, although Kohlberg leaves out the layer of moral rules intervening between principles and particular cases that plays a crucial role in Kant's account. Gilligan, however, has pointed out that women she has studied assign crucial importance in thoughtful moral decisions to a sense of how others might be hurt or otherwise affected by what one does.[7] If this sensitivity is more important than general principles, it leads to a very different view of moral decision from the one Kohlberg provides. It is worth noting that many philosophers of ethics would support a view of moral insight in which Gilligan's women would count as morally more advanced than the men whom Kohlberg places at his highest level. From this point of view, a crucial part of a student's moral education is heightened sensitivity to the details of other people's lives.

Why literature has such a stimulating effect on our awareness of moral, ethical, and values questions is not immediately apparent. We know that intelligent and mature people often have the sense that they have learned a great deal about life from novels and plays. Yet this is puzzling, for they are often hard put to say just what it is that they have learned. In some ways the knowledge gained (if there is any) is more akin to that involved in knowing one's way around a city than it is like having mastered certain information. Moreover, it usually seems difficult to relate what may have been learned to any overt "message" in the novels and plays.

This puzzle has been solved, at least partially, by Ira Newman. His contribution is this: In many disciplines a crucial activity is that of modeling, in which a complex and unwieldy reality is dealt with by means of inspection of a somewhat smaller-scale version of it, one in which perhaps certain details are accentuated or made easier to focus on. Newman has pointed out that many novels and plays do this for life. The role of the work of art thus is heuristic rather than didactic. The novelist or playwright does not tell one what is valuable, or right or wrong; rather, the author puts one in a position to *see* certain things about values that one might not have seen otherwise.[8] In this way there can be learning without there being an explicit message. What is learned may simply be an ability to respond intelligently to certain situations, or to perceive features of them in a way that leads to certain value judgments, rather than an orderly set of ethical truths to store in one's memory.

Let me suggest one example of this process, in relation to Sophocles' *Antigone*. In that play Creon, the proud and implacable king of Thebes, denies burial rights to rebellious Thebans. He is opposed by Antigone, who feels keenly a sisterly obligation to bury her dead brothers. The result of this confrontation is ultimately disaster for everyone concerned. An intelligent student can gain from this play a wariness of insisting on one's point of view against stubborn opposition, whether or not one's point of view is in fact justified. Whether Creon's original judgment was right or not hardly matters; sometimes it is more dangerous to be in the right than in the wrong, because being in the right can encourage one to discount the attitudes and feelings of others. To have gained an appropriate wariness of this sort is to have learned values, but it is not to have learned and memorized a didactic sentence or paragraph; instead it takes the form of acquired dispositions to feel and behave in certain ways. Philosophers from Plato to Hare, and novelists such as Jane Austen (especially in *Mansfield Park*), have pointed out that genuine acceptance of ethical insights requires such dispositions.

We have still to consider the way in which learning about history can contribute significantly to learning about values. There are, to be sure, a number of important reasons, both intellectual and civic, why history should be taught in the secondary schools. My claim is merely that there are indirect connections, in the case of history as well as that of literature, between proper teaching of the subject and students' learning of values. The mediating factor is the students' sense of cultural tradition.

Two assumptions support this claim. One is simply that history and literature are the primary vehicles by which students are given a sense of cultural tradition. Thus in a society in which the humanities are not regularly taught or are not taken seriously or come to be widely regarded as irrelevant, students do not acquire a strong sense of cultural tradition.

The other assumption is more complicated. It is that value judgments are generally made in the context of the person one is, so that learning about values is fundamentally a process of learning to be a kind of person who makes intelligent and reliable value judgments. It has been pointed out by a number of philosophers, including both Plato and Aristotle, that ethical problems are at bottom problems of character. Thus choice of character is the fundamental ethical choice, and anything that aids in this choice contributes to learning about values.

It is widely agreed that the adolescent years are a crucial period for the construction of character. There are numerous pressures and constraints on the process, and it is no accident that many adolescents simply construct themselves as the persons that they are expected by others to become. Furthermore, even someone who is determined to be independent does not have unlimited freedom; none of us could have chosen not to be a woman or man of the twentieth century, any more than Rembrandt could have chosen to paint paintings that were not recognizably seventeenth-century Dutch art. Yet the ideal of unlimited freedom, of inventing oneself as it were out of nothing, is beguiling. It can be appealing to imagine oneself as pursuing a style of life in which everything is up for grabs and nothing is taken for granted just because it is part of a tradition or is recommended by others.

A consideration of the role of constraints in the process of artistic creation can be helpful in evaluating this ideal. Many nonartists imagine that the most creative artists also invent their styles out of nothing, taking nothing from tradition or from the artistic practices of others. It is instructive thus to weigh the testimony of artists who have been thought of as revolutionaries in their art. Both Stravinsky and T. S. Eliot went to great lengths to stress the importance of a tradition in creating an original artistic style. Stravinsky's words are especially worth quoting.

> The more art is controlled, limited, worked over, the more it is free. As for myself, I experience a sort of terror when, at the moment of setting to work and finding myself before the infinitude of possibilities that present themselves, I have the feeling that everything is permissible. If everything is permissible to me, the best and the worst; if nothing offers me any resistance, then any effort is inconceivable, and I cannot use anything as a basis, and consequently every undertaking becomes futile.[9]

Stravinsky goes on to depict constraints as sources of creative strength. In the Norton Lecture from which I have been quoting, he speaks of the "faculty of observation and of making something out of what is observed" as crucial to artistic creation. That faculty belongs only to someone who possesses an acquired culture, which artists impose on themselves and also impose on others. "That is how tradition becomes established."[10] Traditions thus supply constraints that help to make meaningful freedom possible. Stravinsky's remarks indicate that the tradition plays a useful and indeed necessary role both in cases in which an artist works within a tradition, and cases in which the artist works against the tradition.

This provides a helpful analogy if we are to understand ethical development. We do not invent in a vacuum the kind of person we are to become. The quality of life we can have depends on the quality of person we can become. This quality in turn is enriched if we are working within, or against, a strong sense of a cultural tradition. To believe that acquiring a sense of cultural tradition through the humanities can contribute to the quality of life is to affirm that there are values available to civilized people that are not available to barbarians.

This is just to touch on the personal benefits in quality of life for students if they acquire, through study of the humanities, a strong sense of a cultural tradition. The benefits for a society if a cultural tradition is maintained, and the losses if it comes to seem irrelevant, form another subject, one related to the civic benefits of the study of history. If the construction of self generally becomes impoverished, one may arrive, in the best case, at a society of amiable, tolerant, and shallow people. If, while the cultural tradition comes to seem irrelevant, other things go wrong as well, the risks can be much greater. This is one of the subthemes of Thomas Mann's great novel *Doctor Faustus*; to pursue it would be to make the transition, which philosophers since Aristotle have seen as natural, from the study of values to that of society.

NOTES

1. Cf. my *The Foundations of Morality* (London and Boston: George Allen & Unwin, 1983), chapter 1.

2. Jonathan Bennet, "The Conscience of Huckleberry Finn," *Philosophy* 49 (1974): 123–34.

3. Max Planck, *Scientific Autobiography and Other Papers*, trans. F. Gaynor (New York: Philosophical Library, 1949), pp. 33–34; quoted in Thomas S. Kuhn, *The Structure of Scientific Revolutions*, 2nd ed. (Chicago: University of Chicago Press, 1970), p. 151.

4. For extended discussion, see my *Ethical Knowledge* (London: George Allen & Unwin, 1970).

5. Albert Camus, *The Myth of Sisyphus and Other Essays*, trans. Justin O'Brien (New York: Knopf, 1955), pp. 50–51.

6. Richard M. Hare, *Moral Thinking: Its Levels, Method, and Point* (Oxford: Clarendon Press, 1981), chapter 5.

7. Carol Gilligan, *In a Different Voice: Psychological Theory and Women's Development* (Cambridge, Mass.: Harvard University Press, 1982).

8. Ira Newman, "Fiction and Discovery," doctoral dissertation at the University of Connecticut, 1984.

9. Igor Stravinsky, *Poetics of Music in the Form of Six Lessons* (New York: Vintage Books, 1956), p. 66.

10. Stravinsky, pp. 57–58.

The Humanities in the Classroom

The Role of Values
in Teaching Literature
in the High School

Patrick Welsh

The effort now underway to improve the quality of education in the high schools will have little success without the active participation of students in their own education. But engaging high school students in their classes is no easy task for today's teachers. Over twenty years ago, social scientist James Coleman put his finger on the reason why conventional high school courses so often bore their students:

> Modern adolescents are not content with a passive role. They exhibit this discontent by their involvement in positive activities, activities which they can call their own: athletics, school newspapers, drama clubs, social affairs and dates. But classroom activities are hardly of this sort. They are prescribed "exercises," "assignments," "tests," to be done and handed in at a teacher's command. They require not creativity but conformity, not originality and devotion, but attention and obedience. Because they are exercises prescribed for all, they do not allow the opportunity for passionate devotion, such as some teenagers show to popular music, causes or athletics.[1]

For high school English teachers, the discussion and examination of the value issues inherent in literature is a major element in engaging students. Once students see how the values in the novels, plays, and poems they read relate to their values, once they see that the world of literature is really their own world, that literature is a source of insight—even wisdom—into the human predicament, they are on their way to "owning" their English classes.

James Joyce's novel, *A Portrait of the Artist as a Young Man*, for instance, has, like all good literature, many elements. Certainly students should understand the historical and sociological aspects of *Portrait*—the struggle of the Irish nationalists against England, the role of Charles Parnell in that struggle, the power of the Catholic church, with its strict dogma, over the Irish. The biographical elements are also essential. In many ways Stephen Dedalus is James Joyce, and an acquaintance with Joyce's personal life certainly will contribute to a full understanding of the novel. Furthermore, a student probably cannot grasp *Portrait* without familiarity with its technical and aesthetic elements, especially Joyce's use of the unreliable third-person narrator and stream of consciousness.

The problem that I had when I began teaching *Portrait* was that students could understand all the historical, sociological, biographical, and technical elements in the work, could get A's on all the tests, and still say, "I didn't like it. It was boring. Why did we have to read that?" They weren't "owning" the work, and I wasn't satisfied after teaching it. After two years of struggling with *Portrait* I realized that I had been assuming too much. I had taken for granted that my students understood the values in the novel and how all the difficulties Stephen was experiencing in growing up were similar to their own difficulties.

The next time I taught *Portrait*, I made a deliberate effort to link Stephen's world to the student's world. This involved getting away from the text a bit, and at first I was reluctant to do so. Like most teachers I felt that there was never enough class time, and I wanted to spend the time I did have "covering the material." However, once I loosened up a bit and talked about Stephen in terms of the students' own feelings and experiences I could see more of them responding to the novel. We discussed Stephen's decision to be an artist rather than a priest in terms of their own decisions about what colleges to attend and what fields to major in. We compared the fear Stephen felt about leaving his family and country to the anxiety they feel about graduating and going off to college. We examined parallels between Stephen's courage to go against his friends and their struggles to become independent. In the abstract this may sound like an excess of relevance-seeking, but in reality many of the discussions were poignant and, more to the point, they made Stephen Dedalus, living in oppressive Dublin in the 1890s, very real to kids living in liberated Alexandria in the 1980s. This time around far fewer asked, "Why are we reading this?" I felt that I had achieved a breakthrough with *Portrait* and that many students were making it their own. I think it also helped that I finally loosened up enough to tell them about my own youth in a strict Irish Catholic environment. My stories about confession, for instance, helped make that ritual—so crucial in Stephen's life but so foreign even to Catholic students today—a bit more comprehensible.

When I first taught Shakespeare's *Henry IV, Part I,* I had the same difficulty I had initially had with *Portrait.* I felt that I just was not connecting with the class. Even the best students seemed indifferent. After two years of teaching it, I finally realized that at the heart of this great play lies a value question of supreme concern to high school students: How does one strike a balance between work, duty, discipline (all those values represented by Hal's father, King Henry IV) and freedom, passion, play (all those qualities represented by Falstaff)? Now as we go through the play I try to direct the discussion toward that central issue by raising questions like: What causes some kids to be over-achieving grinds who give up a lot of the fun of high school? What is it that causes others to do no work at all and generally waste their lives away? How does one deal with the guilt that comes from disappointing a demanding parent? Is it possible to achieve a balance between work and play, planning for the future and enjoying the moment? To many teachers this kind of discussion may seem a waste of time better spent on textual analysis, but for me it is a successful way to help students to understand and become involved in one of the world's great plays.

Tess of the D'Urbervilles was another work that used to give me trouble. My breakthrough with this novel can be traced to a girl in my class two years ago. I had always assumed that Tess had been seduced by Alec, and few students challenged my assumption until this young woman insisted that Alec raped Tess. She brought in an article from *Ms.* magazine entitled "Date Rape: A Campus Epidemic?" to help argue her point.[2] The article dealt with the insensitive attitudes of college males toward females, how some young men will force a date to have sex, and how the young woman will blame herself. It also discussed the fraternity "gang bang" phenomenon. Was this a fit subject for a high school class discussing a Victorian novel? In retrospect, I would say yes indeed; the discussion provoked by the article—on the ethics, or lack thereof of young people, on the double standard, and on the need for more communication between young men and women—seemed to bind the students to the novel and to give them real insight into and sympathy for Tess's struggles in a male-dominated society. For the last two years, students have loved *Tess of the D'Urbervilles,* and much of that has to do with the discussion of values sparked by the "Date Rape" article.

One of the works I taught successfully from the beginning was

Light in August. Joe Christmas's struggle to find his place in southern society and the constant injustice that society deals him seem to strike a deep chord in young people. Underlying all our discussions of the novel is the basic value assumption that each individual has a special dignity and is entitled to be treated with respect. Our school has an equal percentage of blacks and whites in its population of twenty-four hundred students, and though the races live in peaceful coexistence, there is a great deal of unspoken racial hostility. *Light in August* has prompted many discussions on the often-taboo topic of racism in our school and has made students more sensitive to the pernicious effects of racism both on its victims and on its perpetrators. Of all the novels and plays I teach, *Light in August* seems to engage students the most. Many of them have persuaded their parents and grandparents to read it.

Students also become engaged in poetry, come to experience ownership, if they can see how the values in the poems they study are relevant to their own values. Granted there are some poems that are basically exercises in rhythm and are relatively value-free: Vachel Lindsay's "The Congo," for instance, can be experienced on a purely aural level. But, as poet Robert Lowell said, "Poetry essentially operates in the realm of values."

When I teach poetry, I begin with several works that explore a topic of central concern to the lives of many teenagers—the relationship between parent and child. While we do analyze the technical aspects of these poems, I also emphasize the value issues inherent in them. For instance, John Ciardi's "Boy" and Richard Wilbur's "The Writer" afford teachers a wealth of imagery and figurative language to discuss. But the reason students find both poems so compelling is that they raise the question of how much authority parents should and can exercise in the lives of their children. Both poems have sparked intense exchanges on the values of obedience, authority, and freedom in families. Furthermore, the pain and uncertainty that the speakers in both poems experience as they struggle with their parental roles come as a revelation to many students. They seem to discover that being on the other side of the freedom-and-authority seesaw is not as easy as they thought it was.

Maxine Kumin's "Life's Work" and Phyllis McGinley's "The First Lesson" involve related value issues. In these poems, the speakers are children who must struggle to break away from their fathers to find fulfillment. Young women, especially, respond very strongly to these poems and their common themes that daughters cannot let their fathers live their lives for them.

Adrienne Rich's "The Middle-Aged" and James Dickey's "The Aura" address the natural misunderstandings that arise between parents and children and the profound, unspoken love that exists despite those misunderstandings. "The Middle-Aged" has generated some of the fiercest discussion I've ever seen in a classroom. Philip Larkin's "This Be the Verse," Sylvia Plath's "Daddy," Louis Simpson's "The Goodnight," Peter Meinke's "Advice to My Son," and Robert Mezey's "My Mother" are other poems on family relations in which my students have shown keen interest.

By starting the study of poetry with works dealing with value issues that are important in the lives of the students, I feel I have a much stronger chance of engaging them with the literature, of getting them to experience ownership in the works. Once they are engaged, once they experience poems that speak to them about their lives, students see poetry—and, by extension, all literature—as having worth and meaning. They become much more eager to study and discuss the technical and historical aspects of literature and to tackle poems that at first may not seem accessible. At that point, I feel comfortable moving to more challenging poetry—that of Donne, Keats, Arnold, Yeats, Eliot—with one eye always on the values inherent in the poems and how those values relate to and illumine the students' world.

Poetry can also be used to shed light on novels and plays. For instance, Lawrence Ferlinghetti's poem, "the poet's eye obscenely seeing," can give students who are reading *The Great Gatsby* a clearer understanding of one of the essential themes of that work—the corruption of the American dream. Robert Frost's "Two Tramps in Mudtime" puts Prince Hal's struggles to integrate work and play, vocation and avocation in a new context. "The Love Song of J. Alfred Prufrock" can help a student understand the timelessness of Hamlet's confusion and doubt, as Browning's "My Last Duchess" can illuminate Othello's jealousy. The purists might say that using a poem to illustrate a value in a novel or play is prostituting the poem. I have found, however, that the students' understanding of both the poem and the larger work is often greatly enhanced when the poem is seen in the context of the issues raised by a novel or a play.

In *Horace's Compromise*, Theodore Sizer asserts that "there is opportunity for student ownership in every class in every subject if the teachers value it."[3] It is hard to tell whether some teachers do not value ownership, or whether they just do not know how to help their students achieve it. But the impression I get from talking to students is that ownership is missing in many classes, and that often teachers are to blame. One of the most common student complaints is that teachers merely dispense facts.

"In many classes all that's going on is a transfer of information. Teachers who teach like this don't seem to realize that they are making themselves obsolete," says Yael Ksander, a National Merit Scholar.

"We can get everything they 'teach' just by reading the textbook. In one class the teacher is just a presence up there in front of us. We know it's alive—that it's flesh and blood—but it just goes on babbling, off in its own world, totally out of touch with what we need to master the subject matter."

Teachers who are wedded to factual information usually will not view student ownership as important. The question of values will seldom arise, for once their students grasp "the facts," these teachers see their job as completed.

Another complaint I heard frequently from students was that teachers themselves often do not appear to "own" or to be engaged with or enthusiastic about what they are teaching. "Sometimes it's hard to tell whether it's the subject or the teacher that's boring, but many times it's the teacher," says Elisabeth Orshansky, who was accepted to Harvard and Stanford. "Some of them just stand up there and read their notes, and at times the notes don't even make sense. Maybe these teachers aren't really boring people, but just afraid to show their personalities to teenagers. The problem is that if you're not naturally interested in the subject matter and you get stuck with a boring teacher, chances are you'll never get interested."

Of course some students have such low skills or are so jaded by the video culture that they will find even the greatest teachers boring. On the other hand there are teachers who are, for whatever reason, just plain boring, and boring teachers, as Orshansky says, are deadly. I feel this is especially true of boring English teachers, for they can kill a student's interest in the world's most compelling literature. They seldom spark in their students that exhilarating recognition that the world of literature is one with the students' world. They usually create alienation from, rather than ownership of, the literature they teach.

The biggest gripe of students, however, seems to be that too many teachers just do not understand kids as kids. "So many teachers don't have a very accurate picture of what we're like. Some of them seem to think we're a bunch of degenerates who don't care at all about school, and others feel that our whole life revolves around their subject. Very few really understand us, but those who do get the most out of us," says John Hendrickson, one of four seniors with a straight-A average. English teachers who don't understand kids and their world are obviously going to have great difficulty in helping students connect the values in their lives to the values in literature.

High schools aren't the only places where there is a failure to connect studies with life. In his article entitled "The Shame of the Graduate Schools," William Arrowsmith comments, "The most remarkable and agonizing feature of graduate education is, I think, the gulf between one's studies and one's life, between what we read and how we live. Our studies are alienated from our lives and—such is our professionalism—we are usually required to side with our studies against ourselves, against our lives."[4]

And, apparently, many college English teachers, like their high school counterparts, aren't willing to work hard at connecting literature with their students' lives. In an address to the 1982 Convention of the Modern Language Association, Wayne Booth berated college English professors for their indifference to undergraduates who are not English majors. "We hire a vast army of underpaid flunkies to teach the so-called service courses, so that we can gladly teach in our advanced courses those precious souls who survived the gauntlet. Give us lovers and we will love them, but do not expect us to study courtship," said Booth. Too many English teachers on all levels, it seems, want classrooms full of ready-made scholar-aesthetes eager to soak up whatever literature is assigned. They will not face the fact that, if there is no courtship, especially courtship through the discussion and examination of values, there will be little ownership.

All this discussion of ownership through values is fine, but it will be for naught unless English teachers first solve the very mundane problem of getting students to open their books and read. English teachers too often assume that those kids sitting in front of them deferentially smiling and nodding have read the assigned material. The fact is that many of them will actually fake it with Cliff's Notes or their own cleverness, unless they are prodded to read by old-fashioned scare tactics such as objective quizzes to monitor their reading. I find that when such quizzes are given on a regular basis, most students do read their books. The few who don't may respond to as little additional stimulus as a phone call to parents. In April 1984, when I was pressed to finish teaching *A Portrait of the Artist as a Young Man* before the May Advanced Placement test, I announced that there wouldn't be any quizzes because we needed time to discuss the book. "If I can't trust you at this time of year, it's too bad," I told my classes. It may have been "senior slump" or spring fever or a combination of both, but several students slacked off in their reading and succumbed to the Cliff's Notes temptation once the threat of quizzes was lifted.

The fact that many kids need to be prodded by quizzes and grades discourages the purist in me. Shouldn't the subject matter, the world's greatest literature, be enough in itself to compel them to read? The fact is, however, that many do need the prodding. But the practice is worth the effort. I have taken consolation from seeing students who practically had to be browbeaten to do their reading suddenly become swept up by the power of the work and find themselves unable to put it down. But I have also been told by former students how they have faked their way through English courses in college as well as high school because teachers were too proud—or too lazy—to monitor their reading by giving them quizzes.

In addition to getting students to open their books, another very basic problem facing high school English teachers interested in ownership is the young age of students. Many even of the ablest youngsters just do not have the experience or psychological maturity to grasp the significance of many great works of literature. This is especially true of high school boys, who usually lag a year or two behind the girls in their development. "Ode on a Grecian Urn" is probably included in every high school British literature text in the country. Yet I wonder how many seventeen-year-old boys can truly comprehend or be moved by that profound work—by the antitheses between art and life, youth and old age, passion and permanance that Keats so subtly presents.

How many students have been turned off to great literature simply because it was assigned when they were too young? Some teachers seem totally oblivious to this problem and just forge ahead in the name of "high standards," teaching the literature they like and assuming that there is something wrong with any sixteen- or seventeen-year-old who doesn't share their refined taste. These are usually the teachers who can regularly be heard in faculty lounges complaining about the quality of their students.

I have had students who were soured on *Hamlet* because it was "taught" to them in eighth grade. I also have known youngsters who thought that modern poetry was something totally unintelligible because some junior high school teacher thought that "The Love Song of J. Alfred Prufrock" was suitable material for twelve- and thirteen-year-olds.

Robert Wallace's poem "In a Spring Still Not Written Of" addresses the dilemma posed by the youth and inexperience of students. The speaker in the poem is an English teacher reading poetry to a class of college women. The class is meeting outdoors on a beautiful spring day, but the students are hardly experiencing ownership of poetry:

> . . . all the while, dwindling,
> tinier, the voices—Yeats, Marvell, Donne—
> sank drowning. . . .
>
> Calm, indifferent, cross-legged
> or on elbows half-lying in the grass—
> how should the great dead
> tell them of dying?
> They will come to time for poems at last,
> when they have found they are no more

the beautiful and young
all poems are for.[5]

The speaker in Wallace's poem is, I believe, unduly pessimistic. Even high school students can be engaged by certain works of Donne, Marvell, and Yeats. Yet the poem illustrates so well the difficulty of finding works of literature that will "work" with a particular age group. This is by no means an exact science, and even if one teacher has success with a particular piece of literature, another teacher may not. The critical factor is often the teacher's own love and enthusiasm for the work. As I once heard someone say, the best English classes are those where you can't tell where the book ends and the teacher begins. Because the teacher's relationship to the work is so important, administrators and curriculum specialists must give teachers some latitude in choosing works to teach. Administrators with scant background in the humanities (and very few high school administrators do have a solid grounding in these subjects) might assume that any English teacher can teach one work as well as another work. This is, as teachers know so well, not the case. For instance, I love *Othello* but am lukewarm toward *Macbeth*. Whenever I teach *Othello*, I seem somehow able to interest many students in it. The three times I've taught *Macbeth*, however, I have had little success. Hence I think it would be counterproductive for my students if an administrator handed me a rigid curriculum that required I teach *Macbeth*.

Though the teacher's love of the work is a key factor in engaging students, it by no means guarantees that students will respond in a similar fashion. I certainly love *Moby Dick* and *Joseph Andrews*, but even my best students have found them tedious and boring. There may be teachers who can interest adolescents in these two novels, but I am not one of them, so I gave up teaching *Moby Dick* and *Joseph Andrews*. At first I worried that maybe I was giving in to students, that perhaps I should teach these great novels regardless of how my charges reacted, and that maybe some day in the future they'd look back and appreciate them. In retrospect, though, I think my decision was sound. There is enough great literature that young people can readily make their own that there is no reason to feel bound to works that students find alien.

The question of what literature should be taught to what students is especially vexing in a large urban high school such as mine. Our English department has four academic ability groupings, euphemistically called "phases." At the top are "Phase 4" courses (also called Advanced Placement and honor courses) for those who read above grade level as determined by the Stanford diagnostic test. The brightest kids in the school are in these courses, although there are also a lot of not-so-bright, lazy upper-middle-class kids who are there because of their parents' pushing. There is no question that students in the "Phase 4" courses, as well as those in "Phase 3" (youngsters who read at grade level), should be and are immersed in the study of literary classics. However, when one gets to "Phase 2" (reading one or two years below grade level), the suitability of these works is not so clear. I have seen a few great teachers excite "Phase 2" students about traditional literature. But it does take an extraordinary teacher to communicate successfully the richness of classic literature to students at this level of ability, and there simply aren't many extraordinary teachers. Nevertheless, kids reading a year or two below grade level can, and therefore have a right to, study the humanities. Of course, the choice of works for these students has to be very judicious. They can't really handle some of the more sophisticated works that most students in honors courses can—a Faulkner novel, for instance. But at the same time, they are being shortchanged if teachers limit them to popular novels like *Jaws* and *Salem's Lot*.

A more serious problem arises with what we call "Phase 1" students—high school kids who have the reading ability of a sixth-grader or below. Some educators and policymakers, including several contributors to this volume, are calling for a core curriculum in the humanities for all students. I'm not sure they understand the difficulties involved in transforming that ideal into a reality. I wonder how many of these policymakers ever tried to teach Shakespeare to an eighteen-year-old who could barely read street signs and who could not comprehend paragraphs of the simplest newspaper article. The tragic fact is that there are many such students in American high schools. In my school they make up perhaps 12 percent of the student body. These kids simply *cannot read* the literature that we consider part of everyone's heritage and birthright. Should we try to find, or create ourselves (as one of my colleagues did) condensed, watered-down versions of the great novels and plays so that these kids will at least be familiar with the characters and plot lines of these works? Or should we concentrate on survival skills and on raising the reading level of these students as much as possible before they leave school? Many teachers, myself included, try a combination of both approaches, but few of us feel that we are really accomplishing much. Trying to get these youngsters to experience any sense of ownership in class is the most frustrating aspect of high school teaching. For my part, I am hopeful that the situation will improve as the push for higher standards brings about improved reading proficiency at the elementary level. But we are still a long way from achieving our goal.

Teachers who encourage students to discuss and think about the value issues raised in the study of literature run the risk of being charged with "indoctrination." Sometimes the charge is justifiable. I have seen teachers use the study of literature as a vehicle for their own political, religious, or moral views. Several years ago, our principal came under fire from all sides when one of our English teachers was "teaching" reactionary Christian fundamentalism laced with anti-Semitism, and a social studies teacher was "teaching" value-free, if-it-feels-good-do-it ethics. Needless to say, there are some very strange people in the teaching profession, and any parent would shudder to think of them imposing their objectionable values on children. But there is a real difference between discussing and examining the value claims inherent in a work and using the work as an object lesson in an attempt to force one's own moral code on students. For instance, in Philip Larkin's poem "Church Going," the speaker (and in this case we may assume that Larkin is the speaker) views religion as an outdated social ritual that has little meaning in our time. Teachers could choose, depending on their religious leanings, to attack or defend Larkin's view, and in doing so risk alienating a portion of the class. Or, more profitably, teachers can discuss Larkin's views for what they are—one of many possible responses that people today have to religion. Using the latter approach, I have seen students who are very religious, both Christian and Jewish, as well as students who have no religious beliefs, find "Church Going" absorbing.

I don't believe that open and honest examination and discussion of the values in literature sends students the message that there are no fixed values at all. High school kids are much more sophisticated than many people realize. They know that in our society certain values are open to discussion while others are not. They know that intelligent people can and do disagree about religious beliefs, sexual ethics, and many other value issues. At the same time they know that values like racial justice are fixed. The teacher who openly sides with Faulkner's statement against racism in *Light in August* is not going to be accused of indoctrinating students, for he is simply expressing a moral truth. The teacher who simply explores, without taking a stand, the attitudes toward sex in the "carpe diem" poetry of Catullus, Andrew Marvell, e. e. cummings, or Edna St. Vincent Millay is not advocating hedonism or promiscuity, but is examining various stances toward values that can vary from age to age or person to person.

It is not our job as English teachers to teach particular values to our students. Rather, our job is to use values to teach literature. If values are learned in an English class, they are learned indirectly. For instance, Toni Morrison's novel *Song of Solomon* has probably done more to "teach" my students the value of brotherhood than any work I've taught. Yet this lesson is a byproduct of reading the novel. I did not choose *Song of Solomon* to teach brotherhood: I chose it because it is about a young man's struggle to grow up. When my white students identify with the young man, "Milkman" Dead, a black, they experience a sense of brotherhood that is too often lacking in their everyday school life. An insensitive, meddlesome teacher, determined that students "learn" the brotherhood lesson of *Song of Solomon*, could negate the experience that comes from the book itself. Likewise, I know that students of mine have gained insight into parenting and a stronger respect for their own parents from Adrienne Rich's poem, "The Middle-Aged." But I never said, "This poem teaches you that you should respect your parents because . . ." etc., etc. I merely discussed the poem and the values in it. Those who "learned" values did so simply because they understood the poem.

English teachers must pay attention to the ways in which the values in literature relate to students' values, but not in order to indoctrinate, convert, or save students. We must do it to engage students, to create a sense of ownership in the classroom, or else we will reach only a limited number of them—the high school equivalent of "those precious souls" that Wayne Booth mentions. Moreover, if we teachers of the humanities won't discuss values, it is doubtful whether we should be teaching the humanities at all. We cannot reject the significance of values in the teaching of the humanities without rejecting the humanities themselves. The great works of literature, art, philosophy, and history are rich in values, and students cannot truly understand those works without understanding the value issues inherent in them.

Those English teachers who are not willing to make the effort to show students how the great issues in literature are related to issues in their own lives will perhaps do just as well to limit their attention to "communication skills"—to grammar and composition—and to hope that their students will discover the wonder and power of literature when they are out of school. Better that than to lead students to believe that great literature is so esoteric, so far from their experience, that only a few precious souls can own it.

NOTES

1. James S. Coleman, *The Adolescent Society: The Social Life of the Teenager and Its Impact on Education* (New York: Free Press, 1961), p. 315.

2. Karen Barrett, "Date Rape: A Campus Epidemic?" *Ms.* (September 1982): 48–50.

3. Theodore R. Sizer, *Horace's Compromise: The Dilemma of the American High School* (Boston: Houghton Mifflin, 1984), p. 165.

4. William Arrowsmith, "The Shame of the Graduate School," *Harper's* (March 1966): 51.

5. *Poems on Poetry*, comp. and ed. Robert Wallace and James G. Taaffe (New York: Dutton, 1965), p. 133.

Education Reform:
A Teacher Responds

Claire L. Pelton

In my twenty-eight years in public education, most of them as a teacher, I—like many other teachers—have survived a multitude of reforms. Each of these, presented with appropriate missionary zeal, has pointed an accusing finger at the schools and the teachers therein for the purported failure of elementary and secondary education in our nation. Before accusing the schools yet again, however, the more than 120 education commissions, committees, and self-appointed "experts" of the past several years should possibly have read Samuel Beckett's *Waiting for Godot,* in which Vladimir points out, "There's a man all over for you, blaming on his boots the faults of his feet."

When I was a fledgling teacher, Sputnik was upon us. The nation demanded more rigorous "academic" courses of study from the schools. The demand for change arose from the perception of a menace from without, much as today's impulse toward reform stems more from the dazzling success of the Japanese automobile industry and the decline of General Motors than from any sincere desire to improve schooling in its own right. Today's concern also comes, of course, in response to the much-publicized SAT score decline, which points to still another alleged failure of the schools. But before we launch another flurry of reforms, let us remember what happened between the late 1950s and the late 1970s. The Sputnik-inspired academic curricula were suddenly found to be too cognitive and too confining. Politicians and educational "experts" returned from their Big Sur weekend seminars with a new consciousness; the *affective domain* became the latest educational fad. And teachers, still reeling from the rigors of developing a tougher, more content-intensive curriculum (often during weekend and summer workshops), were told to throw curriculum and text aside and to become "relevant." Many did so gladly, for under Sputnik learning Johnny still read no better, if at all. Teachers became "groovy," the boundaries among academic disciplines blurred in the face of the proliferation of daily demand schedules, individually packaged programs, and team-teaching. Alternative schools and free schools emerged in response to this new consciousness.

And now we find that our elective-rich curricula are held in as low repute as are our teachers. Is it any wonder, then, in light of our past experience, that we veteran teachers view the current call for reform with caution? And, unlike the relatively innocuous innovations created by the Sputnik and Esalen curricula, today's frenzy for tangible, legislated accountability—of schools, teachers, and students—may have lasting and far-reaching implications for public education. For these and other reasons many teachers are less than eager to pledge their support to the new round of reforms.

Another reason for the indifferent response of some teachers is the perception that the reports produced by the panels and commissions represent, in many respects, an ill-supported view of what is wrong with the schools and an inadequate response to the problems that do exist. To some extent I share that perception. Let me cite three problem areas in the current school reform movement.

Many of the reports that have emerged are based on simplistic, even specious reasoning. They seem to assume that *quantity* rather than *quality* determines both what is wrong with our education and what must be done to improve it. What is wrong? Too few hours in the school day and too few days in the school year. The remedy? More hours in the school day and more days in the school year. More is better—it's an old American belief. But does it apply to schooling?

Professor Henry M. Levin of Stanford University observes that although the school year is considerably longer in many other industrialized countries than in the United States—often 240 days or even more—still "there may be little relation between the greater time spent . . . once the elite nature of their student enrollments is accounted for."

Levin stresses—and most teachers would agree—that what is done with the time is of far greater importance in affecting student achievement than are "mechanical increases in the length of the school day or school year or class time spent on particular subjects. . . . Effort may also be reduced by sheer fatigue associated with additional time." Concluding his comments on the quantity approach to educational reform, Levin states: "If teachers are unqualified, books and materials are in short supply, the curriculum is inappropriate, and classrooms are noisy and overcrowded, additional time devoted to instruction may be relatively unproductive. Indeed, it may be more cost-effective to improve the quality of resources than to increase instructional time."[1]

Another problem with the recent reports on educational reform is their shortsighted overreliance on gimmickry and gadgetry to cure our educational ills. These come in two major forms: lavish use of tests and slavish attention to their results, and the acquisition of computers, which, if all the claims about them are to be believed, represent a Second Coming for education.

We have, in fact, become a nation with an almost psychotic fixation on testing. Testing preschoolers to determine which nursery school they should attend is not uncommon in California. And we all know about the minimum-competency tests for our high school students and our teachers. To hear the claims of our politicians and many of our "experts," testing will virtually assure success in schooling and success in teaching. But it should be noted that with a few exceptions—such as the Advanced Placement examinations and some of the achievement examinations that some colleges and universities use for admission or placement—most of the tests whose use has been recommended measure only minimal competency. Successful performance on these tests establishes nothing more than mastery of the lowest common denominator of what our youth and our teachers should know. Although I strongly believe that testing is one of several means to the end of improving education, and that testing can be particularly useful in measuring progress toward that goal, I deny that successful performance on tests is an end in itself.

My experience as a teacher and as a member of test development committees has convinced me that it is a mistake to use Scholastic Aptitude Test (SAT) scores to evaluate the effectiveness of teaching programs. We all have been alerted to the declining figures on the Scholastic Aptitude Test; from 1968 to 1980, SAT averages fell forty-two points in the verbal portion and twenty-six points in the math. Yet it is seldom asked what, in fact, the SATs measure. Certainly the verbal section does *not* test what is taught in school. Although it *does* test command of vocabulary *in context* and reading comprehension in a wide range of subject areas, almost all of the reading passages are from works not commonly found in high school curricula. I have long contended that a person without any formal schooling—one who never-theless had been a wide-ranging, unquenchable reader—could earn outstanding verbal scores on the SAT. Even the College Board's pamphlet, *Taking the SAT*, stresses the importance of "extensive outside reading" and "independent study" in addition to academic course work as part of long-term preparation for college entrance examinations.[2] As for what the SATs actually predict: they explain only 9 percent of the variance of freshman grades in college. And seemingly great score swings may be produced by missing just a few items. The forty-two-point drop in average performance on the verbal portion, for example, is caused by answering only five to six more questions incorrectly. The twenty-six-point drop in math is caused by answering three more questions incorrectly.[3]

Testifying before a House education subcommittee last year, Daniel B. Taylor of the College Board cast further doubt on the prevalent notion that the decline in SAT scores reflects an overall decline in the quality of American high schools. He cited the investigation by a distinguished panel chaired by former Secretary of Labor Willard Wirtz that had examined the score decline of the 1960s and 1970s and had attributed most of it to the significant increase in the number of test-takers.[4] Mr. Taylor suggested four reasons why SAT scores do not provide a fair basis for comparing overall educational performance in schools or districts or states:

> First, the SAT measures skills that develop as the result of experiences both in and out of school, and is sensitive to a variety of social and economic factors. It is, therefore, not a good measure of educational effectiveness as such.
>
> Second, the million or so high school seniors who take it each year are only about one-third of the number of high school graduates, so that the results tell nothing whatever about the rest of the students—including those who do not plan to go to college . . . or about those who plan to attend colleges that do not require the SAT.
>
> Third, the colleges for which students take the SAT are not uniformly distributed across the nation, and the proportion of students in each school, district, and state who take the test varies widely.
>
> Fourth, within each school or district the composition of the student population varies widely, and the educational programs developed to meet their needs vary also—thus making the scores of those college-bound students who take the SAT an extremely uneven indicator of the whole program.[5]

There is, of course, one surefire (if painful) way to raise SAT scores. It is to destroy one's TV set or, at least, to pull out the plug occasionally. More realistically, we should encourage parents to insist on selective viewing for their younsters. At present levels of TV advertising and violence, high school graduates will have been exposed to 350,000 commercials and will have vicariously participated in 18,000 killings. Just as troubling is the sheer quantity of time spent watching TV: today's high school graduates have logged at least 15,000 hours before the screen—more time than they have spent in school or on any other activity except sleep.[6] The time spent in the passive nonparticipatory experience of watching is time taken away from imaginative play, from dinner conversation, from necessary solitude and contemplation, and from reading.

As for our latest gadget, we are now being told that placing computers in every high school and providing an inexpensive Macintosh for every college student will make all students instantly literate; tomorrow's Hemingways will somehow appear as byproducts of Apple and IBM. Joseph Weizenbaum, professor of computer science at MIT and a pioneer in the development of the computer, offers a dissenting view, however, to what he calls the computer fad. In an interview reported in the March 1984 issue of *Harper's*, Weizenbaum observed that

> a new human malady has been invented, just as the makers of patent medicines in the past invented illnesses such as "tired blood" in order to create a market for their products. Now it's computer illiteracy. . . . As for the computer itself, I think it inhibits children's creativity. In most cases, the computer programs kids and not the other way around.[7]

To be sure, the computer is as useful a tool as a sophisticated typewriter. I do not doubt that it can be used to expedite revision of students' papers. It cannot, however, teach students the art of editing or program them to improve their reasoning.

A third problem area involves the blatant omission of adequate teacher and student representation on the various committees, commissions, and panels that have been studying secondary education in America. As a career teacher, I grow weary of being talked at by these various groups who are so sure what's wrong with our schools and who have determined, on their own, what should be done about it. Jay Sommer, a distinguished high school foreign language instructor, was the only teacher on the national commission that gave us *A Nation at Risk*. Other groups had an equally dismal teacher ratio. The Task Force on Education for Economic Growth had thirty politicians and business leaders and only one lonely junior high teacher. Of the twenty-three observers who contributed to Ernest Boyer's study, *High School*, only one, a high school principal, was directly involved in the schools. The much-heralded Goodlad study used teachers as guinea pigs but not as collaborators. Had teachers been an integral part of his team, he would never have made the absurd recommendation that his new position of "head teacher" be filled by someone who had earned a Ph.D. in education. Where is the research, I wonder, that tells us that earning a Ph.D. in education makes one a better teacher?

My point is simply this: These eminent diagnosticians of education, sitting in their sequestered offices, prescribing their favorite nostrums for the ills of the nation's schools, are making the same mistake that countless predecessors made before them. They are treating symptoms rather than causes; they are concocting extraneous, expedient, and flashy "solutions" rather than urging thoughtful, long-term planning. And, as in *all* previous educational reform movements, their recommendations are being imposed from the top down. As Larry Cuban, Stanford University professor of education and former superintendent of schools in Arlington, Virginia, recently noted during a public panel on school reform: "A chronic amnesia plagues all state and national reform movements."[8] Cuban emphasized that the host of previous educational reform movements, which have come from the top down and which have not engaged teachers and other school practitioners, have been doomed to failure.

To get at the heart of what is and what is not working in our high schools today, we must get at the heart of schooling: what goes on *inside the classroom.* We need to understand and perhaps then to alter the approaches and expectations of students and teachers with respect to the subject matter. This will take not only time but also teacher involvement. I cannot be certain that this will be easy to obtain. I was harsh in my criticism of the expert "school physicians" who prescribed their medicine without involving their "patients"—students, teachers, and school-site administrators. Yet I cannot help but wonder whether, if we teachers *were* given the opportunity to change the way things are, we would in fact do so.

The autonomy and relative security of the teacher's classroom have always been among our most cherished possessions. Here we may retreat to the dignity, warmth, and safety of our rooms, where we are interrupted only by an occasional observation by a school administrator or department chair. Here we can sequester ourselves from the most recent diatribes of the public, the parents, the national commissions, and the press. Our classrooms have become our haven and— perhaps—even a cell in which we choose to lock ourselves for five or six hours each day.

Classroom teachers must share the responsibility for having been consistently excluded from major educational reform movements in this country. While teachers have privately thrashed out the problems and promise of their profession, many have been reluctant to work with their colleagues to respond to either. On occasion we will rise from our self-imposed stupor to complain about salaries, dawn faculty meetings, or assembly schedules. After these infrequent outbursts (usually occurring in the faculty lounge before one or two sympathetic listeners), we teachers retreat to our classroom cocoons.

Important issues concerning the teaching profession demand our involvement for their successful resolution. We teachers must become involved in new curriculum development and with the complex and still untested process of teacher evaluation. We must be willing to devote the extra effort required to enroll in rigorous academic courses in our teaching field, rather than settling for those innumerable "basket-weaving" seminars for teachers that enable one to advance on the salary schedule with minimal effort and thought. We and the organizations that represent us cannot afford to shut our eyes to the ineffective teachers on the staff; moves to strengthen the rights of tenure should not overlook its attendant responsibilities.

Teacher involvement is also essential for quality education. Since chances seem remote that a teacher such as myself will ever become a member of a blue-ribbon commission charged with recommending ways to improve education in the American high school, I will take this opportunity to sketch some of my own ideas for enhancing the education of our secondary students.

First, we humanities teachers must confront what it means to be a teacher of humanities, a teacher of English or history or foreign languages. We must concentrate on teaching our discipline with fervor, with unyielding love, with sustained commitment. As teachers of humanities, we have an obligation to share our great literary and cultural heritage with our students; further, we must assist them to develop a writing style that is clear, free from pretension and specious generalities. We must also teach them to become thoughtful listeners who can readily discriminate between spurious grandiloquence and compelling reason.

Exploring great works of literature together provides students and teachers with a shared intellectual adventure in content and in values, in the cognitive as well as the affective domain. I continue to teach Plato, Dante, Shakespeare, Milton, Dickens, Dostoyevsky, Conrad, and Joyce because these and other literary giants speak to the enduring values, the tragedies, the dreams and hopes of us all. Works by writers such as these expand our intellect, our imagination, and our emotion. The works we read have endured because they have something to say to *all* generations and to *all* ages. As Robert Fancher has pointed out, "Great books are great because of what they say about enduring issues, and we should study them not as idols but as sources of wisdom and knowledge, as the best thinking on the central issues that is available to date."[9]

Teaching great literature to adolescents is, however, extremely demanding for both the student and the teacher. Too often the result has been mediocre education. In our well-intentioned desire to "relate" to our students and to their limited experience, we have too often set aside our primary obligation to enrich their present so that they may be better prepared for their future. Too many so-called literature and humanities courses have confined their attention to contemporary literature that reflects the rather limited range of experience and span of interests of our teenage students. To be sure, there are valid reasons for doing so. Students are readily interested in what they find in their own world at present. They—and we—don't have to work very hard since the material in these popular books is readily accessible. But the result is that they read, review, discuss, and write about the obvious and the mundane. Reading, then, becomes almost as passive an experience as watching television.

It is also true that the language of most of the great writers is not readily accessible to many of today's young people who have been bred on pop fads, the empty, repetitive lyrics of rock music, and the vapid dialogues of TV sitcoms. Students and teachers must work hard together to gain access to such writers, concentrating on major passages, probing these with intensity and patience, with shared insight and feeling. When my English class reads James Joyce's *A Portrait of the Artist as a Young Man,* I ask the students to keep a journal of their ideas just as Stephen Dedalus does. Specifically, I ask them to keep a journal of ideas and impressions—philosophical, introspective, creative, personal—that emerge from their reflection on their reading of *Portrait.* I encourage them to relate these impressions to their own lives and present philosophy, their own quests and uncertainties, their many individual perceptions.

One student wrote:

> The insight Joyce gives into Stephen's mind and soul is incredible—I feel as if I *am* Stephen. Sometimes Joyce mentions something that Stephen does, like opening and closing his ear-flaps, and I know that I've felt the same way Stephen has. But Stephen is now bringing me back to realize my thoughts and inward mind-games. It scares me to think that I may be somehow losing the sensitivity I had as a child. Although things still affect me deeply sometimes, there's so much life that passes by me every day, unnoticed. . . . Joyce has a beautiful gift of expressing life and

growth. I just hope and pray that amidst responsibilities, schedules, adult pressures, and change that I will not lose my sensitivity but instead develop it despite the risk—against all odds, it seems.

And another had this to say:

I like the paragraph on the top of page 172. It is really beautiful: "Her image had passed into his soul forever and no word had broken the holy silence of his ecstasy. Her eyes had called to him and his soul had leaped at the call. To live, to err, to fall, to triumph, to recreate life out of life. . . ." Stephen is reborn. The paragraph is so full of life it makes me want to go jogging on the beach, listening to the sounds of seagulls and feeling a fresh cool sea breeze on my face. It's paragraphs like these that make me appreciate good literature.

This class had to work—and to work hard—to understand this novel. But as we struggled together, the novel became accessible to us all. More important, we savored the joy of accomplishment, the "relevance" of novels like this one to our own lives, the enduring truths and beauty of great literature that expand our insights and our imaginations.

As teachers and trainers of teachers, we need to do much more to develop intellectual independence in our students and to inspire in them the habit of inquisitiveness. We need to design courses where students, given the necessary foundation, can formulate problems and develop their own projects, courses that go beyond watered-down textbooks and basic-skills testing. We need to provoke our students to realize that the quest for learning may be more significant than the destination and that it is asking a significant question rather than finding the "right" answer that makes us truly human. As Professor Richard Peters of the University of London puts it, "Educators don't even need to have aims. The function of education is not to arrive at some destination but rather to travel with a new view."[10]

In my own classes, I try to help my students "travel with a new view" by leading them away from discussions that center on *the answer* to a question or *the theme* of a given literary work. (Has any great literary work contained only a single theme, I wonder?) Instead, I encourage them to consider what they think would be the most important question that should be asked about a given work. As for my tests, I avoid asking any essay question that we have already discussed in class. Instead, every test asks students to relate what they have read to a new context. One semester exam in an Advanced Placement class contained the following question:

Strange as it may seem, Fyodor Dostoyevsky, William Shakespeare, Joseph Conrad, Franz Kafka, T. S. Eliot, and Elizabeth Bishop chanced to meet at *Le Boulanger* one afternoon last week. Sipping cappuccino, they bemoaned the state of the world in the 1980s. Although they readily agreed that several dehumanizing forces were working against humankind in the 1980s, they could not agree on which one constituted the single most dehumanizing force. And so, after ordering another round of cappuccino, they decided that each of them would present his or her viewpoint on what comprised the major dehumanizing force in contemporary society as well as offer advice as to how we mortals should resist that force.

What viewpoint did each present? Which of them presented the most persuasive argument and why?

I try also to encourage intellectual independence by having my students explore their own philosophies in light of the philosophers we have studied in a unit on idealism, realism, pragmatism, and existentialism. In addition, students develop end-of-the-year creative projects in which they relate several of the works and the philosophies we have studied to their own artistic and creative pursuits. I have had original piano music adapted to crucial episodes in *Crime and Punishment;* I have had slides, music, and commentary based on a comparison of the lack of humanity found in Conrad's *Heart of Darkness* with that found in our own "civilized" Silicon Valley; I have seen a lovely ballet based on a collection of Eliot's poetry. These projects provide eloquent testimony to our students' ability to "travel with a new view." It is an ability that we need to encourage far more than we have in the past.

Furthermore, we teachers need to affirm the importance of critical thinking and the careful handling of problematic reasoning and even ambiguity in our classes and in our lives. To pay attention to and consider alternative views should be one of our prime requisites for becoming an educated person. We need to develop in the young the ability to think and therefore to listen critically. To encourage careful listening, I prod my students to hear not only the sounds and sense of their own prose but also that which is printed and spoken by others, regardless of the speaker's or writer's position in life. Once my students begin to develop a language awareness, their criticism becomes both contagious and irrepressible; it is directed to the language of their teachers and their textbooks, to the "double-speak" and sometimes blatant illiteracies in the newspapers, on television, in magazines, in statements made by our political leaders. My students display a notable intolerance for passive-verb pronouncements: "It has been decided that. . . ." "So who did the deciding?" they demand.

Local newspapers, the board of trustees' bulletins, notices from the

California State Department of Education—all become prime targets. As a result of my students' relentlessness, I am occasionally chided by some of my colleagues, an embarrassed administrator, or local reporter. I remain delighted. In my most fanciful moments, I imagine my students—past and present—warring against inflated language, pompous prose, and shabby thinking wherever it appears. I even imagine a world with no possibility of another Watergate which, we must realize, was as much the product of dishonest language (e.g., "inoperative") as it was of corrupt human beings.[11] John Milton recognized this danger when he said that "when the language of men in common use in any country becomes irregular and depraved, it is followed by their ruin and their degradation."

Another priority of mine is to educate the public at large—clearly including the press—to the multifaceted responsibilities of the schools and to some of our successes. One dramatic success story that has been too seldom mentioned is the Advanced Placement program. In the year 1955–56, 1,229 students from 104 schools sat for 2,199 exams, sending their scores to 130 colleges. In the year 1983–84, 180,000 students from 6,000 schools sat for 240,000 exams, sending their scores to 2,300 colleges. Unlike the SATs, AP scores have not declined over the years. Nor has the quality of the candidates' writing. Thousands upon thousands of high school students continue to earn college credit for course work successfully undertaken in high school. Many continue while in college to earn strong grades in the subjects in which they had received advanced placement.

Scores on the College Board's Achievement Tests, taken by thousands of college-bound seniors each year for college admission or placement purposes, have not declined over the years either. These scores, too, should be as consistently reported to the public as are the annual SAT scores. Unlike the SATs, Achievement Tests *do measure* what is taught in school. In *High School*, Ernest Boyer suggests that with "some modification, these [Achievement Tests] could form the basis for . . . the achievement portion" of a new assessment program that would "evaluate the academic achievement of the student— linking it to the core curriculum that the student had studied."[12] Of course, the fact that our best students continue to do well is not evidence that the whole educational enterprise is in good health. But it is encouraging to know that effective teaching and learning do occur in our nation's schools.

We need to insist that the media report stories like these as frequently as they describe the sordid details of the latest mugging on campus or the current state of illiteracy of teachers and/or students. Yet too often it seems that good news is no news. For instance, my nearly all-white high school campus became integrated three years ago when we closed one of the other schools in our community. Because of the judicious planning of a sensitive superintendent who maintained that we were not closing one high school but rather closing three and opening two new ones, our integration became a compelling success. We had involved every facet of the school community—parents, teachers, students, retirees, activists, local politicians—all of whom helped to plan for the opening of two new high schools. School mascots and colors were changed at one high school to those of the old school, while the second high school was renamed Mountain View, the name of the school that had closed. Student officers included youngsters from both the closed and the new campus. Even cheerleaders were divided equally. Teachers from all three campuses moved, and former department chairs were asked to resign and go through a new selection process. The result, of course, was that no single set of students or faculty became the "foreigners" on either campus.

The press flocked to Los Altos High the first day of our integration. When I asked one reporter why he wasn't taking any pictures, he said, "No action." I pointed to a group of black, Chicano, Oriental, and white students playing Frisbee on the lawn. His response was, "That's not the kind of action that makes news, I'm afraid."

"Are you disappointed that no one's fighting?" I persisted. But the reporter only smiled and walked away.

Fortunately, the administration, parents, students, and a few teachers did not stop there. We demanded that the local press begin to report the positive effects of our integration—increased academic and cocurricular opportunities for students of all races and economic levels; increased richness provided by various ethnic cultures assembled on the same campus; decreased fears and hostilities as students from quite different backgrounds learned to work together on various school projects. In time, the press responded, but only because various segments of the school community had worked together to insist on fair reporting.

We need also to encourage similar partnerships in education through which the academic community of the university and the academic community of the high school can be brought together to explore common educational concerns and to develop joint approaches for handling some of our common problems. In order to assure university involvement, however, I believe that professors must be granted tenure on the basis of something more than their publications. Furthermore, professors must be assured that working with schoolteachers will not lower their "professional status" in their departments. The Bay Area Writing Project is one prominent example of such a successful partnership. The Study of Stanford and the Schools, a joint project of Stanford University and six local school districts, is another.

Still, these partnerships are too few, especially those involving the *academic* departments, rather than the education departments, of the university. Probably the most durable of these at the national level is, once again, the Advanced Placement program. Each committee member on an AP Test Development Committee, whether affiliated with a high school or a university, has equal status and responsibilities. Indeed, the AP program was born in 1955 when high school and college academicians met together to initiate the development of challenging academic programs for able high school students that would reward them for what they do well, either by granting advanced standing or college credit. Such credit would be validated by taking a national examination.

Aside from those involved in the Advanced Placement program and a number of National Endowment for the Humanities (NEH) summer fellowship programs, many university scholars have been woefully uninterested in working with high school teachers to improve the quality and presentation of the academic curriculum in the secondary school. Still, their lack of involvement with secondary education should not be surprising in light of the fact that very few full professors from prestigious universities are willing to teach even a single freshman-level college course on their own campuses or to have any association with their teacher-training programs. Had I the power to do so—and most university presidents do—I would insist that partnerships be formed with the academic department, the teacher-training division, and the local high school.

High school teachers need the stimulation that such an exchange can bring. Occasional conferences and summer courses simply are not sufficient to yield an ongoing and up-to-date curriculum assessment in the various academic disciplines. As I have learned from working on a number of College Board test development committees, university people can also benefit from such partnerships. After all, we—high school teacher and college professor alike—are a community, and the bell tolls for us all.

Partnerships in education should also involve parents and the community. Belatedly, the business community has begun to realize that only through its own increased involvement in education—both financial and otherwise—will it be able to find the kinds of employees it needs. Partnerships are welcome in times of crisis as well. Recently, a potentially explosive situation at my high school occurred when a small but influential group of parents formed a committee to "review" some of their dissatisfactions with the English curriculum and some of the teaching staff and to make recommendations for improvement. Our English department responded by suggesting that parents could do a great deal to improve their youngsters' reading and writing skills if they would only work *with* the teachers to do so. Some of our suggestions were as follows:

—Turn off the television while students are reading/studying and encourage other parents to do the same.

—Contribute *good* used paperbacks for classroom libraries.

—Discourage the use of Cliff's Notes by students who use them as substitutes for reading novels or researching essays.

—Take their youngsters to the theater, talking with them afterward about the performance.

—Take their youngsters to the public library regularly, checking out books and making reading a regular activity for the whole family. Take them to local bookstores just to browse.

—Discourage their youngsters from taking unnecessary jobs to support their cars, insurance, and stereos.

Thomas Carlyle said, "If I told you I could reach forth my hand and touch the sun, you would say 'that is a miracle,' but the miracle is that I can reach forth my hand at all." Considering all the specialized groups now assessing public education and seeking to mandate this or that, it is a miracle that any of us are able to listen to and communicate with one another. The promise of education depends upon developing a body of enlightened participants—in the community, in the university, in state and federal government, in the press, and ultimately in the public at large—who will recognize that some of the most knowledgeable people in education reside *inside* the classroom, and that to ignore their voices is to ignore the most vital source of educational change and improvement that exists in our nation.

NOTES

1. Henry M. Levin as quoted in *Stanford Educator, School of Education News*, Stanford University (Spring 1984): 1–2.

2. College Entrance Examination Board, *Taking the SAT*, 1983, 7.

3. Elliot W. Eisner, "The Kind of Schools We Need," *Educational Leadership* (October 1983): 55.

4. Daniel B. Taylor, *College Board News* (Spring 1984): 5.

5. *Ibid.*

6. "What TV Does to Kids," *Newsweek* (February 21, 1977): 63.

7. *Harper's* (March 1984): 22.

8. Larry Cuban, Panel on School Reform, Stanford University, June 14, 1984.

9. Robert T. Fancher, "English Teaching and Humane Culture", in *Against Mediocrity*, ed. Chester E. Finn, Jr., Diane Ravitch, and Robert T. Fancher (New York: Holmes & Meier, 1984), 56.

10. Eisner, 53.

11. Claire L. Pelton, "The Sounds of Syntax," *College Board Review* 107 (Spring 1978): 25.

12. Ernest L. Boyer, *High School* (New York: Harper & Row Publishers, 1983), p. 134.

The Excellence
Commission and
the Humanities

Jay M. Sommer

As the humanities are central to the concerns of all who truly care about the quality of American public education, so too is the overall condition of public education an inescapable concern for those of us preoccupied with the fate of the humanities.

My own involvement with education generally and the humanities particularly is inseparable from my twenty-seven years in the high school classroom as a teacher of foreign languages. While at New Rochelle High School, I also had the opportunity to serve as "cooperating teacher" for college students preparing for the teaching profession. As the 1981–82 National Teacher of the Year, I visited many institutions of learning from primary schools through colleges. As a member of the National Commission on Excellence in Education, my own knowledge was supplemented and broadened by our inquiries, by the research done for the commission, and by the wisdom of my fellow commissioners. For the 1983–84 school year, Secretary of Education Bell invited me to be one of the official spokespersons for the commission, in which capacity I traveled to schools throughout the country, and this firsthand contact with other teachers and administrators significantly increased my understanding of our complex educational system.

Serving on the commission was, of course, an extraordinary personal privilege, but for me it was also a powerful reaffirmation of the strength of democracy. Among the voices on the commission I heard one with a German accent; I also heard a southern accent; and when I listened to myself I heard a Czech accent. But all the different accents blended together in our unanimous call for improved public education. The United States is one of the few countries where, despite different accents and diverse opinions, it is still possible to come up with a document such as *A Nation at Risk*. After thirty-five years in America, I am still awed by the fact that opinions are expressed freely and fearlessly at public meetings as well as private ones. I am also still optimistic about the prospects for improvement within our educational system, not least because we can be honest with each other about what is wrong with it.

The commission made a number of unhappy discoveries about our schools, but our findings were in no sense startling. The public, the media, and most practicing educators have long been aware of the inadequacies that beset our schools. We have also long been aware of superb examples of educational excellence—and these the commission noted as well. Ironically, we often found both effective and inferior practices in the same school system, sometimes in adjoining classrooms.

This posed a dilemma for the commission. We found both bad and good. The container was half empty, but it was also half full. After we had held dozens of hearings and closed meetings and had assembled all the data, we had to decide what to do with it. It took long hours of deliberation and some pretty blunt discussion to decide in which direction to go. In the end we agreed that, whatever else the report would contain, it should certainly contain a clarion call that would inspire and move the American public to help us correct the shortcomings of our schools. The commission elected to be brief so that people would read our words, and to be fairly general so that individual states and communities would evaluate their own educational institutions and tailor their own specific recommendations and remedies. The commission never intended its recommendations to be taken as dogma for every school or school system in America.

In large measure, the hoped-for individual state and district evaluations have materialized. Perhaps the most tangible form of activity inspired by our report is the profusion of studies and assessments carried out—and still underway—at the state and local levels.

More than a year has passed since our report was officially released by the White House. Despite a few cynical remarks by the media and some educators, I believe the report will have far-reaching consequences. I believe that America will respond to our plea—our clarion call—and will be generous with regard to its children's futures.

Certainly, it is too soon to pass final judgment on the impact of *A Nation at Risk*. Some improvements have already been made, but the results do not yet signal the conquest of fundamental weaknesses. Having recently visited hundreds of classrooms, my impression is that if the necessary changes are to be made in our educational systems, many large steps have yet to be taken. Unfortunately, some people are claiming victory already.

One insidious impediment to real improvement in schooling has been the deplorable attitude toward teachers prevalent in so many quarters. Correcting this situation is the first of the large steps that remain. As I traveled across the United States, it was all too clear that the general public harbors no great affection for my profession, nor do most people understand the challenges faced by teachers every day. In fact, the public often regards the teacher's task as rather easy—the teacher holding a kind of part-time job with short days and long vacations. Any dedicated teacher can tell you that what is called a vacation is in reality a badly needed rest period, a time of convalescence and regeneration that permits one to go on with what is, at best, a very difficult job.

It has been my good fortune to visit several exemplary school districts where I met contented and enthusiastic teachers who are doing their work with gusto. In these rather special communities, good treatment of teachers prevails not because their residents are uncommonly charitable or fantastically wealthy, but because they enjoy intelligent and practical leadership that understands good business. A wise superintendent, an understanding principal, a well-trained supervisory staff, and a fair-minded school board can engender healthy attitudes toward—and among—the teaching staff. Indeed, they can motivate good teaching and learning. In these communities where teachers are respected and treated well, burnout and related problems are rare. The models do exist. What we need are the impetus and energy to replicate such practices in thousands of other communities.

Poor working conditions, shabby treatment and substandard wages for teachers invariably have adverse effects on the quality of our children's education. That is why our commission urged that teacher salaries and working conditions be improved. The point was not teacher happiness; it was school effectiveness. A year has passed since we said this, but surprisingly few states or districts have paid serious attention to our recommendations in this area. The United States had almost as many unsettled teacher contracts at the beginning of the 1983–84 school year as it did the year before. Nor was our commission the only group to call attention to the dismal teacher situation. Virtually every major education study of the past two years has addressed this grave problem. Almost unanimously, the authors and advisors of these studies have expressed deep concern and empathy for the beleaguered teachers. Theodore Sizer has portrayed the plight of the classroom teacher with special eloquence. But *Horace's Compromise* is more than a poignant depiction of a fate to be avoided; the woes of Horace are a deplorable reality in thousands of schools—a reality that should command immediate attention and correction.

Besides issuing an urgent plea for a thorough review of teacher salaries, working conditions, and community status, our commission addressed the vexing matter of teacher preparation. Here is what we said: "Persons preparing to teach should be required to meet high educational standards, to demonstrate an aptitude for teaching, and demonstrate competence in an academic discipline. Colleges and universities offering teacher preparation programs should be judged by how well their graduates meet these criteria."

The brevity of the commission's report precluded a full account of our examination of teacher education programs. But we gathered ample information that reveals grave problems. To be sure, we also unearthed fine examples of outstanding teacher education programs here and there across the country. But that does not make for a healthy picture of teacher education as a whole.

I had a keen personal interest in these findings. As a beginning teacher, I had suffered the consequences of inadequate teacher education. One of the first things I learned when I started teaching was that I had not been prepared to handle discipline problems. Nor had I been given suggestions as to how to motivate children. I didn't even know how to plan an orderly and effective lesson. At the college where I received my training, the professor who taught me "methods" of foreign language instruction was not proficient in any foreign language!

The commission's inquiries and my own earlier work with students in teacher training programs all pointed to the same bleak conclusion; little had changed for the better since the days when I attended education classes. In the papers written for us on teacher education, I continually encountered "educationese"—words and constructions lacking clarity as well as practicality. Trying to make sense of the writer's words reminded me of what is known in Hebrew scholarship as *pilpul*, a kind of tedious hairsplitting that tends to lead one away from the main point to be made. At the hearings on teacher education, I learned that it is still the case that university instructors teach in areas for which they have neither training nor experience. They purport to teach future teachers that which they themselves do not know.

The commission discovered that there are almost as many different course titles as professors teaching them. In many instances, it was difficult to determine what a particular course of study contained and what was or was not actually learned by way of concrete teaching skills. We found scant agreement concerning minimum standards among teachers' colleges and schools of education across the country. After all these years, we should have a full set of clear and precise goals to guide the preparation of teachers. These should apply everywhere. But they seem to exist nowhere.

Teachers' colleges and schools of education do not deserve all the blame for poorly prepared teachers. A large measure of a teacher's competence should come from on-the-job training in the schools themselves. Yet the commission found widespread problems here as well. Few of the best and most experienced teachers in our schools willingly open their doors to student teachers. Nor, for the most part, are administrators eager to cooperate with the teacher education programs. The student teachers who are allowed into the schools often do not receive the support, supervision, and advice that they need. The situation is not much better for newly hired teachers. Supervisors and department chairpersons who should be mentors to the new teachers instead act almost exclusively as evaluators or judges. Their appraisals are commonly based on the abilities the new teacher brought to the task, rather than on the successful acquisition of new skills under the guidance of the supervisor.

It seems reasonable to expect that one of the top priorities of a supervisor should be to guide and support the new teacher. Yet supervisors frequently complain that other responsibilities prevent them from devoting as much time and attention to new teachers as is needed. Since this complaint is often warranted, an effort must be made to relieve supervisors of less pressing duties so that they can attend to their premier function: the improvement of teaching. The nurturing of new teachers should be their number-one priority and should begin on the very first day of school. I know this is difficult. But I cannot conceive of any function more important for the department chairman than the proper initiation of a new teacher into the profession.

Part of the responsibility for guiding new teachers can be shared by other experienced instructors on the staff who, with a bit of goodwill, could be quite helpful to the newcomers. Collegiality can play a vital role in building personal confidence as well as professional competence. Unfortunately, senior teachers often do just the opposite. They discourage the new teacher, they ignore the new teacher, or they are secretive and parsimonious with the knowledge they do possess. Of course, the new teacher must also shoulder some responsibility for personal growth and professional improvement. Both new and experienced teachers must make the effort to keep in touch with advances in their respective subject areas and in education methods and to make judicious use of them.

The preparation of good professionals should be the collective task of the entire educational community. We face large and urgent problems with respect to the training of our teachers. But we dare not despair or run away from the challenge. Nor can we suppose that with the passage of time the problem will solve itself. The many recent reports and studies have shed considerable light on the problem, but they have not solved it. That task remains to be completed.

Yet recent visits to colleges and my own participation in discussions of teacher education have given me new hope. I do not know whether the schools of education are simply terrified for their own future or have finally recognized how many of their products are tragically lacking in the requisites of pedagogical effectiveness. Perhaps some of both. But I now sense that we are beginning to see a dramatic improvement in the preparation of our teachers.

Another of the large steps that we still need to take is to improve the *content* of the education we offer our children. The first major recommendation of our commission dealt with graduation requirements. We spoke of the Five New Basics. While working on the different drafts of our report, I worried about how this particular recommendation would translate into reality. What, for example, would four years of English actually mean in the New Basics? Will it mean that at long last all of our children will learn how to speak the English tongue and recognize that a common language, spoken, written, and understood by all, is the glue, the cohesive force that holds a nation together? Will our students learn structure and syntax? Will they—each one of them—finally be able to write a well-organized composition? Perhaps it is unfair to ask these questions so soon after the report was issued. Yet I detect signs that give cause for worry. I perceive a certain unwillingness on the part of school districts to recognize the bald fact that English teachers are already overburdened by the number of papers they have to correct. (I speak of good English teachers, of course, the kind who assign papers, make corrections and comments, and offer to read rewritten papers.) Learning to write is learning to rewrite. Many districts seem not to realize that teaching five large classes to write is an impossibility. Pretending otherwise cannot result in good teaching or good learning. It will definitely result in frustrated teachers, though. Boyer makes this point forcefully in *High School*. We all know that rectifying these conditions will take money, but if we are serious about improving education, we will have to find those additional funds.

Fortunately, many other areas in the language arts can be improved without spending more money. Consider something so elemental—and so important—as the restoration of proper speech in our institutions of learning. We are not teaching our children to speak English—their own language. To be convinced of this, all you have to do is listen to conversations among today's young people. For instance, John took Mary to dinner and a movie on Saturday night, and on Monday morning you might hear John ask, "Mary, how's it going?" And she might wobble a little from left to right and say, "Oh, I don't know—I mean, like—oh, you know—okay, I guess." What she wanted to say was probably closer to, "The movie we saw together was impressive. It touched me. But the meal we ate was insipid." It is a sad situation when our young people do not have access to the creative and expressive possibilities inherent in their own language. We must instill in our children pride rather than disdain for good language usage. In our homes and in our schools, we must present students with better models than those offered by popular culture for correct and meaningful language usage. Language is the unique human instrument that distinguishes us from all other forms of life. We must not permit mediocrity to rob our children of that distinction.

English is one of the New Basics; social studies is another. While some high schools already had a three-year requirement in history or social studies, I am encouraged by the additional number who have responded to A Nation at Risk by instituting a three-year program. But the main problem in this area has not been an insufficient number of years of social studies; rather, it has been a matter of faulty approaches, dubious methods, and questionable content. I visited 120 history classes last year. In some schools, little or no real history is taught. In others, I found too much of an obsession with chronology. These classes reminded me of the accusation that Lev Nikolayevich Tolstoy made against the historians of his time. He contended that they took the chaos of the past and put it in chronological order, concentrating their attention on the chronology while neglecting the chaos. I think that our children are shortchanged when we do not explore the chaos with them. But our children are also shortchanged if we fail to give them a sense of how our present came to be out of the past. We must show our children that history relates to their own lives. We must convey to them the idea that history is the collective memory of mankind and that we must perpetuate that memory so as to make sure that we do not repeat the errors and the tragedies of those who preceded us.

All who care about the fate of the humanities must be appalled by the minimal attention that most schools give to the study of foreign languages and foreign cultures. It is surprising that a country like the United States, composed as it is of such a diverse population, should have so little grasp of the value of knowing several languages.

We—educators and policymakers as well as the general public— have a long history of neglect in this area. From time to time, we have perceived some desperate need for experts in foreign languages and have made feeble attempts to resuscitate a foreign language curriculum in our schools. One such shock came during World War II, when we realized how urgently the army needed trained linguists for reconnaissance and for other military and civilian functions. This is how the famous Army Specialized Training Program came into existence, a symbol of the vital importance for our nation's defense of knowledge of languages and cultures outside our own.

But it is almost impossible to compensate quickly for past neglect. The Army Specialized Training Program was excellent, but it could not create the miracle that might have saved many lives. We may never know the cost in human sacrifice brought about by our dearth of personnel properly trained in foreign language. World War II certainly highlighted the meagerness of our linguistic resources. Nevertheless, when the war ended, we sank back into complacency, only to be jarred into renewed activity during the Sputnik era. In our sudden realization that Soviet science had surpassed our own, we generated renewed effort not only in the study of science, but in other disciplines as well. We even made a serious move toward improving the state of foreign language study. Title III of the National Defense Education Act gave thousands of teachers the opportunity to receive excellent training. With such help, I received a masters degree in Russian language and literature. Many high schools and colleges responded to the call for greater attention to foreign language study. According to the Educational Testing Service's report, "Foreign Languages in the Schools," in the sixties foreign language course enrollment in our nation's high schools reached 27 percent of all students. The enthusiasm for language study even filtered down to the lower grade levels as a number of elementary schools across the country began to offer a foreign language program. Unfortunately, the moment did not last. In the late sixties, most foreign language programs in elementary schools were eliminated. The junior high schools did not fare so badly, but quite a few lost or drastically cut their language programs. As colleges eased their entrance requirements, a decline in high school programs was apparent as well.

In 1975, when the Helsinki accords were signed, the United States committed itself to promoting the study of foreign languages and cultures in order to foster international understanding. In an effort to honor this obligation, President Carter established a Presidential Commission on Foreign Language and International Studies in 1978. That commission's findings were not unexpected either. We learned that we faced grave shortages in almost every professional field of persons trained in foreign languages. The commission urged that regional centers be set up in the nation's colleges to foster foreign language studies and that funds be given to teaching institutions for this purpose. Few of its recommendations have been carried out, but efforts continue to put more of them into place.

Today we still find ourselves lagging well behind most other advanced countries in foreign language proficiency. Slack enrollment in language courses in the schools continues both to cause and to document the problem. Studies reported in July 1984 by the National Center for Education Statistics show that the majority of all students graduating from high school in 1982 had studied no foreign language. Only 13 percent of the graduates, and a surprisingly low 27 percent of "academic program" students, had earned more than two years of credit in foreign language study. Indeed, more than a quarter of the academic program students had no foreign language training at all while in high school. Most (79 percent) of the students were graduated from schools *offering* a three-year program in at least one foreign language, but 58 percent of all academic program students emerged from schools with no foreign language *requirements* for graduation.

Should the collective plea of the studies and report be heeded, and should we undertake in a serious way to promote foreign language study in our public schools, many changes will have to be effected. We will, for example, have to change our thinking about when foreign language study should begin and how long it should continue. Research tells us that skills in either the native or a foreign tongue are best acquired at an early age and that children are not confused by learning more than one language simultaneously. Many children are bilingual at the age of four or five. We also know that in most countries where foreign language study is taken seriously, instruction begins in the early grades. We have had a number of good models in the United States that confirm the value of an early start. I recently visited several such schools. The most memorable to me is in Cincinnati, a program supervised by Mrs. Mimi Met. In this immersion approach, young children learn history, art, and other subjects *through* the foreign language. It was impressive to see how well these youngsters dealt with language structure and how fluent they were, even in first and second grades.

There are two compelling reasons to begin language learning early.

First, younger children really do absorb languages more easily and naturally than do adolescents. Second, this is the only way to eke out enough years of study and practice to yield real language proficiency. At least six or seven years are required for this process. In addition, foreign language learning must be continuous, like studies in the native tongue, from the primary grades through high school and into college. Whatever the chosen method of instruction, continuity and structure are essential. The accomplishments of years of instruction can be nullified by an interruption of even one year.

A successful language program has other requirements. Most obviously, we need to use trained and expert language teachers, not, as some schools do, teachers of other subjects who may speak or read a foreign language. Emphasis should be placed on *all* the communication skills: speaking, comprehension, listening, reading, and writing. Even in the early stages, the study of culture should provide the background against which language instruction takes place so that each enriches the other. We also need to coordinate stages of language proficiency with the level of schooling. By the end of junior high school, language students should be able to demonstrate functional proficiency, displaying the capacity to converse on topics related to their age level and experience as well as the abilities to understand native speakers and to be able to read and write on that level of competence. In high school, concentration can then shift to more complex and abstract uses of the language and to a deepened understanding of the art, history, and literature reached through the language. By the time the student enters college, his or her language proficiency should have reached quite an advanced level. But that is a far cry from the recommendations of most contemporary reformers (including our own commission) and still farther from the reality to be found in most schools. Requiring two years of high school Spanish or French for college entrance will rarely produce competent linguists. Nor do two—or three, or sometimes even four—years enable the student to gain the level of proficiency at which foreign languages truly become part of the humanities, the level at which the student is able to grasp ideas and literature and history and values as well as syntax and vocabulary.

It is clear that American public education faces difficult challenges. We must raise our standards of performance for both teachers and students. There is no alternative to the improvement of teacher salaries if we want to attract competent young men and women to the profession and retain the good teachers that we now have in our schools. This challenge will not be easy to meet, but it is in the service of a still greater goal, that of preserving public education in America. The Commission on Excellence in Education might have titled its report *Public Educa-tion at Risk*, for that is the reality. The survival of public education is threatened by those who do not comprehend or appreciate its value in a democratic society. Persistent blows have come from those who harbor malign political motives. (Others have been struck by public educa-tion's well-meaning but sometimes foolish friends, who assign it bur-dens it cannot possibly bear with any success.) The distrust and fear engendered by the attacks on this vital institution have prompted many to defect. Happily, however, there are still sane voices to speak for the viability, value, and vitality of public education.

I count myself one of these. I am deeply concerned with the fate of this precious national institution. I know that my interest in its survival is shared by millions who, like me, have been its beneficiaries and are consequently in its debt. My experience is similar to that of other immi-grants to this country.

I was born into a very poor Czech family and had to work from childhood to add to our meager resources. At the age of eight, I was a ball boy on the tennis courts, getting up at five in the morning and working until eight at night. My mother used to wait impatiently for me to get home because my earnings for the day often provided the meal that the family would have that night. Poverty forced me to drop out of school at the age of ten with less than a fourth-grade education. There was no public education for the very poor in my part of Europe, and no one cared whether I attended school or not. The fact that I was deprived of education at such an early age still remains one of my most painful and humiliating memories.

At the age of twelve, I became a mechanic's apprentice. When, after three years, I finally had a chance to earn a decent living, Hitler inter-vened, and I was taken to a labor camp where I spent two years. Ten days before I was to be moved to Auschwitz, I escaped to Budapest and managed to hide out, using an assumed name, until my somewhat dubious liberation by the Russian army. On the second day of my new "freedom," I was made a "volunteer" in the Russian army, given a machine gun, and told to go out and fight the enemy. It was like going from one concentration camp into another, for, despite the horrors I had witnessed, I could still not understand how one human being could point a gun at another and fire. I subsequently learned enough about my liberators to realize that I would have to engineer a second liberation if I ever wanted to live as a free man.

Happily, I was able to take a permanent furlough from the Russian army. After a miraculous reunion with my brother, the only other sur-viving member of my immediate family, we decided to leave the place where so much tragedy had been perpetrated upon our people and which we suspected would soon be under the heel of the Soviet Union.

After months of wanderings and illegal border crossings we came to the displaced persons' camp in Cremona, Italy, the city of Stradivarius. My experience with the Italian people showed me that humanism had not died; their kindness revived in me new hope for my life. Learning to speak Italian, to sing Italian songs, and eventually to read Foscolo, Alfieri, Leopardi, Dante, and other great Italian writers was an expression of my gratitude to this good and generous people.

Displaced persons' camps, however, provide only temporary shelter for the homeless, and my plan was not to overstay my welcome. As a child, I had heard about the wonders of America and had even heard that one could find gold on the streets. Although I no longer entirely believed those stories, I still fervently wished to get there somehow. Thrilled with my decision, I ignored all the obstacles in my path, including the fact that thousands of other refugees with similar aspirations had relatives in the United States who could act as sponsors. Again, I had to rely on a miracle. After two and a half years in Cremona and many unsuccessful efforts, a stranger with a charitable soul agreed to send me documents enabling me to come to America.

On February 16, 1948, I first laid eyes upon the Statue of Liberty and a snow-covered New York. On the second day of my arrival, I discovered the real gold to be found on the streets of America—its public school system—represented for me by P.S. 149 on Sutter Avenue in Brooklyn. Here I could realize my long-awaited dream to gain the formal education of which I had been deprived. I was then twenty-one and had a fourth-grade education, but neither my age nor my background mattered. What mattered was that I wanted to learn. I was told that I could attend classes at night to learn English, and then go on to high school. And it was all free of charge! My English teacher was brilliant: she understood that refugees learn much better when they are well fed. She took me home and prepared the best steak I ever ate. Indeed, within six weeks I spoke English well enough to register for courses at Thomas Jefferson High School. I spent six months there, one year at Washington Irving High School, and many long hours studying at home, preparing to enter Brooklyn College, another public institution that generously opened its doors to me. By 1950, I was a fully matriculated student in the school of general studies, majoring in Russian language and literature. Six years later I received my B.A.

My experience with the American public school system can be echoed by millions of immigrants as well as native-born Americans whose lives have been transformed by the free education available to all regardless of their backgrounds. My felicitous experience and theirs give testimony to the vast accomplishments of American public education.

In recent years, public education has been attacked by those who seem to have forgotten the crucial service it delivered to America and its children. There is no doubt that, beset by a multitude of social and economic problems, public education today is not performing well enough. Our reaction, however, should not be to add to its burdens by unfair attacks, much less to abandon it, but to come to its aid through measures to restore its glory. The time is right. There is at present a resurgence of interest in and recognition of education as an irreplaceable component of American democracy. This is a development of which we must take proper advantage for the benefit of all our children and for the well-being of our nation.

The Policy Context

The Challenges of
Educational Excellence

Chester E. Finn, Jr.

Most essays in this book focus—as they were meant to—on particular challenges that beset the humanities in American schools, challenges that in somewhat altered forms also confront the humanities in our colleges, our cultural institutions, and in the norms and expectations that the broader society sets for its members.

There is, however, a risk in plucking the humanities from the larger context of American schooling in the mid-1980s, a risk that we shall thereby fail to understand the ways in which the tide of reform now washing over the entire educational system could lift—or swamp—our fragile crafts.

This essay therefore undertakes to limn that context, both because the "excellence movement"—as I shall call it—is interesting and important in its own right, and because its implications for our more specific concerns are immense. It is written from the perspective of a social critic and public policy analyst, not that of a school practitioner or humanities scholar.

The United States is in the midst of a vast educational reform movement. "Excellence" is its rallying cry, its watchword, and its buzzword.

Higher standards are its central precept. As I write, this movement is shaking the school policy foundations of most of the fifty states and of a great many local school systems. It has become an issue in national elections. It is the object of extraordinary media attention, the subject of innumerable books, reports, commissions, task forces, and conferences, and a matter of intense interest on the part of a great many "important people" who had not previously been noted for their concern about elementary and secondary schooling.

Where did this movement come from? Contrary to the impressions of many, its source was not the April 1983 report of the National Commission on Excellence in Education, nor the many other reports and studies that accompanied and followed that one. Though the stirring rhetoric of *A Nation at Risk* surely helped articulate and legitimize the concerns of the "excellence movement," the United States had long been accumulating a vast reservoir of public discontent with the overall performance of its educational institutions.

There was ample evidence of this: deteriorating "approval ratings" of the public schools; mounting interest in private schools, home schooling, and other "alternative" arrangements; tax limitation referenda, the main effect of which was to constrain school revenues; and a flood of books, newspaper articles, magazine cover stories, and television documentaries about "our failing schools."

There was also ample provocation: falling scores on such standardized measures as the Scholastic Aptitude Test; well-publicized instances of semiliterate or functionally illiterate high school (and sometimes college) "graduates"; testimony by employers who found themselves obliged to equip their new workers not only with job-related training but also with basic cognitive skills and elementary knowledge; reports of the armed forces having to simplify their manuals and instructions to match the faltering educational levels of their recruits; unmistakable signs of dwindling productivity and international competitiveness in the American economy, combined with accounts of the superior educational standards of countries that were outproducing us; and innumerable reports of crime, disruption, indiscipline, and apathy within the schools themselves.

Reasonable people can differ about the extent to which these and other problems are fairly laid at the schoolhouse door and the extent to which they may be aspects of larger social and cultural phenomena that have beset all our institutions. Schools cannot reasonably be expected to withstand all the shock waves rumbling through the society, much less to cure all of its diverse maladies. Indeed, at least a measure of public dissatisfaction with the schools can be traced to unrealistic expectations about their efficacy as all-purpose "social improvement" institutions—and to the willingness of educators to let them be thought of that way. Still, within the domain of responsibilities that are *properly* entrusted to the schools—certainly including the transmission of intellectual skills, substantive knowledge, fundamental values, and general cultural understanding from one generation to the next—the public is within its rights to expect the schools to do well. Yet the public has been saying for some time that in that central domain (as well as in others) the schools are not doing nearly well enough.

The key to understanding the relationship between this cumulative negative appraisal and the fervor of today's "excellence movement" is to realize that the American public never lost its fervent belief in the importance of education, both for the individual receiving it and for the larger society. The poll data could not be clearer.

What we have been experiencing, then, for at least the past decade and possibly for two, is a widening gap between the value that the public assigns to good education in the abstract, which continues to be extremely high, and the perceived quality of American educational institutions and offerings as they are in reality. When such a gap exists in a democracy with regard to a major public institution, political action is all but inevitable—and it is precisely that kind of action that I believe we have been witnessing for the past several years.

In fact, we began to see it in the late 1970s, as the "back to basics" movement gathered steam and as one state legislature after another mandated high school "proficiency" tests that students must pass before receiving their diplomas—in effect establishing minumum standards of intellectual skills and knowledge and imposing these standards on the schools.

Two developments of the early 1980s lent considerable added force to the emergent excellence movement. First, an array of governors and business leaders analyzed the unsatisfactory economic circumstances of their states and communities, seeking to identify the preconditions for prosperity in a postindustrial age, and concluded that near the top of their policy agendas must be placed the need for dramatic improvements in the general level of educational achievement and skill training. For the first time in the history of American educational reform, this awareness dawned initially in the southern states—and it is no accident that such southern governors as North Carolina's James Hunt, Florida's Bob Graham, Tennessee's Lamar Alexander, Mississippi's William Winter, Arkansas's Bill Clinton, and Virginia's Charles Robb have been some of the most visible and effective leaders of the excellence movement.

Second, as noted above, the past two years have witnessed an extraordinary outpouring of solemn studies, pronouncements, reports, and recommendations by scholars, commissions, and task forces, all attesting to the sorry state of American education, particularly at the high school level, and all urging that school standards be raised and conditions improved. Though *A Nation at Risk* and its ilk did not manufacture a crisis where there was no problem, they put words—often bluntly eloquent words—to the public's frustration, they legitimized the principle of educational standards—often before deemed an elitist, even discriminatory notion—and they articulated a series of clear policy recommendations by which such standards might be established.

In combination, these developments produced a huge wave of interest in—and efforts toward—educational quality improvement and school reform. Weary observers of many earlier reform movements may fairly ask, however, whether this one differs in any consequential ways from its predecessors and whether there is reason to expect it to yield different, better, or more durable results.

One cannot be certain in advance about the quality or permanence of the reforms that may result, but it appears to me that today's "excellence movement" can be distinguished from earlier educational reform efforts along three dimensions.

First, it manifests an almost single-minded interest in cognitive outcomes, rather than in school inputs or processes. How much and how well do children learn? The excellence movement does not much care whether more or less money is spent per pupil—it is willing to do either to obtain the results it seeks—or how large the classes are. It has minimum interest in the number of books in the school library, the ratio of guidance counselors to students, the success of the softball team, or whether the youngsters "feel good about themselves." Rather, it seeks evidence of measurable improvements in cognitive skills and knowledge (and, sometimes, in the acquisition of sound values and correct behavior). In pursuit of those ends, the excellence movement is startlingly open-minded as to means and resources, willing to organize, staff, and pay for schools in ways heretofore deemed heretical. But this very catholicity gives pause to cautious professionals who are at least as much concerned with educational means as with ends and who are apt to ascribe great significance to established practices.

Second, the excellence movement is decentralized. The federal government had practically nothing to do with starting it (except for establishing the national commission and—fortuitously—basking in the reflected glow of its celebrity) and will have very little to do with sustaining it. The national organizations of educators have, with rare exceptions, been surprised bystanders (or even hostile witnesses) rather than leaders. Save for the media—which have certainly aided the excellence movement by publicizing the conditions that provoked it— the other national private institutions have likewise contributed little. Rather, the current reform movement is centered in the fifty statehouses and the fifteen thousand local school systems—not in every one of them, to be sure, but it is at that level that it is operating and at that level where it is having an effect.

Third, rather than being dominated by the education profession, the excellence movement is led by elected officials, business leaders, citizen activists, and other laymen. Previous education reform movements in the United States were heavily influenced by—sometimes wholly controlled by—leading members of the profession. Though this one relies for some of its intellectual firepower on a handful of education analysts and writers (and, in a few cases, state and local school administrators), and though it owes a debt to scholars who have been distilling the characteristics of "effective schools," the excellence movement is a laymen's movement, populist in its impulses and energy sources, albeit steered by the elites of government, industry, and the media. If one had to point to its key leaders, one would doubtless single out the governors, legislators, and other elected officials who seem to have received a message from the public that this is something people feel strongly about, that there is political reward in boldly responding to those feelings and political cost associated with disregarding them.

It is therefore perhaps not surprising that the reformers who spearhead today's excellence movement are using the same kinds of tools that are familiar to elected officials in other substantive policy domains: mandates, prescribed minimal standards and prerequisites, standardized tests, licensure and certification procedures, conditions attached to funds, etc. The educational excellence movement is following a regulatory strategy more than an institution-building strategy, and in so doing it is blithely altering a great many long-established institutional patterns, practices, and governance arrangements.

Sometimes these alterations are crude and simplistic, sometimes imaginative and sophisticated. Most of the time, they seem to unite the clumsy with the sublime. But such are the mechanisms that public officials are familiar with and the policy tools that they are accustomed to finding in their workrooms. The primary reason that they have been using those tools rather than the subtler instruments of traditional education reformers is that the education profession, by and large, is not part of the excellence movement. The profession did not initiate it, is not leading it, and in many instances is opposing key elements of it. Despite some recent—and often opportunistic—attempts by parts of the profession to climb onto the "excellence bandwagon," we must understand that that very bandwagon is rolling over some of the best-loved (if also most vulnerable) beliefs of the education profession.

So far as I can tell, there are five points of particular friction between the values and assumptions of the excellence movement and those that characterize the education profession.

First, the excellence movement holds that the principal way to assess educational performance in schools and colleges is in terms of student learning outcomes, preferably the measurable kind. It has little patience for the cherished indices of the profession: extent of services offered, the degree of individualization of instruction, pupil sense of self-worth (or even "happiness"), the newness of the curriculum, or the faculty-student ratio.

Second, the excellence movement holds that someone needs to prescribe *what* students ought to learn—and then enforce the prescription. This point of conflict follows from the previous one; the education profession has a long history in the United States of providing students with lots of choice and individualization, sometimes of letting people learn what they want—or think they "need"—to learn, and of being reluctant to specify what everyone must know and particularly to decide for them what "values" they should hold, even when these may be the most central tenets of American democracy. The excellence movement, after recovering from its shock at discovering how diffident the profession is with regard to what many laymen assume is its most elemental obligation, has simply gone on to say, "Okay, then we the legislators, lay governing boards, and other nonprofessionals will specify who must learn what." The result is the already visible surge of course requirements and, sometimes, more detailed curricular prescriptions, mandated by lay policymakers.

Third, the excellence movement has a higher tolerance for failure than does the education profession, which has accustomed itself to the belief that schooling can and should be organized so that everyone will be judged to have succeeded at it (save perhaps those who truly refuse to participate at all). This is a commendable human sentiment, but it flies in the face of any real conception of standards, certainly of uniform standards, so long as we live in an imperfect world populated by individuals with different capacities for learning and different degrees of motivation to succeed. The excellence movement believes in standards if it believes in nothing else and is accordingly realistic about the likelihood that some will not, or cannot, meet those standards, and thus will be judged to have failed. Though it is not yet clear, as a matter of practical politics, how *much* failure the excellence movement can endure without weakening its populist base, certainly it does not share the education profession's view of any failure as unjust or immoral.

Fourth, consistent with its emphasis on measurable outcomes, the excellence movement has a keen sense of accountability: a firmly held belief that the child, the school, and even the individual teacher are fairly held to account for the educational results that they produce. By contrast, the education profession (like others) instinctively rejects the proposition that its institutions and individual members should be deemed responsible for their results.

Fifth, the education profession—again like other professions—tends to assume that in order to do anything differently, certainly in order to do anything better, more money must be committed. The excellence movement, by contrast, has deduced that setting—and even enforcing—higher educational standards does not necessarily cost any more; indeed, under certain circumstances might even cost less. What may cost more, perhaps quite a lot more, is to organize and staff the schools such that an acceptable proportion of students meet the higher standards. But that logic is very nearly the opposite of the profession's reasoning. The excellence movement is saying—and, if poll data are reliable, the public is agreeing—that we are unwilling to commit another dime for "more of the same" but will gladly spend what is needed on condition that things be done in significantly different ways that we can be reasonably confident will achieve the desired results.

Those five clashing attitudes—and their corollaries and consequences—may begin to explain why there has been some cultural lag, not to say overt resistance, on the part of the education profession with respect to the values and emphases of the excellence movement. I do not contend that the education profession is the only obstacle to the attainment of excellence in American education, and certainly not that all members of the profession are obstacles. But I do suggest that the old Pogo formulation has some applicability: We have met the enemy and he is—at least partly—us.

In addition to attitudinal differences between today's reformers and many of the professionals, we find within the educational enterprise the predictable "vested interests" that for all the predictable reasons are wary of change—and the more radical the changes, the warier they become. Most of these are so obvious as not to warrant extended attention here. They include the teachers' colleges and unions, the local school boards and superintendents, the curriculum directors and teacher supervisors, the textbook publishers and vocational educators, the various ethnic and minority groups that have obtained special programs or standards of their own, the devotees of particular subjects (or special focuses within subjects), even the bureaucracies of the state education departments, now in many cases expected to adopt norms and procedures quite different from those to which they have long been accustomed. Each of these deserves to be understood for what it is and to be appraised in terms of its compatibility (if any) with the public interest more broadly construed. But I shall forbear and in the balance of this essay turn instead to the identification of a dozen challenges to educational excellence that seem to me both less obvious and far less easily dismissed as expressions of self-interest. They might more accurately be termed "dilemmas" that the excellence movement must confront and, if possible, resolve.

The first of these is a rather basic contradiction between the central tendency of the excellence movement—which is to employ a regulatory strategy to mandate certain kinds of uniformities among schools—and one of the premier findings of recent research into the characteristics of unusually effective schools: namely, the extent to which most such schools enjoy a high degree of building-level sovereignty; have developed a distinctive ethos and climate of their own; have, in the argot of modernism, "invented themselves." Excellence in educational practice tends to be school-specific and homegrown. Yet the excellence movement seeks—with the best of intentions—to make educational practice more uniform, in effect requiring ineffective schools to adopt the practices that typify their more successful counterparts. The problem is that the best schools seem to have a secret ingredient that cannot be mandated. Increasingly, in fact, uncommonly effective principals (and sometimes individual teachers) seem to be "outlaws," to have figured out how to succeed in spite of the mandates, rules, and procedures that they are ostensibly obliged to follow.

Second, the excellence movement is devoted to measures of student performance as gauges of success, sometimes almost as ends in themselves. Yet at the present time we have terribly primitive means of assessing student performance in the ways that policymakers crave most, namely, in comparing achievement among schools, school systems, states, and whole nations. That there are reasons—some scientific, some political—for the shortcomings of our comparative educational assessment tools does not much simplify matters. Policymakers tend to draw their conclusions from such indicators as they can get their hands on, including some that were never designed for this purpose, and they tend also to construct their goals around those educational outcomes that are most susceptible to measurement and comparison. This can lead to particularly unsatisfactory handling of the humanities, subjects whose lack of obvious and immediate utility already made them suspect in the eyes of many laymen. When it is also explained to those laymen that the acquisition of humanistic knowledge and understanding is particularly hard to measure with the available instruments *and* that intense controversy surrounds the definition of such concepts as "cultural literacy," they are apt to turn back to easily measured cognitive skills and to subjects such as math and science that are less discordant.

Third, the excellence movement has had great difficulty specifying "learning objectives." This can be traced in part to the problems with testing and measurement, in part to the detachment of the education profession from today's reformers, and in part to age-old arguments about what knowledge should be expected of everyone and what should be elective. The result, however, is that the policymakers often end up settling either for a simple test of cognitive skills or for the specification of so many years of such-and-such a subject before one can graduate from high school. Even the National Commission on Excellence in Education fell into this trap, substituting crude measures of "seat time" for any clear statement of what young people should know—and know how to do—before exiting from school into college, employment, or whatever. The excellence movement is moving into what E. D. Hirsch, Jr., calls "educational formalism" rather than into the (admittedly arduous) specification of cultural literacy. This, too, is very damaging to the humanities—and to other subjects that are knowledge-based rather than skill-based. To require a youngster to take four years of English and two or three years of "social studies" is not necessarily to expose him to a high-quality education in the humanities!

Fourth, the excellence movement is ambivalent to the point of schizophrenia in its attitude toward two radically different visions of what an ideal educational system would look like (and, of course, toward the associated conceptions of the nature of society and the role of schooling within it). On the one hand, we encounter the boldly democratic proposition—manifested most clearly, I think, in *The Paideia Proposal*—that all youngsters should attend essentially the same schools, learn essentially the same things, and be held to essentially the same standards, with minimum regard for differences in aptitude, interest, or heritage. On the other hand, we find the conviction that educational quality is most surely achieved—and the values of a pluralistic democracy best honored—if schools are encouraged to be as unlike one another as possible, if children (and their parents) are free to select the form of schooling that they think suits them best, and if competition rather than homogeneity becomes the premier organizing principle of the educational system. I do not know whether a workable synthesis of these seemingly opposed "visions" is just over the horizon. I do know that I, like the excellence movement as a whole, am sorely vexed by having to choose between two models of reform that are both enormously appealing in their very different ways.

Fifth, educational reformers are generally much better at agreeing to the abstract proposition that schools have tried to do too much, that the curriculum is out of control, and that a general whittling down and simplification should occur than they are at deciding precisely what to discard in favor of what. One person's notion of a subject that can easily be jettisoned turns out to be another's highest educational priority and the source of another's livelihood. Nor are public and private social agencies rushing forward to assume the health, welfare, counseling, nutritional, employment, and other noneducational services that the schools have in the past been expected to provide, even though in many cases the schools cannot provide them satisfactorily, at least not without compromising their central educational functions. Hence the long-term impact of the excellence movement on the schools could turn out to be as inconsequential as that of the doctor on the obese person who agrees that he really needs to lose weight—but who just can't seem to stop eating several desserts every evening.

Sixth, can we deal honestly with the alleged tension between educational "excellence" and "equity"? This much-debated trade-off is, so far as I can tell, both a perverse distortion of the language and—if we're not careful—an invitation to the most damaging form of liberal racialism. I do not contend that no problems will arise if a sudden, sharp escalation of educational standards, especially one unaccompanied by adequate efforts to assist people to meet those standards, leads to failure rates that are both absolutely high and disproportionately experienced by members of low-income or minority groups. But to allow that concern to argue us away from raising standards or into having multiple standards is to succumb to the ugly suggestion that some parts of the population simply cannot be expected to learn as much as other parts. As for the linguistic carnage, observe that "excellence" and "equality" are not antonyms in any dictionary. The opposite of excellence is mediocrity; the opposite of equality is inequality or perhaps injustice. To pose them as contrasts with one another is to rob each principle of much of its power. Yet the contemporary debate about educational reform commonly assumes that they are opposites—as if daring the excellence movement to abandon the doctrine of equality of opportunity in pursuit of some elitist fantasy.

Seventh, can we solve the "teacher problem"? The excellence movement is disposed to assume that if intellectual standards and salaries are elevated, a large number of capable people will enter the teaching profession, thereby rescuing it from the sorry state to which it has sunk. This may be a little naive in the face of several awkward realities: the huge number of new teachers that we will need very soon—if the federal projections are reliable, some 1.16 million of the 2.64 million people who will be teaching in public and private schools in 1990 were people not teaching in 1984; the iron grip that traditional teachers' colleges and state certification procedures have on entry into the occupation, notwithstanding a few recent attempts to loosen it; and the low status into which school teaching has fallen during the course of at least two decades of declining educational performance, increasing unionization, and widening opportunities for the ablest members of teaching's historically "captive" populations of women and minority group members. It is simply unknowable whether the measures now being contemplated (and in some cases undertaken) at the state and local level, sensible and meritorious though they may be, can bring about the needed transformation of the profession of public school teaching. For most of our history, the average parent has seen in his child's teacher a person smarter and better educated than himself; if the aforementioned transformation does not occur, we may be entering an era in which the average parent regards himself as smarter and better educated than his child's teacher. The implications of such a shift are sobering to contemplate.

Eighth, have we any hope of arresting the processes of intellectual decay that continue to afflict much of the conventional wisdom about education within some of its largest institutions, and that thereby weaken the profession itself? I offer a single example that seems to me to speak volumes. The March 1984 edition of *NEA Today*, the primary publication of the education profession's single largest organization, carried on its inside back cover a deadly earnest pro-con "debate" about the proposition that it is time to abandon the teaching of English grammar in American schools. I do not suggest that this—or any other— issue should be taboo. But ponder the implications of a nation captivated by the prospect of educational excellence in which the dominant teachers' organization is seriously willing to quit trying to teach—or expecting children to learn—the way the national language works.

Ninth, are we not expecting too much of the high school? This concern may be a natural consequence of the preoccupation with secondary education that has characterized the school reform movement thus far; perhaps elementary schools and colleges will soon come under equally intense scrutiny. (I believe they should.) But at the present moment it seems to me that we are expecting the high school both to rectify the shortcomings and the failures of the primary and middle grades *and* to supply the rudiments of a broad "general education"— the latter partly because we (correctly) feel that every citizen should have an education even if he's not going to college, partly because the colleges and universities appear to be either incurably vocationalized and specialized or entirely nondirective about what their students should learn. These tendencies combine to place far too heavy a burden on the three or four years we assign to high school. They also combine to create a special challenge to the humanities: if high school is both the last chance we have to ensure that everyone masters the basic skills of the three Rs *and* our last reliable opportunity to prepare everyone for entry into a world obsessed with science and technology, what hope have we of eking out the time for thorough exposure to things seemingly as unworldly as literature and history?

Tenth, can education defy the general lassitude of a laid-back society, a leisure-minded population, and a political culture that favors "no-fault" policies? This is a very general point, but it's important. For the purposes of the excellence movement to be realized, a lot of people—teachers, students, parents, taxpayers, principals, board members, etc.—are going to have to put themselves and their institutions onto something akin to a stern training regimen, a "get-back-into-shape" routine of hard work, self-discipline, and denial, complete with increased risk of failure. There will not necessarily be any greater compensation for enduring this regimen than the sense of success associated with doing well at it and thereby meeting its (explicit or implied) standards. (There is, of course, huge long-term compensation for the individuals and for their society, but this will not be obvious to many on a Monday evening when it is necessary to shun television football in order to write—or grade, or help one's child to write—another theme.) Are we up to it? A totalitarian regime might tell us we have no choice. In the absence of compulsion, this must be an act of will.

Eleventh, have we the patience? It took twenty years and more to slide to the bottom of our educational ditch. If we are steadfast, energetic, and purposeful, maybe it will take only half as long to climb out. But ten years is longer than we ordinarily devote to "reforms" (the civil rights revolution being a welcome exception), especially the kind that demand a lot of effort. At present, the excellence movement has considerable momentum and lots of popular support. But can it be sustained? Or will the governors, the business leaders, the newspaper editors, and the others who are leading it decide either that the problem is well on its way to being solved or, alternatively, that it's hopeless and cannot be solved, thereupon turning their attention to other matters? Will the colleges, beset by enrollment problems of their own, keep up their newly raised admissions requirements? Will the present—still rather modest—forms of cooperation between school people and university people endure, or will each slide back into old routines? Are we in the early stages of something durable? Or nearing the end of an epiphenomenon?

Twelfth, and finally, will we redefine "the problem" into insignificance and then convince ourselves that matters are really fine pretty much as they are, save perhaps for a few minor adjustments and expansions here and there? Will we empty the term "excellence" of any real meaning? This seems to me particularly likely as the lay leaders of the present excellence movement turn their attention to other issues, leaving the responsibility for fine-tuning, implementing, and evaluating the processes of educational reform in the hands of the education profession—the self-same profession that I criticized a few pages back for posing a series of (principled and self-interested) obstacles to the achievement of educational excellence. Will the profession come out of its bunkers, relieved that the air war is over and that life on the ground can return to normal? There is already visible within the profession, besides self-interest and philosophical resistance, a sense of weariness, apathy or futility, as if "this, too, shall pass," as well as the beginnings of an authentic backlash to such modest successes as the excellence movement has thus far achieved.

Confronted with twelve such vexing "dilemmas," the reader may fairly ask whether I have any grounds for optimism, either about the excellence movement or about the possibilities of improving the humanities as they are understood and taught and studied in our schools. Conceding that I may be indulging in unconscious self-delusion, I feel more hopeful than ever before. Educational excellence has the attention of the nation. It is, at least for now, both an honorable concept and one invested with real political energy as well as moral power. A number of influential actors who have not previously been known for close attention to—much less taking risks in pursuit of improvements in—elementary and secondary schooling are now deeply involved. The pollsters say that as a public issue this one is apt to have a longer run than most. Here and there in the education profession itself, one encounters thoughtful and articulate figures who have "signed up" with the excellence movement, even at some considerable personal risk of repudiation by their professional peers.

As for the humanities, we cannot be certain that they will fend off the challenges identified in this volume (and elsewhere), emerging stronger and better understood as a consequence of the engagement. But when well learned, the humanities, while they certainly do not make us human and may not make us good, do enable us to grow in wisdom—as well as in the knowledge that they, along with other disciplines, can provide. Wisdom is not the same as virtue, nor knowledge equivalent to decency. But if one is gambling on the future of the nation that has correctly been termed the last best hope of mankind, one is going to get better odds if he puts some money—and some confidence—on the humanities.

Epilogue

William J. Bennett

The preceding chapters have both described and responded to some of the most pervasive and troublesome challenges to the humanities in contemporary American education. Their discussions are insightful, illuminating, and for the most part encouraging. But what if, notwithstanding the cogent arguments presented in these pages, key participants in the educational enterprise—school boards, principals, state curriculum committees, teachers—decide that the game is not worth the candle? Suppose many of them come to believe that grave challenges to the humanities should be ignored because there are more compelling priorities for the schools or conclude that the defense and teaching of the humanities simply take too much energy, time, and resources relative to their pedagogical benefits. Suppose, then, that in many places the humanities go untaught, either for lack of interest in them or lack of ardor in their defense against these and other challenges. What will we have lost?

First, we will have lost a truly convincing and complete idea of education. We do not serve our students well if we believe, or invite them to believe, that the major purpose of education is preparation for a job rather than preparation for a life. H. G. Wells termed life "a race between education and catastrophe." Perhaps so. But whether we think of the alternative to education as catastrophe or as something less severe but still unwelcome—say, an impoverished view of self, or a self not equipped with important skills or good habits of thought and work—in either case, the terms of the alternative remain serious, and the humanities have a substantial part to play in the ultimate outcome.

An argument for the humanities is an argument neither against practicality nor against "practical" education. Education ought not to be severed from matters of job, training, and career. "It is not enough," wrote Dewey, "that a man be good—he has to be good for something."

While no one can prudently abjure the practicalities of becoming employable, the larger issue is how also to prepare students for the practical tasks of living well, thinking wisely, and acting sensibly. The study of the humanities cannot guarantee such results, of course, but because we still (thank the Lord) believe that such things matter greatly, we attend to them by all the means at our disposal, including the humanities.

In framing the educational goal for the long run of a practical life, perhaps no one has given a better example or more specific direction to the sorts of things the humanities ought to teach than Montaigne in his essay, "On the Education of Children":

> A pupil should be taught what it means to know something and what it means not to know it; what should be the desire and end of study; what valor, temperance and justice are; the difference between ambition and greed, loyalty and servitude, liberty and license; and the marks of true and solid contentment.[1]

Are these practical matters? Indeed they are. Can the humanities help in making these things one's own? Yes, if they are taught well and studied intelligently. Should all students be given the opportunity to become knowledgeable about these matters? Surely, yes. For all whose lives will be touched by these matters, some preparatory guidance will be helpful, indeed will be practical. To sacrifice such preparation by scorning or omitting the humanities is neither smart policy nor considerate adult behavior. We and our students are not free to be or to know those things we have never learned. Were students to part from us without an inkling of the matters Montaigne describes, the consequences would be severe, for they would not be ready for the world and life they enter. In short, the loss of the well-taught humanities would be considerable.

Once this practical matter is settled—and it likely will be, for our education system does not by and large want to bury the humanities—other practical questions remain, including many addressed in the essays that constitute this book. What should we teach? How do we select? How do we match up low-ability students with the highest-ability thinkers and writers of our civilization? How do we overcome resistance, hostility, and indifference to the enterprise? All of these matters have been well treated in the preceding pages. Let me add just a few thoughts on each.

We should teach the best we have to offer. The "we" includes at least two parties. First, it is the author or artist in question—Mark Twain or Jefferson or Hemingway or Flannery O'Connor or Ecclesiastes or Emily Dickinson or Rembrandt or Thucydides. In deciding what to teach, we must draw from what is better or higher than average, from the best and most compelling material we have. Why? Because one purpose of teaching the humanities is to invite students into the company of great souls and to have them linger there awhile. We do not have to invite most students into the company of their peers, to television or to movies and popular music, for most can already be found in that company. In teaching the humanities, something else is involved. We should offer something different, something better. The humanities—history, philosophy, literature, the classics—are a record of, to paraphrase Matthew Arnold, the best thought and said and done. They are a repository of compelling questions and compelling answers presented in ways admittedly unfamiliar to many of the young but for that all the worthier of a close look.

The other party of the "we" is the teacher. We offer the best that we, as representatives of the world our students will enter, have to offer them, the best that we can muster. The teacher must teach of the humanities what *that* teacher knows and loves of the humanities. If the teacher knows nothing he should teach nothing; if he knows much he should strain to teach it. Most teachers find themselves between these extremes. "I am my students' greatest limitation," a teacher recently wrote the National Endowment for the Humanities. "Where my knowledge stops theirs must stop. Sirs, I seek the opportunity to take my knowledge, and my students', further." As this comment makes plain, teachers must maintain an intellectual life of their own, as difficult as that sometimes can be. Yes, great teaching is contagious for learning, but the contagion can begin only with someone who is himself thoroughly infected and repeatedly bitten by the bug. We do not today need—we never did need—the dull, deadening, didactic, droning on to another generation of students a lifeless *Julius Caesar*, immunizing them for life against Shakespeare. Successful teaching of the humanities does not take genius; it does not even take a Ph.D. It does take good material, a lively mind, a firm grasp of the subject matter, and contagious enthusiasm.

Of course, it also takes students. In my experience over the last twelve years as consultant to more than fifty secondary schools, I was always saddened when I learned that the humanities program consisted of a single course called "humanities," and my sadness deepened when I found that it was a course only for honors students or for the "gifted and talented." The first saddened me because that solitary course usually represented a mishmash: In one school I visited, it included literature, art, music, fairs, carnivals, body painting, and gymnastics (the humanities as "fun group activity"). In another school, it was equally depressing to find that the humanities course comprised units of sociology, interpersonal relations, philosophy, and environmental crises (the humanities as "consciousness-raising" about contemporary societal maladies). The problem is that neither of these, whatever its benefits (dubious at best), was the humanities. In this observer's judgment, it is usually better to teach the humanities by teaching literature or history. Normally, we should teach the humanities in the same way that, once past the primary grades, we teach science, not by teaching a course called "science" but by teaching physics or chemistry or biology.

Further, we should try to make the teaching of literature and history a common experience. If the "practical" argument I made earlier is right, then middle-ability and lower-ability students must be included along with the bright and able. Life's vagaries and choices do not scan individual intelligence and then descend only on the top ten percentiles of the human race. As Ishmael in *Moby Dick* reminds us, "The universal thump is passed 'round." The questions the humanities ask are everybody's lot, the answers everyone's birthright. In our society, everyone is invited to full citizenship. If the humanities truly are a sound part of preparation for these practicalities, then everyone should have a chance, an invitation to thoughtfulness about them. And if we do not extend that invitation to all, those who are not "gifted and talented" may, though they may not tell us, resent us for not providing it for them. Albert Shanker of the American Federation of Teachers tells of visiting with a group of average-ability students and asking them what they thought they should be studying. "What do you think we should be asking you to read?" he asked. After a short silence, a student raised his hand and said, "What are the smart kids reading, Mr. Shanker? That's what we want to read, too."

The same point is evident when we examine the great works of the humanities and ask what audience they address. We at the National Endowment for the Humanities recently polled educators, members of

Congress, writers, scholars, and journalists, asking each to give us a list of the books he or she thought every high school student should read. The top four choices were Shakespeare, the Bible, *Huckleberry Finn*, and the "founding documents" of the nation: the Declaration of Independence, the Constitution, the Gettysburg Address. Now, what is the intended audience for these? Who is addressed by the Bible? The gifted and talented only? Who learns from *Huckleberry Finn*? Only the brilliant? For that matter, who identifies with Huck? Certainly not your typical academic high-achiever. Do Shakespeare's lessons about the struggle between good and evil for the possession of a soul apply only to those with a high IQ? And finally, were the Declaration of Independence and the Constitution written to be read and followed only by the ablest? Obviously, these are matters of common property, of the shared heritage of every American, and should be distributed as such.

Some will agree that the intended audience is quite properly all, but will still contend that the actual works of the humanities—even these four works—are beyond the intellectual grasp of "all." Of course there are some with no ability to read, some with severe learning disabilities, and in every school some who simply don't show up. Nevertheless, in the hands and through the mind and will of a good teacher, almost all our youngsters can become students of the humanities. Consider Homer's *Iliad* or *Odyssey*. First, are they worthy of study? Yes. They certainly do teach about honor, temperance, loyalty, justice, and injustice. Second, they can be taught or "made accessible," as some say, to students in many ways. In a recent conversation with a group of middle and high school teachers, I found that many of them taught Homer. For some with very precocious students, their reading was from a recent edition of an excellent translation; at one school, a teacher even reported that a few of her students were studying Greek in hopes of reading the *Iliad* in the original.

But others with less able students successfully taught Homer, too. I recall one teacher in particular, from a rural school system with many students of low ability and poor background. There, she said, easier editions were read slowly with the aid of pictures and slides. The teacher told the students parts of the story before they began reading, helped them through difficult passages, and avoided very difficult parts altogether.

To all but the purist, this is a perfectly acceptable, indeed laudatory, way to proceed. One can be brought to greatness slowly. The point is to get there. As Patricia Graham has said, vary the pedagogy but retain the substance. Many a child of my generation had his first taste of the humanities in *Classic Comics Illustrated*, a taste that whetted one's appetite for more substantial treatment later on. We should never forget that for generations of humanities students, indeed for most of us, the enterprise of the humanities began at a very early age with the familiar and modest words, "Once upon a time."

To this point, I have assumed that works of the humanities will be read by "all." But some dispute this on grounds that have lately become familiar. Does not the heterogeneity of our student body, they ask, argue against any common set of readings in the humanities? This question too has been well and clearly treated in the preceding pages, but I would offer an additional word of my own. To refer once more to the recent survey we conducted, it revealed that literate Americans from all walks of life believed, by a landslide preference, that four "books"—Shakespeare (Macbeth, Hamlet), selections from the Bible, the "founding documents" (the Declaration of Independence, the Constitution, and the Gettysburg Address), and Huckleberry Finn—should be read by all American students before completing high school. Does that near-consensus bespeak an act of intellectual imperialism, an attempt to force intellectual conformity, a mindless disregard of student ethnic or racial differences, or a violation of pluralism? I think not, for several reasons. First, the humanities at their best—and these four works are bona fide candidates for that distinction—speak to us as men and women and to our condition as human beings; they speak to us in terms that we share, if not as a species, then at least as a nation. The great works of the humanities are neither gender, race, nor ethnicity specific. A people's commonly held knowledge is the basis of their ability to communicate with each other. The humanities offer a wealth of resources for developing a language of common experience, a language capable of markedly more elevated style and considerably deeper insight than the language employed by the mass media.

Second, in E Pluribus Unum we salute plurality as well as unity. There is a time for the noting of what makes us different, and there is a time for the recognition of what we share as a people and as fellow sharers in the human condition. The humanities offer insight into both what is shared and common, and what is particular and individual. They should be taught for both these worthy ends. Today in some places the tide is running against teaching that which holds us together, against that which unifies us and give us ideas and cultural reference points in common. We want never to obliterate or to ignore variety, particularity, or cultural diversity, but we do not serve these ends by obliterating unity and digging up the common ground. After all, to be able to speak to each other about differences among us requires that we have a common language. The ability to recognize the importance of things foreign to our experience and the dignity of persons different from us also requires a shared vision, the elements of which include a common code of tolerance, sympathy, empathy, openness, and a belief in human equality. There are some things we must all learn and learn together. The humanities, as exemplified in these four "books" and other great achievements, can be our allies and helpers in this attainment. Yes, there should be some common reading.

I close on a note similar to where I began. Granting the value of the enterprise, can we, in today's schools, actually pull it off? Is it practical to encourage the study of the humanities when at times so much seems allied against it? In our world, challenges to the humanities are usually met—when they are met—by more than the conviction of mind and heart. Often, personal resoluteness is not sufficient to the task of institutional betterment. One needs allies. "In the campaign for character," Harvard's Charles W. Eliot wrote, "no auxiliaries are to be refused." So too in the campaign for sound teaching and instruction in the humanities, not only are auxiliaries not to be refused, they must be sought. Organizational and political courage are often required; there are days in some schools when it seems that the entire educational enterprise is in conspiracy against the kind of reflective learning the humanities represent. So attention must therefore be paid to the selection of principals, the election of school-board members, the involvement of parents, and the nurturing of professional leadership—all these influences can be crucial, both to local circumstances and to the national climate for learning. The humanities need defenders and they need advocates. It is welcome and important news when the kinds of people represented by the Educational Excellence Network become such advocates, when the distinguished contributors to a book such as this pull together, making the impact of the whole greater than the sum of the parts, arguing as intelligently and persuasively as in the preceding pages to the importance of humanities study. In the seemingly endless and often fractious public debate on education in America, a moment can arise in which a good case for exemplary teaching of real history and good literature can be presented with a chance that it might be heard. Many believe—I among them—that one of these moments is now before us. It is important to seize it and bring others into the debate before the moment passes, perhaps not to recur for another ten or twenty years. (Though it will return! Everything returns sooner or later in America!)

In meeting the challenges to the humanities, one finally has to remember that the defense, the teaching, and the learning of the humanities are all fraught with difficulty. There are many obstacles scattered across this terrain. In talking about the humanities, there are temptations to overstate, understate, misstate; in the background are always lurking suggestions of irrelevance, corruption, "cultural imperialism"; in practice there are tendencies in the teaching to make things too easy, too difficult, too much a matter of feeling and not enough one of thinking; there are student complaints about homework, difficulty of material, even boredom. Sympathetic readers of this volume are all too familiar with these and other excuses, equivocations, and authentic difficulties. So what comfort may we take? We can remind ourselves that things worthy are often things difficult. Meeting the challenges to the humanities is like the study of the humanities themselves. Trying to follow Socrates' arguments, assessing the issues in the *Debates* of the Federal Convention, penetrating Shakespeare's language—all are genuinely difficult, but many have learned that the effort is warranted. With regard to the humanities themselves—the serious study of literature, philosophy, and history—as well as to the challenges to the humanities, we may do well to remember Josiah Royce's observation: "Yes, it's hard to wrestle with angels, but there are some blessings that can't be won any other way."

NOTES

1. The quotation was translated by Marvin Lowenthal and published in his collection of selections from Montaigne's writings, *The Autobiography of Michel de Montaigne* (Boston: Houghton Mifflin, 1935), p. 33.

Conference Participants

Titles and affiliations as supplied by the participants
at the time of the conferences

Phoenix Conference (March 14–17, 1984)

Bill Abernathy, Superintendent, Mena Public Schools, Mena, Arkansas

Mark S. Auburn, Professor of English and Dean of the College of Arts and Sciences, Arkansas State University, State University, Arkansas

Mark William Ballantyne, Mathematics Teacher, Gonzaga Preparatory School, Spokane, Washington

Rose Barden, Chairman, English Department, Lincoln High School, Tacoma, Washington

Barry Bauska, Associate Professor and Chairman, Department of English, and Adjunct Professor and Director, Tutorial Writing Program, School of Law, University of Puget Sound, Tacoma, Washington

Bill Beasley, Superintendent, Jonesboro Public Schools, Jonesboro, Arkansas, and Member, Arkansas State Council of Economic Education

Mike Bowler, Reporter, *The Baltimore Sun*, Baltimore, Maryland

Diane L. Brooks, Manager, History-Social Science Unit, California State Department of Education, Sacramento, California

Irving H. Buchen, Dean, School of Humanities, California State College, San Bernardino, California

Jim Burton, Teacher, Page High School, Page, Arizona

John J. Burton, Social Studies Supervisor, Pinellas County School System, and Social Studies Teacher, Pinellas Park High School, Largo, Florida

Dorothy P. Cheatham, English Teacher, Pinellas Park High School, Largo, Florida

Gwendolyn J. Cheatham, Foreign Language Teacher, Booker T. Washington High School, Atlanta, Georgia

Louise Allen Cobb, Section Chief, English Language Arts, Louisiana State Department of Education, Baton Rouge, Louisiana

J. Scott Colley, Associate Professor of English and Associate Dean of the College of Arts and Sciences, Vanderbilt University, Nashville, Tennessee

Maria C. Collins, Foreign Language Specialist, Kansas State Department of Education, Topeka, Kansas

Mark Curtis, President, Association of American Colleges, Washington, D.C.

Michael H. Davitt, Principal, Cajon High School, San Bernardino, California

Elizabeth K. Doenges, Member, Executive Committee, State Arts Council, Tulsa, Oklahoma

Ronald C. Duncan, English Teacher, Page High School, Page, Arizona

Thelma Elliott, Member, Oregon State Board of Education, Portland, Oregon

Elizabeth L. Feely, Superintendent, Area III, Atlanta Public Schools, Atlanta, Georgia

Denis M. Fitzpatrick, Chairman, English Department, Pinellas Park High School, Largo, Florida

Larry E. Frase, Superintendent, Catalina Foothills School District, Tucson, Arizona

Margaret Ann Furr, English Teacher, Mena Public Schools, Mena, Arkansas

E. Nicholas Genovese, Professor of Classics, San Diego State University, San Diego, California

Joanne Hackman, Humanities Teacher, Clarksville High School, Clarksville, Tennessee

Loretta M. Hargroder, History and Language Arts Teacher, Brame Junior High School, Alexandria, Louisiana

Gary J. Hoban, Assistant Superintendent, Ramona Unified School District, Ramona, California

Bobby L. Hogue, Member, Arkansas House of Representatives, Jonesboro, Arkansas

C. E. Holladay, Superintendent, Mississippi State Department of Education, Jackson, Mississippi

Richard L. Hopper, English and History Teacher, Clarksville High School, Clarksville, Tennessee

Nathan I. Huggins, Professor of History and Afro-American Studies, Harvard University, Cambridge, Massachusetts

Shirley Ann Jackson, English Teacher, Leesville High School, Leesville, Louisiana

David M. Kennedy, Professor of History and Associate Dean of the School of Humanities and Sciences, Stanford University, Stanford, California

Ralph L. Ketcham, Professor of History, Syracuse University, Syracuse, New York

Karen S. Kutiper, President, Texas Joint Council of Teachers of English, and Language Arts Coordinator, Alief Independent School District, Alief, Texas

Berkeley W. Latimer, Upper School Principal, St. Andrew's Episcopal School, Jackson, Mississippi

Paul M. Levitt, Professor of English, University of Colorado, Boulder, Colorado

Rita C. Manning, Lecturer in Philosophy, California State College, San Bernardino, California

Philip N. Marcus, President, Institute for Educational Affairs, New York, New York

Bernard Martin, Veterans and Education Programs, Office of Management and Budget, Washington, D.C. (Observer)

S. R. Martin, Jr., Professor of English and Chairman of the Faculty, Evergreen State College, Olympia, Washington

Bernard H. McKenna, Program Development Specialist, National Education Association, Washington, D.C. (Observer)

Jacqueline F. Meadows, History and Social Science Teacher, North Carolina School of Science and Mathematics, Durham, North Carolina, and Area III Coordinator, The Governor's School of North Carolina

Harriett Meloy, Member, Montana State Board of Education, Helena, Montana

Fay D. Metcalf, Executive Editor, *The Social Studies,* and History Teacher and Coordinator of the Secondary Assessment Project, Boulder Valley Public Schools, Boulder, Colorado

Susanna Mosley, English and Speech Teacher, Mena Public Schools, Mena, Arkansas

Paralee F. Norman, Assistant Professor of Language Arts, Northwestern State University, Fort Polk Campus, Leesville, Louisiana

Sidney B. Poellnitz, Adjunct Professor of Education, University of Alabama, and Assistant Superintendent, Tuscaloosa County Board of Education, Tuscaloosa, Alabama

Carol A. Pope, Assistant Professor of English Education, University of Texas, University Park, Texas

Alice H. Price, Chairman, English Department, Sullivan High School, Chicago, Illinois

Juanita D. Quick, Director of Language Arts, Tacoma, Washington

S. Ann Rece, English Teacher, Wheatley Senior High School, Houston, Texas

Paul W. Rosier, Principal, Page High School, Page, Arizona

Gayle St. John, English Teacher, Norman High School, Norman, Oklahoma

David Savage, Reporter, Los Angeles Times, Los Angeles, California (Observer)

Martin E. Segal, Chairman of the Board, Lincoln Center for the Performing Arts, New York, New York

G. Sue Shannon, Assistant Principal, Timberline High School, Lacey, Washington, and President, Policy Board, Professional Certification Programs, Central Washington University, Ellensburg, Washington

Robert T. Shaughnessy, English and Social Studies Teacher, Patrick Henry High School, San Diego, California

English Showalter, Executive Director, Modern Language Association, New York, New York

David Sinitiere, Member, Louisiana State Board of Education, New Orleans, Louisiana

Hildreth Spencer, Chairman, Social Studies Department, Highland Park High School, Highland Park, Illinois

Lynn Stinnette, Coordinator, Department of Curriculum, Chicago Public Schools, Chicago, Illinois

Philip B. Swain, Member, Washington State Board of Education, Seattle, Washington

Jerry B. Talley, Humanities Teacher, Washington High School, Tulsa, Oklahoma

Jean H. Teel, Foreign Language Resource Teacher, Shawnee Mission School District, Shawnee Mission, Kansas

Sharon Thomas, Chairman, Language Arts Department, Timberline High School, Lacey, Washington

June Thompson, Social Studies and Foreign Language Teacher, Riverside Junior High School, Northport, Alabama

Gary Tisdale, Assistant Professor of History, Louisiana State University, Alexandria, Louisiana

Patricia Tubiola, Chairman, English Department, Cajon High School, San Bernardino, California

Stephen R. Van Luchene, Director, Graduate Institute in Liberal Education, St. John's College, Santa Fe, New Mexico

Jon S. Vincent, Professor of Portuguese and Spanish, University of Kansas, Lawrence, Kansas

Ron Voeller, Education Division, Dependents Schools, Department of Defense, Alexandria, Virginia (Observer)

Nobuo Bob Watanabe, Director, Curriculum and Instructional Services, Contra Costa County Superintendent of Schools Office, Pleasant Hill, California

Jeanette H. Whatley, Instructional Coordinator, Booker T. Washington High School, Atlanta, Georgia

Penny B. Williams, Member, Oklahoma House of Representatives, Oklahoma City, Oklahoma

Aubrey J. Womack, Associate Professor of History and Political Science, Stillman College, Tuscaloosa, Alabama

Celeste P. Woodley, Executive Director, Educational Programs Division, Boulder Valley Public Schools, Boulder, Colorado

Frank A. Word, Columnist, *The Vernon Journal*, Vernon Parish, Leesville, Louisiana

Minneapolis Conference (April 8–11, 1984)

Duncan W. Alling, Headmaster, Miami Valley School, Dayton, Ohio

Phyllis A. Bailey, Coordinator of Social Studies, Baltimore County Public Schools, Towson, Maryland

Ann Bardwell, Member, Kentucky State Board of Education, Lexington, Kentucky

Jim Bencivenga, Education Reporter, *The Christian Science Monitor*, Boston, Massachusetts

Margaret M. Bronder, Head of Social Studies Department, Peters Township High School, McMurray, Pennsylvania

Gordon L. Burstein, History Teacher, Des Moines Public Schools, Des Moines, Iowa

Mary F. Butz, Chairman, Social Studies Department, Murrow High School, Brooklyn, New York

Gabriella B. Canfield, Assistant Museum Educator and Lecturer, Metropolitan Museum of Art, New York, New York

Elaine Cantor, History and Social Studies Teacher, Utica Free Academy, Utica, New York

Harold Cantor, President, Community College General Education Association, and Professor and Chairman, English-Humanities Department, Mohawk Valley Community College, Utica, New York

W. Robert Carr, Member, School Committee, Hingham Public Schools, Hingham, Massachusetts

Peter F. Clark, Assistant Principal, Cold Spring Harbor High School, Cold Spring Harbor, New York

Barbara A. Cleary, English Teacher, Miami Valley School, and Member, Centerville Board of Education, Centerville, Ohio

Paul Cole, Vice-President, American Federation of Teachers, Albany, New York (Observer)

Marguerite Collesano, President, Western New York Society for the Preservation of Italian Folklore, and Social Studies Teacher, Cleveland High School, Buffalo, New York

Carol Collins, Secondary Supervisor, Dinwiddie County Schools, Dinwiddie, Virginia

Audrey Cotherman, Deputy Superintendent, Wyoming State Department of Education, Cheyenne, Wyoming

Charles J. Curran, Assistant Professor of Political Science, Sinclair Community College, and President, Montgomery County Commission, Dayton, Ohio

Cecelia M. Daher, Chairman, English Department, Cold Spring Harbor High School, Cold Spring Harbor, New York

Jolly Ann Davidson, Member, Iowa State Board of Education, Clarinda, Iowa

Margaret Q. Dietemann, Associate Professor of Modern Languages and Assistant Vice-President for Academic Affairs, Iona College, New Rochelle, New York

Roland Dille, President, Moorhead State University, Moorhead, Minnesota, and Chairman, National Humanities Council Education Committee

R. W. Doepner, Assistant Superintendent for Curriculum and Instruction, Winston-Salem/Forsyth County Schools, Winston-Salem, North Carolina

Susan J. Donielson, Director of Curriculum, Des Moines Public Schools, Des Moines, Iowa

David A. Durfee, Chairman, Social Studies Department, Sleepy Hollow High School, North Tarrytown, New York

Joyce M. Follman, Member, Board of Education, School District of the City of Ladue, St. Louis, Missouri

Kevin Free, Member, Delaware House of Representatives, Wilmington, Delaware

Norman L. Frey, Chairman, English and Humanities Department, New Trier Township High School, Winnetka, Illinois

Peter Gibbon, Director, Upper School, Hackley School, Tarrytown, New York

Ann Goodwin, Editor, *Dispatch-Pioneer Press*, Minneapolis, Minnesota

Dennis Gray, Program Director, Council for Basic Education, Washington, D.C.

Henry Halsted, Vice-President, The Johnson Foundation, Racine, Wisconsin (Observer)

Patricia F. Hamner, Member, West Virginia State Board of Education, Buck Hannon, West Virginia

James M. Hare, Director of Instruction and Assistant Principal, Richfield High School, Richfield, Minnesota

James L. Heizer, President, Kentucky Association of Teachers of History, and Professor of History, Georgetown College, Georgetown, Kentucky

William A. Heyde III, Chairman, English Department, Watkins High School, St. Louis, Missouri

Kenneth V. Hilton, Member, Delaware State Board of Education, Newark, Delaware

Jerome Hughes, Member, Minnesota State Senate, St. Paul, Minnesota

Jay K. Jarrell, Director, Peters Township School Board, McMurray, Pennsylvania

John H. Jones, Superintendent, Murfreesboro City Schools, Murfreesboro, Tennessee

Patricia Keegan, Education Editor, Gannett Westchester Rockland Newspapers, White Plains, New York

Theodore W. Kotsonas, Social Studies Teacher, Richfield High School, Richfield, Minnesota

David A. Lacatell, Social Studies Teacher, Hingham High School, Hingham, Massachusetts

Daniel C. Leclerc, Director of Social Studies, Hingham Public Schools, Hingham, Massachusetts, and Vice-President, Massachusetts Council for the Social Studies

Mrs. Arnold Levy, Member, New Trier Township Board of Education, Winnetka, Illinois, and President, Illinois Association of School Boards

Viola Luginbuhl, Member, Vermont State Board of Education, South Burlington, Vermont

Robert B. McCarthy, Headmaster, Brookline High School, Brookline, Massachusetts

William J. McGill, Professor of History, Washington and Jefferson College, Washington, Pennsylvania

Joseph B. Michel, Director, Northwest Area Foundation Gifted/Talented Program, and Science Teacher, Richfield High School, Richfield, Minnesota

Joseph O. Milner, English Department, Wake Forest University, Winston-Salem, North Carolina

McLean Mitchell, Chairman, Advanced Placement Department, and History Teacher, Career Education Center, Winston-Salem, North Carolina

S. Rex Morrow, Assistant Professor of Social Science, Department of the Model Laboratory School, College of Education, Eastern Kentucky University, Richmond, Kentucky

Joe Nathan, Research and Development Fellow, Public School Incentives Program, St. Paul, Minnesota, and author of *Free to Teach*

Dennis C. O'Brien, Associate Professor of Geology, Drake University, Des Moines, Iowa

Joseph O'Connor, Assistant Professor of Classics, Georgetown University, Washington, D.C.

Amy F. Pace, Curriculum Coordinator, Henderson County Schools, Hendersonville, North Carolina

Daniel E. Pace, English Teacher, West Henderson High School, Hendersonville, North Carolina

Joan M. Palmer, Curriculum Consultant, Baltimore County Public Schools, Towson, Maryland

Marion B. Polsky, Director, Latin Cornerstone Project, and Assistant Professor of Classics, Brooklyn College of CUNY, Brooklyn, New York

James W. Robinson, Curriculum Coordinator, Cody Public Schools, Cody, Wyoming

Donald Rogan, Social Studies Teacher, New Trier Township High School, Winnetka, Illinois

Murray Sachs, Professor of French, Brandeis University, Waltham, Massachusetts

Mary Ellen Saterlie, Associate Superintendent of Instruction, Baltimore County Public Schools, Towson, Maryland

Michael G. Sams, Social Studies Supervisor, Virginia State Department of Education, Richmond, Virginia

Anthony A. Schepsis, Principal and German Teacher, Utica Free Academy, Utica, New York

Walter L. Schneller, Chairman, History–Social Science Department, Hackley School, Tarrytown, New York

Arnold D. Sgan, Communication Skills Coordinator, North Carolina State Department of Public Instruction, Canton, North Carolina

Nancy M. Shambaugh, Member, Cold Spring Harbor Central School District Board of Education, Cold Spring Harbor, New York

John T. Shaughnessy, Jr., Associate Superintendent, Board of Education, School District of the City of Ladue, St. Louis, Missouri

Robert L. Smith, Executive Director, Council for American Private Education, Washington, D.C.

Donald Thomas, English Teacher, Brookline High School, Brookline, Massachusetts

Joseph M. Vocolo, Director of Foreign Language and Bilingual Education, Buffalo Public Schools, Buffalo, New York

Richard G. Weeks, Dean of Instruction, Northwest Community College, Powell, Wyoming

Susan Weliky, Consultant, Latin Cornerstone Project, and Latin Teacher, Murrow High School, Brooklyn, New York

Ronald C. Wheeler, Associate Professor of Education, College of William and Mary, Williamsburg, Virginia

Angene Wilson, Associate Professor of Curriculum and Instruction, College of Education, University of Kentucky, Lexington, Kentucky

Carolyn Q. Wilson, Director of Planning and Development, Woodrow Wilson National Fellowship Foundation, Princeton, New Jersey

Stephen S. Winter, Professor of Education, Tufts University, Medford, Massachusetts

William S. Woodside, Chairman and Chief Executive Officer, American Can Company, Greenwich, Connecticut

Betty Jo Zander, Public School Incentives Program, St. Paul, Minnesota

About the Authors

Biographical information as supplied by the authors in the summer of 1984

JOSEPH ADELSON is Professor of Psychology at the University of Michigan. He is the coauthor (with Elizabeth Douvan) of *The Adolescent Experience* (1966) and the editor of *Handbook of Adolescent Psychology* (1980). A collection of his essays, largely on education, will be published in 1985 under the title *Inventing Adolescence*.

WILLIAM J. BENNETT was appointed Chairman of the National Endowment for the Humanities in 1981. He has served as president and director of the National Humanities Center at Research Triangle Park, North Carolina. He is the coauthor (with Terry Eastland) of *Counting by Race: Equality in American Thought from the Founding Fathers to Bakke* (1979).

CHESTER E. FINN, JR., is Professor of Education and Public Policy at Vanderbilt University, where he is also co-director of the Center for

Education Policy. He is director of the Educational Excellence Network. In addition to many articles, he has written *Education and the Presidency* (1977) and *Scholars, Dollars and Bureaucrats* (1978) and has coedited (with David W. Breneman) *Public Policy and Private Higher Education* (1978) and (with Diane Ravitch and Robert T. Fancher) the predecessor to this volume, *Against Mediocrity: The Humanities in America's High Schools* (1984).

PAUL GAGNON is Professor of Modern European History at the University of Massachusetts, Boston, where he previously served as Dean of Faculty. He is the author of *France since 1789* (1972) and has published widely on French educational reforms enacted since 1945, including articles for the *New Republic, Commentary,* and *Change Magazine.* He is currently engaged in research on the teaching of the history of Western civilization in secondary schools and universities.

BERNARD R. GIFFORD, Dean of the Graduate School of Education, University of California at Berkeley, was graduated from the University of Rochester with a Ph.D. in radiation biology and biophysics. He was Professor of Political Science and Vice-President at the University of Rochester and has served as Deputy Chancellor of the New York City public school system.

E. D. HIRSCH, JR., Kenan Professor of English at the University of Virginia, has written *Validity in Interpretation: The Aims of Interpretation* (1967), on the theory of reading, and *The Philosophy of Composition* (1977), on the theory of writing. He is currently pursuing research on the connections between literacy and specific background information. He has served as advisor to several educational boards, including the National Institute of Education and the New York State Board of Regents.

JOEL J. KUPPERMAN is Professor of Philosophy at the University of Connecticut, where in 1973 he won the Alumni Association Award for Excellence in Teaching. His publications include *Ethical Knowledge* (1970) and *The Foundations of Morality* (1983). He is currently engaged in an extended study of the topic of character.

CLAIRE L. PELTON, who served as English Department chairperson for twenty years at Los Altos High School in Los Altos, California, currently teaches English part-time at Los Altos and is working at Stanford University on a three-year study of the American high school. Mrs. Pelton is the author of numerous articles, and for three years she wrote a monthly column for *Literary Cavalcade.* She has served on a number of test development committees for the College Board. In the year 1978–79, the California State Superintendent of Schools and the California state legislators honored her as one of four outstanding teachers in California.

DIANE RAVITCH is Adjunct Professor of History and Education at Teachers College, Columbia University. She has published more than one hundred articles and is the author of *The Troubled Crusade: American Education, 1945–80* (1983), *The Revisionists Revised: A Critique of the Radical Attack on the Schools* (1978), and *The Great School Wars: New York, 1805–1973* (1974). A collection of her essays, *The Schools We Deserve*, will be published in the spring of 1985. She has also coedited four books, including (with Chester E. Finn, Jr., and Robert T. Fancher) *Against Mediocrity: The Humanities in America's High Schools* (1984). Professor Ravitch is the codirector of the Educational Excellence Network, and she is a Phi Beta Kappa Visiting Scholar for the year 1984–85.

P. HOLLEY ROBERTS is Research Assistant in the Center for Education Policy at the Vanderbilt Institute for Public Policy Studies. She is a graduate student of philosophy at Vanderbilt University, where she was a teaching fellow in the year 1982–83. She was assistant editor of *Soundings: An Interdisciplinary Journal* from 1980 to 1983.

JAY M. SOMMER taught foreign languages at New Rochelle High School in New York for more than twenty-five years. In 1981 he was named National Teacher of the Year and was appointed to the National Commission on Excellence in Education, which issued the report *A Nation at Risk*. During the 1983–84 school year he was invited by Secretary of Education Bell to serve as an official spokesperson for the commission. Mr. Sommer is currently a Visiting Professor in the School of Education at Long Island University.

STEPHAN THERNSTROM, Winthrop Professor of History at Harvard University, has also taught at U.C.L.A. and at Brandeis University. He was the Pitt Professor of American History and Institutions at Cambridge University and Professorial Fellow in Trinity College in the year 1978–79. He is the author of *Poverty and Progress: Social Mobility in a Nineteenth-Century City* (1978), *The Other Bostonians: Poverty and Progress in the American Metropolis, 1880–1970* (1973); and *A History of the American People* (1984). Professor Thernstrom is editor of the *Harvard Encyclopedia of American Ethnic Groups* (1980) and coeditor (with Richard Sennett) of *Nineteenth-Century Cities: Essays in the New Urban History* (1969).

PATRICK WELSH has taught English for fifteen years at T. C. Williams High School in Alexandria, Virginia. He is the author of a nine-part series of columns entitled *Tales Out of School* for the *Washington Post.* Mr. Welsh is also an attorney and a member of the Virginia bar.